EMOTIONAL HEALTH:

THE SECRET for FREEDOM

From DRAMA, TRAUMA, and PAIN

An owner's manual describing practical methods to release your physical and emotional chronic pain, suffering, and emotional stress

Michael David Lawrience

B.A. Natural Theology in Sacred Healing

B. Commerce

Professional Bowenwork Practitioner

Lawrience Publishing

Sedona, Arizona

I dedicate this book to inspire YOU, the reader.

May the concepts and stories of over 15 people's life experiences, plus some of my own story, spark a desire in you to step into your own healing journey.

We experienced many physical, emotional, energetic, psychological, and spiritual challenges.

We persevered and now share parts of our lives for your healing and elevation of consciousness.

As all of us know, massive changes now shake our planet, lives, and consciousness to the core.

For the first time in the history of the planet, we all have the opportunity to move beyond feelings of separation into greater joy and experience of our life purpose.

Michael David Lawrience

Table of Contents

ACKNOWLEDGMENTS

I am grateful for the assistance and support of the people who shared their journey and life experience toward greater emotional wellbeing in this book. I applaud their efforts to heal their emotional suffering to gain greater freedom. I offer my heartfelt thanks to them.

I thank Lyn O'Hara, a core energetic healer, Julie, a patent lawyer, Joanna, a retired CEO of a major soft drink company, Shivani, a former nurse, Shannon Nelson, a quadriplegic, Julianna, a therapist for teenagers, Jacqueline Stone, an author and spiritual coach, Viola Bergeron, a former paralegal administrator, Oceanna, a Living Water Medicine woman, Sinnet Olina Tiwaz, a horse whisperer, Kathryne-Alexis, a life consultant coach, Anita Bear, a transpersonal therapist, Pat Gurnick, a psychotherapist and lifestyle counselor, Sharon Lund, an author, producer, and international speaker, and Tiara Kumara, the founder of Children of the Sun.

I thank Monica Hagen, artist, teacher, and writer, for her professional editing assistance to make this book clearer and more readable. I thank my wife, Lyn, for her ongoing support in my own personal healing as well as her profound insights on the cutting edge of energy healing and the Awakening experience.

Lastly, I am deeply grateful to Sri Bhagavan and Amma at the Oneness University http://www.onenessuniversity.org for their divine mission of awakening humanity to Oneness.

FOREWORD

I, like many of you reading this book, suppressed my emotions for most of my life. I took on the role of the invisible child in my alcoholic family and kept everything inside because I felt unsafe and afraid of my father's violence. Through years of suffering low self-esteem, unrecognized low-grade depression, and unhappy codependent relationships, I gradually discovered my high degree of codependency and the inner child inside me sad, lonely, and buried in agonizing pain.

Stone faced, appearing unemotional on the outside and protected by layers of energetic armor to numb my feelings for most of my life, you may ask how I would be qualified to teach about healing the emotions. Challenged by doubt of my self-worth and continuously swinging back and forth between the two poles of the victim, anger or powerlessness, I emerged from a long journey of forty years learning how to recognize, feel, and express my emotions in a healthy way.

Researchers now show the link between emotions and physical health. I find the following study amazing.

We've known for a while now that emotions play a critical role in physical health, said Sarah Pressman, assistant professor of psychology at Kansas University in a 2009 study from the Gallup World Poll.

The findings with adults in more than 140 countries provided a sample of 95 percent of the world's population.

Participants reported their physical health issues and answered questions about their basic survival needs for food and shelter. Pressman described positive emotions being linked to better health, even with the lack of basic needs being met.

The study showed the association between positive emotion and physical health being more powerful than the link between health and adequate food.

Christine Northrup, M.D. quotes from *Acupressure for Emotional Healing* by Gach and Henning, *Today, the mind/body research is confirming what ancient healing traditions have always known: that the body and the mind are a unit. There is no disease that isn't mental and emotional as well as physical.*

My experience has taught me that gaining greater emotional health involves the courage and willingness to face and go through the pain of our emotional suffering. As the poet Robert Frost says, *Very often, the only way out is through.*

Current terms such as *energy medicine* and *energy psychology* have appeared to indicate the connection between our emotions/mind and body. Energy medicine includes methods, such as Emotional Freedom Technique (EFT), to heal the emotions and body. Energy psychology, in a similar way, relates to energy therapies based on the Chinese meridian system of medicine, which clear emotional traumas from the mind/body through holding or tapping acupressure points on the body.

By learning to accept and staying present with our emotional states rather than avoiding or repressing them, they transform, we gain more energy, insights may come, and we become more serene and joyful.

In my experience, three areas need addressing to improve our emotional health: trapped emotions in the body, traumas and abuse from our childhood, and emotional issues in our DNA.

I wrote this book over a period of fifteen years and based it on my life experiences and learning's, as well as those of other people. Our healing, which includes the emotions, involves finding what works best for us from all the natural healing methods, as well as methods from conventional medicine. The joy of the journey rests on discovery of our own tailor-made program.

May you be inspired by the concepts and stories in *Emotional Health: The Secret for Freedom from Drama, Trauma, and Pain* as you step into your own personalized healing journey. Also, may you awaken to your next level of moving beyond feelings of separation into greater joy and experience of your life purpose. Michael Lawrience, Sedona, Arizona

EMOTIONAL HEALTH

INTRODUCTION:

ACHIEVING EMOTIONAL HEALTH/WELLBEING

I f you picked up this book, you probably want a way out of your pain and suffering. If you choose, you can start to find freedom from your suffering and improve your emotional health and wellbeing.

In this book you will read stories of people who healed their emotional suffering to gain greater freedom, including a former CEO of a major company, a therapist for teenagers, a Science of Mind minister, a Living Water Medicine woman, an author and spiritual coach, a horse whisperer, a quadriplegic, a life consultant coach, a core energetic healer, a psychotherapist, a former nurse, a transpersonal therapist, and the founder of Children of the Sun.

MY JOURNEY

This book birthed out of my own journey from an unconscious desire to free myself from suffering. In my mid-twenties, I began exploring self-growth with a psychiatrist, then studied psychology and participated with countless encounter groups. I also studied Western esoteric systems of development like Kabala for many years. Then I uprooted myself and moved from Alberta, Canada to Los Angeles to live in a psychological community, The Center for Feeling Therapy, for two years. After that community disbanded, good fortune guided me to study hands-on energy healing at The Healing Light Center Church for three years. Since then I have dedicated my life to self-growth, studying and practicing many forms of energy healing, systems of esoteric psychology, as well as yoga and different forms of meditation.

Even after all my study and growth, I still carried many unhealed emotional patterns of suffering. Victim and lack consciousness like *I can't have* plagued me for most of my life until recently. Although I continually identified patterns and received energy healings, I remained unaware of when I would fall into the hopeless pit of the victim. Anger and feeling powerless, believing I was unable to make a difference, fueled my victim. Fortunately, I have a wife, who as a gifted energy healer pointed out when she saw the victim overpowering me. My biggest discovery occurred when my wife told me one day to stay present with the feeling of the victim rather than sinking into it. At that moment, I had a choice. I stayed present with the feelings, holding a focus on them, and after a short time I experienced a shift and more energy entered my body. I felt emotionally stronger. Now each time the victim emerges I still have to choose. It gets easier.

Eckhart Tolle talks about being present with emotions and whatever occurs moment to moment. I knew and respected his concept for years, yet I needed a professional to teach me, like my wife did for her clients, how to focus and contain my feelings without unconsciously losing the focus because the discomfort felt too painful. I also wanted to come out of my pain rather than remain attached to it.

BENEFITS of IMPROVING OUR EMOTIONAL HEALTH

Our emotional patterns of suffering confront us throughout our lives until we identify and become aware of our unconscious patterns and heal the core issues through our choices and the assistance of professional healers.

These patterns contain our life lessons, which once learned allow our special talents and strengths to emerge. We can then use our gifts in assisting others, thereby fulfilling our life purposes as many of the people in this book describe.

Did you know that our cells hold memories of our emotional patterns of suffering? For instance, have you experienced similar situations that emotionally trigger you? Would you like to identify these triggers? Would you like less emotional drama in your life? Are you tired of being in unsatisfying codependent relationships? Would you like an owner's manual for improving your emotional health?

You may be wondering, what is good emotional health? Simply, it refers to our level of emotional wellbeing. This wellbeing relates to our feelings or personal experiences of our emotions to thoughts and to our behaviors, which can be unconscious reactions to our feelings.

Recent research by such people like biologist Bruce Lipton shows that our emotional health directly affects our physical health. For instance, depression can correlate to heart attacks and anxiety can create digestive issues. Anger overstresses our heart with fight or flight hormones.

Most of us refuse to recognize our emotions, take action to heal toxic emotions, and realize change takes time. First, we need a desire to change. This desire can sometimes emerge out of years of being in an abusive relationship or relationships.

Western medicine tends to ignore the effect of emotions on physical health. As a Western society, we also deny the expression of our emotions and push them away when they rise to the surface. Improving emotional health remains unimportant, until intense suffering forces us to look deeper at our feelings.

Rather than being a powerless victim, would you like to feel more empowered? Improved emotional health involves changing our nonworking emotions into positive emotions that work in a more healthy way. Rather than getting hooked into emotionally reacting to repeating upsetting situations, we can develop the ability to be proactive as we become aware of our unconscious critical thoughts and feelings.

As we reclaim power over our emotional reactions, emotions no longer run our lives. We no longer live in fear that our emotions will erupt like a child in a temper tantrum and hold us hostage to suffering. We can discover ways to heal our emotions and critical thoughts such as "I am not good enough." This will decrease the pain in our bodies.

My thirty-five years of practicing and receiving various types of natural energy healing has emphasized that improving emotional health and achieving freedom from suffering involves connecting, at an energetic level, to the core cause of our emotional suffering. When we learn how to accept our emotions and stay present with them, they transform on their own. Energy increases in our body, insights come, and we may experience calm and peace.

As our emotional health improves, we gain greater awareness of our emotions and how they affect our thoughts and behaviors. We learn more about our strengths as well as our weaknesses and how to turn weakness into strength. We increase our self-esteem and confidence. We gain skill in taking charge and managing our emotions in healthier ways. Most important, we have greater choices to be proactive rather than continuing to suffer as victims at the mercy of our emotional dramas. In addition, we also understand the emotions of others, which give us greater social awareness. We can have and maintain healthier relationships with better communication and less conflict.

WHAT YOU WILL FIND in THIS BOOK

- Questionnaire to access your present state of emotional health
- Basic three-part formula to lessen suffering.
- Stories of people who used different methods to achieve freedom from pain & suffering.
- Tips at the end of each chapter to begin to improve your wellbeing.
- Description of Energy Medicine techniques and links for further information.
- Importance of healing your wounded inner child who otherwise runs your emotional life.
- Healing your unconscious shadow aspects, that can sabotage every effort for success.
- Recognizing and healing codependent relationships
- Method to heal soul splits – Soul Retrieval.

As we heal our emotional states and eventually reach a place where we still have intense feelings, yet no longer emotionally react, we can begin a journey of awakening into Oneness i.e., experiencing the connection/unity with all life around us.

The following questionnaire gives you the opportunity to discover your level of Emotional Health.

EMOTIONAL HEALTH QUESTIONNAIRE

Rate each statement on a scale from 1 to 5:

1 = Never true

2 = occasionally true

3 = 50/50

4 = Mostly true

5 = Always true

1. I express my emotions with ease.

    1   2   3   4   5

2. I express anger without projecting it onto someone.

    1   2   3   4   5

3. I stay emotionally neutral when someone pushes my emotional hot buttons.

    1   2   3   4   5

4. I take charge of my emotions in upsetting situations rather than reacting.

    1   2   3   4   5

5. I often feel powerful rather than a victim to emotional dramas.

    1   2   3   4   5

6. I have healed repeating behaviors, addictions, or unhealthy emotional patterns.

    1   2   3   4   5

7. I take responsibility for my behaviors rather than blaming or judging others.

    1   2   3   4   5

8. I am aware of my critical thoughts and feelings.

    1   2   3   4   5

9. I love myself enough to leave abusive or unsatisfying relationships.

    1   2   3   4   5

10. I take charge and manage my emotions in healthy ways.

    1 2   3   4   5

11. I live in the present, aware of my feelings in the moment.

1   2   3   4   5

12. I communicate my feelings and needs easily.

1   2   3   4   5

13. I have intimate positive relationships.

1   2   3   4   5

14. I communicate well and handle conflict easily.

    1 2   3   4   5

15. I love myself.

    1 2   3   4   5

16. I experience inner peace or joy.

    1 2   3   4   5

17. I am grateful for being alive.

    1 2   3   4   5

18. I learn from my mistakes.

    1 2   3   4   5

19. I do work I enjoy.

    1 2   3   4   5

20. I am fulfilling my life purpose.

    1 2   3   4   5

Scoring:

80 – 100: High level of Emotional Health

60-79: Good level of Emotional Health

40- 59: Average Emotional Health

Under 40: Lots of opportunity to begin improving your emotional wellbeing

Regardless of your score, you can start to improve your Emotional Health by reading this book and practicing the tips. Take the questionnaire again after you finish the book and practice some of the tips for a while

PART ONE

- Improving emotional health
  - Easing pain
  - Healing ourselves
- Healing physical & emotional abuse
  - Facing our fears
  - Stabilizing our minds

CHAPTER 1

HOW CAN DIVINE GRACE EASE OUR PAIN?

Creation is light and shadows both ... Without suffering he (man) scarcely cares to recall he has forsaken his eternal home. Pain is a prod to remembrance. The way to escape is through wisdom.

Yogananda, Autobiography of a Yogi

In this chapter I describe a general three-part method of lessening suffering/pain.

An energetic healer describes how we can begin to face our suffering and two people tell about life experiences involving the manifestation of grace. The chapter ends with a Master of Wisdom offering greater understanding of Divine Grace.

Would you like to freedom from your suffering? Yogananda, an Indian yogi, points out a three-fold method to do so.

You must make an effort with all your heart, which makes up 25% of the requirements for lessening suffering. This includes in the Western world improving ourselves through personal inner emotional and spiritual work. Another 25% involves the guidance of inner and outer teachers, which can include angels, friends, situations, books, seminars, healings, etc. All these help our own efforts. The last 50% involves Divine Grace, which according to some spiritual teachers such as El Morya, a Master of Wisdom; *Grace surrounds us all the time as a part of creation.*

To receive this grace, however, involves the surrender of our minds, fears, and illusions of what we believe to be reality or truth. As Yogananda says, *All surrendering love draws His Grace.* I will speak more of grace later.

Human suffering exists on national and group levels through war, destruction, violence, and disease in war inflicted areas around the world. I am, however, going to address only suffering in areas related to women, men, parents and teenagers, people living with friends or family in pain or pain experienced from loved ones passing over, and mainly individual physical and emotional pain and suffering.

Other people, as well as I, will describe experiences of suffering and methods we have used to lessen it.

The example below shows how energetic healing and outside assistance aided the overcoming of suffering when the client chose to face their pain.

HOW MY CLIENT OVERCAME SUFFERING

Lyn, as a Core Energetic Healer, guides clients through life challenging issues to assist their empowerment.

Overcoming suffering takes courage. Each client I have seen who begins to face suffering has courage. This means the courage it takes to face the unknown – namely being without suffering. Who would think this actually takes courage to be without suffering? It does. What drives us to want to face this suffering and overcome it?

For each person the answer to this question is different. Courage remains the one thing they all have in common. Sometimes when they begin to face this suffering or fear they turn away by taking drugs, often given by a doctor. Some doctors will keep them on these drugs for years or the client will find another doctor to continue the drugs.

Truthfulness comes to the person with courage, courage to face the truth and a willingness to state the truth to someone else without blaming. When someone begins to step out of either the perpetrator or the victim role, they also begin stepping out of suffering. Until they realize their choices that have brought them to this learning, they will stay in the vicious circle of victim or perpetrator. Both of these patterns create harm to themselves and others, which perpetuates suffering.

The path begins with claiming truth of oneself and the right to have a self. This occurs in the body's core beginning with the central pillar within the body, which makes up the spinal column and cranial sacral fluid running along the spine. This also includes all of the places where the nerves connect up the spine.

We have to energetically claim, as our own first, the spinal column and the above part of our bodies. Once claimed, then we can begin to contain our emotions through the nervous system. As emotions activate, so too our nervous system activates in the body. As we contain and allow the fire of emotions to receive love, our nervous system heals with love along with our emotions.

Containing our emotions allows self-healing to occur. Containing emotions challenges highly emotional people or those of us who prefer suppressing rather than expressing our emotions. Both of these will affect our nervous system and then the whole body including organs. This can lead to many illnesses. So learning how to contain and allow the love to hold the emotions eventually heals the whole body and mind.

An emotion activates with a thought. Suppression of emotion or constant emotional reacting buries the belief behind it. As we contain our emotions and heal them with love, the pain of emotional events begins to burn away. Choosing to refuse to contain our emotion creates more pain and the cycle of suffering continues.

This pain affects so many things, physically and emotionally. It clouds our brain; it drives us to eat unhealthy foods, and to avoid the pain we already experience. This leads to more pain. As magnetic beings, we can create our lives with this pain, bringing more circumstances to give us a choice to heal or add to the levels of pain already held in our bodies. The majority of humanity lives daily with this cycle of suffering.

This also leads to the discussion of choices. Do we make conscious choices in our lives or choices to avoid suffering? The latter actually creates more suffering through choosing drugs, alcohol, watching television, playing video games, etc. Think of your favorite ways of escape. Quite often, we make these choices without even thinking. We have habituated ourselves to the suffering.

It takes an effort to take ourselves out of the suffering. Developing good habits is the beginning. You may find when you begin, a struggle persists within you. Is this the higher choice or does it come from the part of you unwilling to face pain? Often this is the inner child. Like all children, they do well with discipline and soon learn this leads to joy. All children love joy. Depending on how much pain you experi-

ence within determines how much struggle you will face with this discipline.

Lyn describes an example of how she assisted a client to overcome her suffering. *Julie, a lawyer, faced depression and extreme codependence her whole life causing her to stay in a loveless marriage, pay all the bills, receive verbal abuse, and take prescription drugs, for many years. This took its toll on all aspects of her life, including intimacy with family and friends. She found herself unable to say no, so people constantly used her as she sought love and approval. She escaped into prescription drugs to put her to sleep and antidepressant drugs just to make it through the day. She did nothing that nourished herself. Her husband kept hold of her emotionally; after all, she paid the bills, allowing him to have his own life. Unable to discern between her adult self and her child self made her easy prey for an abuser. She often considered suicide.*

Finally, Julie found a friend that introduced her to me. At first, she refused to make the changes I advised, beginning with time away from her husband and establishing her own sense of self. Eventually she did leave her husband and her friend advised her to go to Oneness University in India and attend the 21-day intensive. This experience gave her time away in an atmosphere of love. This love gave her a foothold to begin to face what she had been avoiding her whole life.

One day when she had been in tears for several days, she called me. I helped her face her fear and enter it. As she entered, the fear dissolved. When this occurred, in her head also dissolved and she had more clarity for her work. She could not believe this life-long agony had changed so quickly. She still experienced bouts of sadness, but they no longer overwhelmed her into thoughts of suicide. She began to laugh and make new choices for her life. This took great courage on Julie's part all along the way.

Through this courage she allowed hope to enter her life. She described the difference as feeling "life" for the first time.

The following two stories illustrate examples of suffering and the intervention of Divine Grace.

JOANNA: SUFFERING and DIVINE GRACE

Kidnapping for profit has become a growth industry in some Latin American countries. A national sense of insecurity reigns. A wide gap between the rich and poor contributes to the suffering. Only about five percent of the criminals ever end up in court and the press only reports accounts of wealthy victims.

In one country in 2006, people reported 10,000 dial-a-kidnapping scams. Highly-organized kidnaper's observe their intended victim's office routines and routes to and from work.

The following describes Joanna's experience living in South America. As a CEO of a major soft drink company, one of her employees, set her up to be kidnapped for a large ransom.

One night as Joanna left her company in a car with her driver two cars cut them off at an overpass. Armed men forced Joanna and her driver out of their car and commanded Joanna lie down in the back seat of one of the drug dealer's cars with a black cloth thrown over her. They arrived at a small brick house and hustled Joanna and her driver into a room with a bare bulb dangling from the ceiling. A mattress on the floor and a bed filled the room.

On the eighth day of her kidnapping, nothing had been resolved between the kidnappers and   Joanna's company.

Joanna in spite of a lack of religious upbringing silently cried, pleaded, and screamed within for help from God. Why do we only scream for God in life-threatening situations?

Then Joanna heard a Voice inside her left ear. *Don't worry. We will get you out.*

In a sarcastic voice Joanna replied to the disembodied voice. *Sure. How?*

The Voice said, *We will send you an illness.*

Yeah, right. Any little cold and they will let me go.

Trust, said the Voice.

Wait a minute. No permanent damage please.

Just trust.

Within thirty seconds, Joanna experienced something strange in her body, weakness and tingling.

Daily her condition worsened as the right side of her body developed partial paralysis.

Five days went by. Then the exchange for two of her directors to take her place allowed Joanna to be released. Maybe the kidnapper's considered *Dead merchandise to be worthless.*

Joanna had had a series of mini strokes. In times of stress, blood vessels can close off, so no hemorrhaging occurred. In Joanna's case the blood vessels did not rupture, so after two weeks of physical therapy, she recovered fully.

Divine Grace/miracles do occur. We can attribute this Divine intervention to the work of God, angels, or a Higher Power. The event occurred. The mystery remains.

In the deepest night of suffering
You are granted entry . . .
Yes,
The Invisible
Will see you through.
Alison Stormwolf

SHIVANI: DIVINE GRACE

The following relates Shivani, an artist and healer's, experience of grace.

Later at a New York hospital a nun said, "Trust,
He's in Mary's hands My son lay on the ground, un-
moving. Someone had pulled him out of the water. I
had told my son Luke, age five, that morning to stay
away from the waterfall. Later, I heard his voice in
my heart calling me. I rushed through the woods to
the waterfall now."

My son lay in a hospital bed linked to life sup-
port.

I went outside and lay upon the grass. Although
non-Catholic, I felt the grace of Mary. Calm spread
all over me from a place of silence. I prayed for Luke
to stay, yet on another level, I sensed the futility of
this act. God had a bigger plan.

That night I slept at the hospital and dreamt of
playing in the playground with my son.

The next morning, with no support from family members, who focused on heaping blame upon me, I made the heart-wrenching decision to turn the life support off. My brain-dead son's heart stopped even before the machine shut down.

I went up on a roof to face the storm and rain that had continued from the time of Luke's drowning. I spread eagled my arms and gave all to the Grace of God.

Again I heard Luke speaking inside my heart, "Mommy now you can go study with Bhagavan – my spiritual teacher in India." At that moment the clouds opened and the sun emerged as if giving me permission to live.

My teacher Bhagavan said, "Death is an illusion. Look inside your heart you will feel him there. Society teaches us some things are good and others are bad, but I teach you all things are a gift from God."

Some weeks later, an Edgar Cayce psychic told me, "Your son came to give you love. When his mission finished, he left."

Luke gave me the grace of his life. Luke gave me grace by his death.

Alice Bailey, a spiritual writer and teacher in *The Destiny of Nations,* describes the lesson of surrender, which can be learned through our children. *Through pain and suffering . . . their love enters into a newer, a higher, and truer phase. They rise above the personal and find again . . . after feeling loss and suffering – those who they loved as souls . . . it is through their children that the lesson is learnt . . . did they but know and see aright, they would realize that to hold, one must detach, and to keep, one must release. Such is the law.*

I believe, through personal experience, we have a choice of lifting ourselves out of the mud of unhappiness and physical and emotional suffering. We can begin placing our feet upon the steps of an inner stairway to the Light of Grace. Have you ever experienced Light when you close your eyes in meditation? Imagine each step upward choosing the inner Light over remaining stuck in unhappiness.

Choices include turning inside through meditation and prayer to connect with the intuition of our spiritual Higher Self. These choices also include the gentle releasing of past disappointments, sorrow, and unconscious emotional pain through the intervention of physical hands-on healing and other methods of healing. We can begin searching for and eventually discovering our unique creative gifts. These gifts can be used in work we love doing in the fulfillment of our life purpose.

The above choices take us on our personal journey up the inner stairway of Light to grace. Along the journey we experience challenges which, when over-come, develop greater spiritual Light within us. Teachers and friends help, just as we too have oppor-tunities to uplift others.

Our journey leads us on a progressive alignment of a physical, emotional, mental, and spiritual nature. This alleviates aspects of our suffering.

Grace raises all of our individual expressions and experience up through all levels of consciousness to the Divine Source. Numerous pathways exist through suffering to remembering and finally to grace. Grace awakens all of us, as humanity, to the truth of our real nature of wisdom and compassion.

EL MORYA: MASTER of WISDOM

The Path of Grace allows people to learn the path of service to come out of selfishness, which occurs grad-ually. The path of service is the same as the path of Grace.

El Morya

El Morya explains in greater detail the path from suffering into grace with a further explanation of Di-vine Grace and also the connection of synchronicity with grace.

Suffering, as a gift, allows humanity to break through patterns out of the personality self to truth, which is Grace. People tend to avoid suffering, which only creates more suffering. The smallest suffering can bring awakening if we choose to allow the awakening.

Grace surrounds us all the time as a part of creation and love. Yet grace tends to be unrecognized when we stay caught in suffering. We can choose to bring the suffering in our bodies into the Body of Grace. We can choose to awaken the love in our bodies. Then our whole body becomes grace walking on Earth. Then we grace everything and everyone we touch.

How do we awaken love in our bodies? When we encounter physical or emotional pain, we withdraw. We say or think; "I hurt and want to avoid the hurt." What if we could love the pain by embracing it like a baby in our arms? What if we could just be present with the sensation in our bodies without wanting to stop it, fix it in some way, or figure out the reasons for it? What if we could just love our pain? Then it would have an opportunity to transform.

Loving our pain presents a major challenge. I have learned to do this with coaching from an energetic healer. I have felt the tension; heaviness, tightness, and congestion in my physical body as well as emotions such as grief well up inside me. Yet when I contained the sensations like cupping water in my hands rather than letting them spill out, the sensations lessened and relief followed.

Our greatest enemy to learning to transform pain and suffering lies with our minds. El Morya has this to say about the mind: *Our minds have no control over grace so they block it by examining, for our minds have their basis in fear. Grace dissolves fear. Our challenge lies in receiving the grace. Our lower personality mind thinks it understands grace, yet fear allows suffering to inhabit our bodies. Therefore, we cycle from suffering to fear back to suffering.*

Grace exists in the higher invisible worlds all around us. As all parts of us awaken the invisible world becomes visible. Then we can see grace all around us. Our hearts will know grace.

Divine Grace can be defined as benevolence, giving, and love. Divine Grace manifests as God's everflowing loving kindness and compassion by which souls awaken to their true divine nature. Yet, to many of us, this grace remains invisible until we mature to a certain level spiritually and discover the grace *all around us* as El Morya said. Then we see all of God's actions as grace, whether pleasant or otherwise.

Bhagavan, founder of Oneness University, describes the importance of our level of perception to be able to recognize grace. *Realize that anything you experience in this life is by God's grace. Supposing you slip while walking, try to realize that as God's Grace too. If you see God in everything, your life will become wonderful.*

The Divine Grace dictionary comments how Divine Graces enters our lives without any effort on our parts. *For him – the mature soul, his very love of God, the power to meditate or worship, and the spiritual urge which drives his life are entirely and obviously God's grace, a divine endowment, an intercession, unrelated to any deed or action he did or could perform.*

Finally, Siddha Yoga talks of grace as *the infinite power of divine love that creates, maintains, and pervades the universe. When awakened within a seeker by a Siddha Guru, this power leads the seeker to Self-realization.* A Siddha Guru has attained enlightenment wherein his body has filled with light and he can pass on a blessing of Divine Grace through a spiritual initiation – shaktipat or as it is called at the Oneness University, an Oneness Blessing.

Now let us look at the relationship between synchronicity and grace. Carl Jung, a Swiss psychiatrist, described synchronicity in psychological terms as an experience of two or more unrelated events occurring in a meaningful way.

El Morya says, *Synchronicity has many components of which the psychological remains only as a small part. Synchronicity like grace exists all around us. The more we understand synchronicity the more it occurs. Everything around us is the coming togeth-er of a moment – synchronicity. Move from one mo-ment to the next. Grace occurs in every moment like walking through a waterfall, constant drops falling upon us. In those moments, we have the ability to dissolve suffering through grace. We have only un-derstood synchronicity through the mind. Do we un-derstand this moment from the mind or the heart? From the heart, it is synchronicity. Do ideas bubble up from the heart into the mind? This dissolves the suffering of the mind, which tends to grasp. Syn-chronicity becomes lost in the grasping. The heart only feels the beauty of every moment. Our hearts teach our minds how to be.*

Finally, do we believe what we describe as mira-cles as another way to show us the power of grace manifesting without any effort? Author Katherine Anne Porter says, *Miracles are instantaneous, they cannot be summoned, but come of themselves, usual-ly at unlikely moments and to those who least expect them.*

Can you think of some experiences of grace, syn-chronicity, or miracles in your life?

CHAPTER 2

WE CAN HEAL OURSELVES

DO YOU BELIEVE THERE'S SOMETHING WRONG WITH YOU?

T he most important choice in lifting me out of my misery occurred at age fourteen. A visiting vocational counselor spoke in our grade ten classes. He sparked the question, what did I want to do with my life?

In looking back upon a quest to better myself emotionally, mentally, and spiritually spanning over forty years, I now realize how each challenge strengthened and prepared me for my next step in self-growth.

Friends pointed me in the right direction. I also felt powerful intuitive urges to make certain critical choices. Now, in retrospect, I realize this came from my Higher Self. Later as a hands-on healer and teacher, I became aware of more spiritual light flowing through me after mastering particular challenges.

If I had stayed in the small farm community in Alberta, Canada, where I grew up, I may never have gotten out of my cycle of suffering. Boys tended to work and eventually take over the family farm or business. Life involved laboring on a small dairy and grain farm of eight hundred acres. We had no electricity during the first few years on the farm, water came from a well, and we read by kerosene lamps. We used an outside toilet. In the wintertime, I used to brush the heaped-up snow off the seat. My wife who grew up in the city in an upper-class neighborhood sees my boyhood as hardship.

My life for twelve years consisted of a constant routine of going to school, milking cows, weeding gardens, tending and cleaning up after animals, and in the late summer, harvesting hay and grain. I abhorred the never-ending cycle of tedious work, which I endured with reluctance and suffered in silence.

I felt like a victim without any power to complain. The thought never occurred to me that I could complain, be defiant, or refuse to do the chores. My strong connection to nature, however, allowed me to enjoy the clear blue skies, fresh country air, clusters of green maple trees, and flowing pale yellow grass in the pastures.

My mother, a small woman, toiled on the farm and raised five children without any emotional support and sometimes little physical help. She had been brought up on a farm and served as a surrogate mother while very young when her mother and older sister abandoned the family. I honor my mother for the emotional stability she provided the family. If she had chosen to drink like my father, all of our lives would have been much different and filled with a lot more suffering.

With toxic shame there's something wrong with you and there's nothing you can do about it; you are in-adequate and defective. Toxic shame is the core of the wounded child.

John Bradshaw, *Healing the Shame That Binds You*

Unlike my mother, my father spent the majority of his time in town drinking at the local beer parlor. In Alberta in the 1950's beer parlors had small tables loaded with glasses of beer and mostly men would sit around them and drink as much as possible. When on the farm my father had an inexhaustible supply of rye whiskey stashed away in our two-story barn. To my knowledge, my father seldom went a day without being drunk, sometimes staggering drunk. I remember feeling so ashamed one day as my father staggered up from the barn through a gate toward the house and collapsed on the ground in a heap.

Every man carries a deep longing for his father and his tribal Fathers.

James Hollis, Jungian psychotherapist

Even when physically present, my father always seemed emotionally absent. Except for giving instructions for work, he never engaged in conversation. I yearned for him to see me, to talk to me, and to explain how to run machinery and share the skills of working a farm. Later in life, I imagined that other farm fathers had spent time with their sons and taught them. Deep within I still thirst, like a boy without water wandering the desert, for my father's contact. My father paid attention to me only one time; the day I give the valedictory speech for my high school graduation.

In my deep longing for contact with my father, I used to sit outside the farmhouse on the summer grass. Staring in expectation across a sixteen-acre field at the brown ribbon of road in the distance, I waited for him to return from town. He never returned until late at night after I had gone to bed.

I never knew some fathers tell their sons they love them and appreciate their accomplishments. I believe my father felt threatened by me from certain events I experienced. For example, I spent, during the end of Grade 12, most of my time at night studying for finals. One night my father commented to my mother as we sat at the kitchen table, *That boy will go crazy studying so much.*

He treated me as if I were invisible. It hurt yet I ignored the comment and continued my regime of study. Rather than complimenting me, my father chose to criticize my efforts. He had only finished grade three.

Another time when I came from living in Hawaii for nine months, with $4000 in savings and a desire to share my experiences, my father refused to sit down with me. He'd never traveled. Rejected, I shared my Hawaii adventure with a visiting uncle.

The greatest burden a child must bear is the unlived life of the parent. So each man must examine, without the motive to judge, where his father's wounds were passed on to him. Either he finds himself repeating his father's patterns or living in reaction to them - in both cases a prisoner.

James Hollis, *Under Saturn's Shadow*

Because of lack of skills in communicating, I socially and emotionally withdrew. I locked all feelings of shame and inferiority about my father as a drunk within myself. I loaded myself with toxic shame and took on my father's pain as my own. As Hollis says, I lived in reaction to my father's drinking by at first resisting, then falling into a pattern of drinking during college, and then stopping by choice.

Codependence is a very vicious and powerful form of Delayed Stress Syndrome. The trauma of feeling like we were not safe in our own homes makes it very difficult to feel like we are safe anywhere. Feeling like we were not lovable to our own parents makes it very difficult to believe that anyone can love us.

Robert Burney, codependence counselor and therapist.

I felt unsafe with my father's unpredictable behavior and anger. About five feet ten inches tall, well-muscled, with rugged features like the Marlboro man, his drunken anger shook my tranquility. Calmness, unlike true inner peace, resulted from intervals when my mother refrained from fighting with my father about his drinking.

The family atmosphere could change in an instant from depressed silence, which everyone in the family lived in as a false cocoon of safety, to an all-out vicious verbal combat between my parents. Adrift in a sea of uncertainty, I kept myself out of the line of attack. I learned to become invisible without a voice. For years after, I believed I had nothing to say.

My mother, like me, tended to be shy and quiet and valued inner peace. It never occurred to me to talk to her about my unhappiness and fears. In later years she told me, *I thought you were okay because your never said anything.* She also said, *I saw on your face sometimes that something bothered you and I remained uncertain how to talk to you.* Neither of us knew how to communicate our feelings.

As a state of being, shame takes over one's whole identity. To have shame as an identity is to believe that one's being is flawed, that one is defective as a human being. John Bradshaw

Feeling separate and alone in the world, I wallowed in a pit of unhappiness and worthlessness known only to me. So at fourteen, besides secretly choosing a career, I also made a silent pact with myself. I would somehow leave the miserable family situation as soon as possible. At sixteen, I realized going to university after high school graduation would be my escape ticket.

Every day, I dreamed about breaking loose.

The key to success is to just want it bad enough. If you want it bad enough, you'll figure out a way to get it. All other factors are irrelevant. Upbringing, IQ, genetics, environment, and possessions - all don't matter. It comes down to drive. If you have the fire, then you'll get what you want guaranteed.
Brian Buchner, Video Game Programmer

To attend university required a minimum grade average for admission. In grade twelve, I picked the smartest student, Stuart, as my role model. My secret goal: to attain grades as high as Stuart. School never came easy for me. Unlike Stuart, I studied every night. Our IQ scores indicated a thirty-point difference, which added to my feelings of inferiority and motivated me to work harder.

At Easter, the high school principal revealed to Stuart and me, in his office, that we both had the same grade average. A warmth of accomplishment swept through me. Then to my utter amazement, the principal announced I would be the valedictorian at graduation! This meant giving the valedictory speech at a special dinner.

Walking outside on the farm in the clear May air, spontaneous creative ideas began pouring into my head. The flood of inspiration uplifted me in joy as if I floated on air. Writing down ideas, I began memorizing them, unaware that the valedictorians before me had read their speeches.

The Higher Self is the voice of the Soul. Creating a best friend relationship with your Higher Self can provide immediate and insightful help for the challenges of everyday living.

Susan Lupton, author

Finally, the evening for the delivery of my speech arrived. In the white-walled banquet hall, all the tables stood arranged in one rectangular formation. The school superintendent sat on my right. Directly opposite and beside me were seated some of the most influential people in the community. Queasiness fluttered in my stomach. Even though I sat, my legs trembled. My throat clogged. My body shook as I stood up. Opening my mouth by an act of will, I began talking. In a brief second, the banquet room and all the staring faces vanished. Before finishing the last few sentences of the speech, I came back into consciousness. Fear had taken me beyond the conscious mind into a special place, which allowed my Higher

Self, unknown to me at the time, to speak. My Higher Self, an aspect of my soul, revealed a different side from the shy, emotionally withdrawn, and inexpressive teenager.

After graduation, only Stuart and I left to attend university. Leaving my sleepy town of eight hundred people to move to Edmonton, the capital city of Alberta with half a million people became the next significant event in my inner transformation. University life and a thronging city would be a complex, exciting maze of experience, maturity, and learning for me over the next few years.

I thank my father as a pivotal person in my life for presenting with me the challenge to develop greater compassion, which has taken most of my life to achieve. He probably remained unconscious of the reasons for his suffering. I know he had no idea how to heal himself. I appreciate the knowledge and opportunities to heal much of the pain, conscious and unconscious, in my own life.

SHANNON NELSON: A QUADRIPLEGIC: LEARN to LIVE WITH YOUR PAIN

Shannon tells her story. "Your daughter will never walk again." When my mother heard those words from the neurologist at Maine Medical Center, she fainted. Nothing could have prepared her. She still mourned the death of her beloved husband, Bob, who had died two months earlier after a long battle with colon cancer. I broke my neck in the summer of 1995 in a swimming pool accident. When I regained consciousness, I found I would never walk again.

Elisabeth Kubler-Ross, author of On Death and Dying, describes the five stages of grief when we face a terminal illness or experience a major life change. We can experience these stages in order, out of order, a few of them, or all of them.

The Stages:

Denial - *This isn't happening*

Anger - *Why me? It's not fair.*

Bargaining – *Give me just a little more time.*

Depression - *Why bother with anything?*

Acceptance - *It's going to be Okay.*

Shannon continues. *I went through the typical stages of grief after such a life-changing event, at first denial, then anger - mostly with myself, and finally depression and resignation to my new life as a quadriplegic.*

The neck supports the head. It connects the head, symbolic of the Spiritual plane, to the body, symbolic of the Material Plane. Therefore, it represents the need for balance between the two.

Michael Schwartz, author, Health & Disease/Symbology Handbook

Shannon continues. *I know for sure I lacked balance in a big way at the time of my accident. I experienced confusion about some decisions I had made and sadness about a relationship that had just ended.*

Before the accident, I experienced an identity crisis. I wanted a change in the course of my life. Unknown to me, I sent forth a desperate plea on an inner level. I never expected the change meant breaking my neck.

If I never had the accident, I would probably be married with children. I always wanted to be a mom. I still do. I would love to adopt or have foster children.

Emotionally distraught for some time after my accident, I went from an active twenty-four-year-old to a wheelchair-bound quadriplegic.

A quadriplegic normally loses sensation and movement in all four limbs and the trunk. This generally results from a spinal cord injury to the neck. The loss of sensation and movement, however, may be incomplete with some sensation and movement being retained in parts of the arms and legs.

Shannon continues. *After coming to terms with my accident, I had a few years of relatively good health with no complications typical of people in my condition. Then I began experiencing severe health problems in late 1999. Chronic pain and depression became my constant companions for about six years. Throughout these years doctors prescribed many different pain medications and anti-depressants with side effects horrible beyond words. Barely able to function, I felt constant dizziness, tiredness, and nausea.*

I also developed recurrent bladder infections and severe lower-back pain. Tired of my constant visits to the emergency room, and following my doctor's advice, I had bladder surgery in 2001.

I would love to say that ended my health problems, except nothing could be further from the truth. The infections stopped, yet the pain persisted, including severe back pain, to where within months I could no longer get up in my wheelchair. I became completely bedridden and suffered deep depression.

My body, unable to handle pain like a regular person, goes into a state of dysreflexia – an autonomic reflex with spinal cord injury at T6 - mid back - and above. My blood pressure goes sky high, my head feels like it's going to explode, and my heart threatens to jump out of my chest.

I had been prescribed pain medication after pain medication, even Botox injections to paralyze my back muscles that shot off pain. Nothing worked.

My doctor, a spinal cord specialist, finally said, "Nothing more can be done. Learn to live with your pain."

Talk about a life sentence! With this final blow, emotionally and physically exhausted, I gave up all hope.

Before her life sentence, Shannon had kept putting faith in the next magic pill, and the next one, and the next one. Have you done this too? With the final blow from her doctor, she dipped back into another stage of Elisabeth Kubler Ross's stage of grief, depression/apathy, *It's hopeless; Why bother?*

In my experience if we want, we can heal ourselves. See Shannon's continuing journey of healing in chapter 14.

In the next chapter, Joanna, a retired CEO of a major soft drink company, talks about repression of memories of abuse, depression, and the saving grace of a good psychiatrist.

CHAPTER 3

WE CAN HEAL OUR PHYSICAL and EMOTIONAL ABUSE

JOANNA: SEXUAL ABUSE

*A*s a child I suppressed memories of sexual abuse. This abuse delivered upon me by my father occurred from the age of three to nine. The abuse stopped at nine because, diagnosed with TB, my father lay critically ill in a hospital for thirteen months.

Dominating and controlling, he lost his temper often. He heaped verbal abuse upon my brother and me by calling us stupid, lazy, and sitting on our fannies. My mother's life focused around serving my father.

I continued into adulthood lacking confidence. Any new situation created immense fear. When I wanted to express anger, my throat seized up and I began to cry. My father never allowed me permission to speak up in the family. In high school, college, and married life, insecure and lacking self-esteem, I sought men to fulfill the role of father.

At twenty-four with a three-year old son, I re-married. I sank into a deep depression and wanted to end my life. Why did I feel so depressed? I remained ignorant of the sexual abuse.

After two months of depression, I swallowed a bottle of anti-depressants. While in intensive care I met a good psychiatrist. I call this a saving grace. After leaving Intensive Care, I received a referral to another psychiatrist.

A floodgate of bottled-up emotions and memories broke through my depression. I spent three months crying in therapy. After three years in therapy, I moved from the U.S. back to South America.

In South America, I remarried for the third time after divorcing an alcoholic. I had a lot to heal and yet I continued in my dysfunctional patterns. I sought psychiatric help for another three years.

In my experience psychotherapy, which consists of mostly talking, does have some value. It, however, deals mostly with the mind and seldom addresses the core emotional issues which need healing.

After my last psychiatrist, at the age of forty, I began to explore alternative therapies and energy healing. In one such session, lying on the therapist's couch, I suddenly looked at the therapist's face. I froze in terror. My father's face superimposed itself over the face of the therapist. I curled up into a ball in *a fetal position. When the therapist brought me back I stumbled out of the office.*

My husband took one look at me and said, "What happened?"

"Something happened between me as a child and my father," I said.

Psychiatrists and psychologists can assist us in mental and emotional crises. We can become aware of unhealthy patterns, yet, regardless of the skill of the therapist, the therapy ball remains in our hands to make the changes to improve our lives.

Joseph Wardy writes on the value of psychotherapy, If the therapy is effective, the patient is looking in the mirror and seeing the scars in his soul. He is hurting from the inquiry and what it might mean with the great possibility to heal from the experiences.

Rob Bryant, a spiritual counselor, also expresses an important point to consider, I believe that ultimately we have all of the answers we seek, inside. A good therapist will successfully bring those answers out of us.

Julianne, a therapist, like Joanna describes years of suffering from repressed memories of sexual trauma.

JULIANNE: MOLESTATION

A dry drunk, a non-alcoholic drunk intoxicated with his own abstinence.

Dr. Curtis T. Prout

I grew up in an alcoholic family. My father, as the result of being a dry drunk, held the family hostage with depression and a bad temper. My dad gave me affection yet, at the same time scared me with his anger which he took out on my older brother, the hero of the family. Fearful and shy, I kept a low profile.

My twenty-two year old uncle molested me at the age of two. This trauma stay buried in my memory until my 40's. I became frightened of people and stopped smiling at two and a half years when my dad's friends laughed at me for smiling.

I also suffered molestation from my older brother and at the age of 16 I passed out from drinking and again became the victim of sexual abuse.

In India at the age of 42 while practicing Siddha Yoga at the ashram of Gurumayi, I woke up from a dream in terror. I only remember hiding in a closet and recognized something bad had happened at a young age. The terror burned in my body like electricity.

Siddha Yoga, which Julianne practiced as a spiritual path since the age of 27, involves mastering the mind. Gurumayi's guru, Swami Muktananda who founded Siddha Yoga said, Meditate on your own Self. Worship your Self. Respect your Self. God dwells within you as you.

Grace surrounds us all the time. It's connected with innocence. Grace enters when I am innocent, said Julianne.

Cecilia, an ordained minister and energy healing practitioner, now describes her journey out of suffering through dance, art and design, and spiritual hands-on healing.

CECILIA: EMOTIONAL ANOREXIA

My mother liked to tell of my arrival into this world. When the nurse brought me in to meet her, she stared in amazement as I slept with one hand extended up into the air. This always remained a mystery to her how a child could sleep with a hand extended. I understood this mystery many years later.

It is necessary to own and honor the child we were in order to love the person we are. And the only way to do that is to own that child's experiences honor, that child's feelings, and release the emotional grief energy that we are still carrying around.

Robert Burney, counselor and therapist.

Cecilia continues. *My mother grieved for my absent father and as a four-year-old sensitive and empathic child, I refused to eat, developed an eating disorder, and allergies. My mother at that time, with three children, also suffered great financial stress. To help with expenses she rented out a room to two young women*

The meals of canned vegetables and hastily overcooked meat after Mother returned from work tasted most unappetizing. I gagged on canned spinach and could not chew the hard meat. Looking back I realize my mother did the best she knew for me.

In desperation my mother attempted to force feed me tonic and employed the help of the young women she rented to. Now I understand she feared losing me as she had lost another child six years before my birth. In retrospect, I realize I showed symptoms of anorexia before it became known.

I believe Cecilia become codependent by taking on her mother's feelings and possibly her emptiness in a desire for connection and love, thus her anorexia.

Codependency is a condition which sets us up to be starved for emotional nurturing - to be emotionally anorexic . . . Codependence allows us to survive physically but causes us to feel empty and dead inside.
Robert Burney.

Cecilia continues. *My mother took me to the doctor for a checkup and advice. He recommended I be given physical activity to stimulate my appetite. By this time, at five years of age, my mother enrolled me in dance classes. By coincidence, my father returned from the Armed Services and I began to thrive and enjoy free expression in dancing. Talented, I advanced rapidly. At eight years old, I received point shoes and began a life as a ballerina. I had been a quiet and introverted child up until this time. Given the license to be sensual and expressive, I became engrossed with dance as an answer out of my suffering.*

Still verbally restrained, dance allowed physical freedom of movement and as I excelled dance also brought recognition of my talents through advancement.

I heard of a Russian ballet teacher who had recently come to Kansas City to start a ballet company. I begged my mother to let me change dance schools. After much pleading, she relented and the lessons, however, became limited to once a week as my mother could afford no more.

The dance activities accelerated and my first professional dance experience occurred at age 16 when I danced the solo in the opera "Carmen." My Russian ballet teacher, Tania Dokoudavska found me a work-study at the Conservatory of Music to pay for my increasing dance classes and encouraged me to pursue a career as a professional dancer.

The dancing gave me a vehicle to express myself as well as to travel. At the age of 18 years I moved to

New York City to pursue a career in dance. I followed this career until the age of 30 when I decided to start a family.

Believing my husband had all the qualities I lacked, I now recognize the codependency in my marriage. He exhibited a clever quicksilver tongue while I had little confidence in my own verbal abilities. He said my astrological characteristics, Sagittarius Sun and Mercury, showed my verbal affliction.

Together for three years of courtship and five years of marriage, my husband demonstrated his unfaithfulness many times.

In the sixties, the years of free-love, many partners had other sexual relationships; however, it eventually broke our marriage. In a bizarre drama my husband began an open affair with a neighbor. His lover attacked me physically. Like a soap box drama, my husband flaunted his 21-year-old lover for all to see.

I had been educated as a Catholic, believing marriage endured for better or worse. Thirty years old, bereft of any self-esteem and with my once-perfect athletic dancer's body large and pregnant, I broke and exited the marriage including all illusions.

I studied art and design and became interested in motion picture work. Like the dancing, art became a meditation and release for stress and fear. When I

*became involved with art I would be completely en-
thralled and could forget myself in the creative process as in meditation. Again I gained recognition, acceptance and advancement socially through my art
and dance. My self-esteem improved and I coped
with the critics. I then channeled this talent into lu-
crative work in the Hollywood movie industry for
many years as an art director and set decorator.*

Osho – an East Indian spiritual teacher - has used
dance as a meditation because he says that dance is
the only activity in which the ego can disappear easily,
says Amrit Sadhana. Dance until only the dance remains without any dancer. Allow the dance to flow as
we play with our life energy. We merge until we become both the dancer and the dancing.

Cecilia continues. *With my advancement in the
industry came stress due to the accountability of
budgets and handling employees. A fellow worker
introduced me to spiritual hands-on healing to relieve stress. These spiritual energy treatments revealed scenes of the traumatic events of my childhood. The most vivid scene revealed being force-fed
tonic by my mother while held down by the young
women who rented a room in our house during
World War II. I forgave my mother, knowing she only wanted to help me in her own primitive way.*

*Famous healer Dean Kraft reports that Energy Heal-
ing activates the mind/body connection and can un-
block and balance the patients natural energy fields*

in order to jumpstart the individual's own healing system.

Bob Kish.

Cecilia continues. *I found the work so astounding I became inspired to learn healing methods myself. Thus, I began the journey of a Spiritual Healer. I began to learn the hands-on energy methods of healing such as La-Ho Chi from the healing facilitator who had treated me, Michael David Lawrience.*

Along the way, I asked Spirit to show me my work and words. I continue in amazement by the revelations imparted to me through Spirit. In meditation I would ask Spirit to reveal the words and the work I should use. Shortly after, healing modalities and teachers would appear. I studied with a channeling coach, attended channeling groups, and worked with many other teachers. Finally, I came upon Science of Mind at the Agape Center for Truth and began studies.

During the practice of spiritual energy work I realized Spirit had guided me all my life holding my hand even as an infant as I entered this world and in all the stages of my life.

Have you recognized the working of Spirit or Grace in your life?

In the next chapter abuse survivor, Jacqueline, explains the events that led her to believe she deserved being a victim. How many of us get caught up in the cycle of victim without seeing any way out?

CHAPTER 4

WE CAN FREE OURSELVES FROM ABUSE

JACQUELINE: VICTIM to VICTORIOUS: A SURVIVOR'S STORY

Much of my life has been governed by the unconscious belief that I deserve to be a victim.

Jacqueline Stone, author of *Awakening Consciousness*, and spiritual coach
http://recoveringfromabuse.blogspot.com

A t thirteen, my boyfriend and six of his friends molested me. Until that moment I had been an innocent, a trusting person. In shock, once released, I wandered across a freeway; please let a truck hit me, let it all be over.

Back home my mother shouted, "Look at those grass stains on your clothes."

When I told her what happened she said, "You dress like a slut; you act like a slut. You deserved it." *Nothing could have been farther from the truth for I had no desire for sex. Being shy, my inhibitions prevented me from flirting, even if my life depended upon it.*

After my mother's comment, I believed in my state of shame and self-loathing of victim consciousness, I deserved being molested. I took a shower, went to the basement, lay on the cold cement floor, and listened to Tchaikovsky. Unrelenting tears streamed down my cheeks. Inside, my soul screamed. I lay still, my body numb.

I imagined my mother's footsteps on the stair, as she came to soothe me. I needed her acknowledgement of my pain and assurance of caring. She never, however, left my father's side in front of the television upstairs.

Heyward Ewart, a psychologist, who devoted 20 years treating victims of child abuse, wrote in his book, *The Lies That Bind: The Permanence of Child Abuse, Such an event begins to mangle the personality so that the victim believes that it is his or her fault . . . . The original abuse will lead to further abuse, because of the attraction of predators. Predators, by their nature, attack wounded individuals.*

Jacqueline continues. *I got the message loud and clear: I am a bad person. I deserve to be treated badly. I had done something wrong. I gave those boys a reason to do what they did. It was my fault.*

After the molestation, I swore I would never let a man hurt me again. How could women stay with men who beat them? I certainly would never tolerate it or so I thought.

How could I ever fully trust anyone again? No one would comfort, defend, or help me.

I stopped expecting love and started being what others wanted me to be so they wouldn't be mean to me. Realistically how could I expect love? Good treatment and acceptance had to be earned. I understand now everyone wants love, yet, we may remain unaware of how to love.

As a former victim of domestic and sexual violence, Jacqueline commits herself to assisting others to recover from mental and emotional abuse. In a future chapter, Jacqueline continues her story of her journey out of codependency and victimhood into freedom and empowerment.

Like Jacqueline, another victim of abuse, Viola travelled the path from abuse into empowerment.

VIOLA BERGERON: ABUSE to EMPOWERMENT

In the 1980s it became clear to psychiatrists that victims and survivors of domestic abuse suffered from the same post-traumatic stress symptoms as

shell-shocked veterans of Vietnam and other wars,
says Wynona Ward – *Have Justice Will Travel.*

*Look deep inside yourself and light the lamp in your
soul and let it lead you. Learn to listen to your inner
voice, it never lies.*

Viola Bergeron, Paralegal Administrator

*I met my husband at age twelve, married him at
nineteen, and started a family at twenty-five. At
twenty-six I had my second child and at twenty-eight
my third. At thirty-nine, I found myself a single
mother and a widow,* explains Viola.

*Before the age of 18, approximately one in four chil-
dren is exposed to family alcoholism or addiction, or
alcohol abuse.*

Alcohol Free Children

Viola continues. *My husband, an alcoholic,
crawled so far into his disease that his own children
never knew him sober. They witnessed scenes they
never should have. Many other families have had
similar experiences. I have chosen to learn and grow,
find peace, and an ability to love and forgive.*

*I had a marriage like many others for about five
years, then came the drinking and abuse, physical,
emotional, and mental. After the children came, it
became worse. I did my best to hide the abuse from*

the children all under five, yet it became more than I could handle.

I had nobody to turn to, nobody to talk to. I acted as if everything was okay in front of family and friends. I lived two different lives. Who was I? I felt lost and alone in this world with three children. I searched for a way out twenty-four hours a day.

Desperate, I came up with the idea of taking the lives of my children and myself. Now all day long I questioned, how? How could I take us all out at once? Maybe running a red light but then I pondered all the ways it could go wrong. What if I died and my children survived disabled?

What if we all survived and the other innocent person died? What would that do to their family? I passed on that idea. What about getting hit by a train? What about hitting a brick wall? You can see the wildness of my thoughts.

Victims feel worthless, dependent, fearful, anxious, stressed, burned out, left out, angry, jealous and betrayed. Victims, believing they have no choices, frequently use should, have to, must, supposed to. They expect to make mistakes, mistrust themselves and others, and believe they don't deserve.

Judith Joyce, Life Coach

Viola continues. *I felt worthless, belonging nowhere. I wanted out of my marriage, the abuse, and the* pain. *Yet it remained out of the question to leave my children with an alcoholic. I had to take them with me.*

I would see news clips on others killing their children and I could relate to what they felt. I saw myself in them. I understood the shock the world experienced. Yet I struggled to get through each day alive.

Our Guardian Angels will intervene when necessary to overcome unforeseen events that could jeopardize our soul's learning experiences. Our Guardian Angels have access to unlimited power to help us.

Mark Stallabrass, Intuitive Healer

Viola goes on. *Then the day happened. I know an unseen force of an angel or inner guide intervened. I drove down the street with all three children in the car. My daughter of four sat in front without a seat belt, my three year old son in the back seat, and my one year old in a car seat.*

I watched my daughter from the corner of my eye as I watched the two boys from the rear view mirror. I thought I saw the light turn green. As I put my foot on the gas pedal just enough to go forward, I slammed into the back of the car in front of me.

The boys suffered no injuries while my daughter shattered the windshield. Fear seized me for I saw what the impact had done to my windshield and imagined the worst for my daughter.

When the EMS came they put my tiny girl on a huge stretcher with a brace around her neck. I refused to have her go alone to the hospital so a police officer offered to take my boys home to their father. A wave of fear swept over me as I agreed. What would my husband do when the police came home with the boys? What would he say? Worried for my daughter as well, I experienced fear to the depth of my being.

Once at the hospital I waited for the doctors when 'he' came through the doors. "Look I began explaining. . . .

"Shut up," my husband yelled with a boozy breath.

I realized I would receive no support from him. I felt the fear in my bones again. To this day I remember five little words; I hope you learned your lesson.

Yes, I replied with no hesitation.

Angels, according to Terry Lyn Taylor – author & angel expert - *help us look for the opportunities in life, to turn in directions that are right for us to grow and expand . . . The angels move us, if we will listen, to follow the pulse of what is largely invisible, but still quite potent for our lives, to sense the inner impulse and follow its direction.*

Viola continues. *From that day forward my life changed. I look back and I know now the words of spirit came through him.*

> *Loving an alcoholic is not about taking care of them, but about taking care of you . . . . Setting boundaries for you is how to become healthy, mentally, emotionally, and spiritually . . . . All the boundaries I suggest are always detaching from the alcoholic in a loving way.*

Angie Lewis, author of three marriage books

Now I refused to allow my husband to have control over me. I refused to allow him to take my self-esteem away from me any longer. I refused to allow him to control how I felt about myself. I refused to allow him to take my soul and destroy it. I began to build my self-worth back again, comments Viola.

I made the joyous discovery that ten minutes of genuine belly laughter had an anesthetic effect and would give me at least two hours of pain-free sleep. Norman Cousins, *Anatomy of an Illness,* healed himself of arthritis by watching Marx Brothers films.

I sat up alone at night and watched comedy shows, laughing out loud, to teach myself how to laugh again, said Viola.

> *End your day by privately looking directly into your eyes in the mirror and saying, I love you!*

Mark Victor Hansen, co-author, *Chicken Soup of the Soul*

I stood in front of a mirror and stared at the person looking back. I started telling myself, I am worth something. I am loving, giving, and a wonderful person. I can do it alone. I will survive. I am a wonderful mother and my children will grow into wonderful adults, Viola reports.

The only thing we can do to change and to heal our self-worth is to change what's in our minds – the self-talk.

Carolyn Ball, *Claiming Your Self-Esteem*

Viola continues. *I had to convince the person looking back at me the truth of the statements. I did my own therapy because I had no one to assist me with the negative thoughts running wild inside my head. I had to believe within myself. I would have believed my own self-talk over whatever anyone else told me. I taught my daughter the same method after her father died. Guilt filled her over the last words she had spoken to her father. I told her to sit in front of a mirror and talk to the person looking back.*

Over time the person looking back at me in the mirror talked to me in my quiet moments. Then I knew I had beaten the personality ego.

I decided to get my life in order to prepare living on my own. I started planning my divorce.

It took me almost ten years as I kept pushing forward, getting stronger within myself. I first went back to school and got my degree. I would work midnights and then come home in the morning to get my children to school. To avoid my husband, I went to school during the day and when he came home, after putting the children in bed, I went to work. This way I suffered less abuse at my husband's hands.

I made preparations for my new life. I started getting credit in my name with my first car. I opened my own savings/checking account as well as a savings at my work with automatic withdrawals from my check into stocks and savings.

During these preparations, my children and I still walked on eggshells every day.

Even thought my children knew, I continued hiding the issue of abuse from them. Then one day my daughter asked, "Why don't you divorce Father?"

I got the wake-up call. I looked into legal help from my work insurance. I saw a lawyer and filed the paperwork. Yet before the lawyer filed the papers with the court, I needed a place to live with my children. I searched apartments, rentals, everywhere. I searched every day.

Then on the day before Thanksgiving in 1999 I suffered the last of my husband's drunken abuse. The drama had developed in full swing when my children arrived home so they waited outside. My son had come in twice to pull his father off me, my daughter came in once. When I finally struggled outside, dazed and bloody, my daughter ran to a neighbor who called the police.

I know without the intervention of the police, I would probably be dead. My husband had gotten the shotgun and searched for the bullets, which I had hid.

The police took my husband away and prevented him from coming back for several weeks. For the first time in all the years of abuse, the police had been called.

Taking this opportunity as a way out, the next day I had the lawyer serve the divorce papers at my husband's sister's house.

I exchanged everything I had, all my stocks and savings, for a one-bedroom apartment for my children and myself.

Determined to take my life back, the fear evaporated. I needed only to pick up the pieces of my life and put them into order. The divorce finalized in August 1998.

I had controlled my husband's drinking, when we lived together, by finding the alcohol and pouring it out. Then he went out and bought more.

Five months after leaving my husband, he lay in a coma from drinking, his organs shutting down one at a time. He came out of the coma for six months before arriving back in the hospital again.

On December 16, 1999 his family took him off the life support machines, letting him go. Now my children had lost their father. My daughter of fourteen suffered deep emotional scars. A son of thirteen receded into withdrawal and my ten-year-old son lacked understanding of the whole situation. I shone full attention on them in an effort to assure their well-being. I had faith to move forward. I continued on track with a will to survive.

James Hollis, a Jungian psychotherapist, explains in *Under Saturn's Shadow* the wounding and healing of men. As Hollis explains, I believe many men and boys, including myself, experience grief for the loss of our fathers as companions and sources of wisdom. This remains particularly true when our fathers become alcoholics or other types of addicts and remove themselves emotionally or even physically from their sons. We also have no tribal elders to initiate us from boyhood into manhood.

We suffer in silence as I did or act out in rage as my brother, Wayne, choose to do and became an alcoholic and out of pain disowned himself from the family. *If men are to heal, they must activate within what they did not receive from without,* says Hollis.

Viola continues. *We lived in the one-bedroom apartment for a year with the legal fight for my husband's insurance money so I could buy a house. He had taken my name off the insurance policy as a punishment for the divorce. I fought with his family for what belonged to my children and won.*

I now have stable grown children and a beautiful granddaughter and grandson. I have a normal family. We escaped the cycle of abuse. I know in my heart and soul it all came about with those five little words in the hospital waiting room, I hope you learned your lesson.

The more difficult the adversity, the more valuable will be the lessons it offers to teach.

The lessons we are meant to learn will reappear until we learn them completely.

Steve Brunkhorst, Life Success Coach

Viola continues. *Yes, I learned my lesson in many ways. I also have no regrets. I am grateful for the lessons my children's father gave me the opportunity to learn. I have no hate or ill feelings toward him. I learned what drinking can do to someone, how it can take over someone's life without their awareness. I learned the difficulty for an alcoholic to take back their life. I knew this man before it took over his life. I also know he wanted to beat it when he came out of his first coma, yet it had already gone too far and I think he knew.*

My husband grew up with alcoholism in his family. He watched his own father die of alcoholism at forty-five, six years longer than himself. I knew he loved his children and I did everything to make sure they knew, no matter what went on between us. He never abused them physically. I know, however, it affected them on an emotional and mental level.

Helping children heal from the effects of domestic violence means we have a chance to break the cycle of abuse in future families.

Sharon Hunter, Counseling Coordinator

Viola continues. *I knew to be honest with my children and I refused to allow them to blame themselves. For their sake I choose to end the cycle of abuse to prevent it spilling over onto their children. I made this promise to their father's spirit and his memory. Rather than thinking of him as a monster, I yearned for them to know him before his alcoholism. Whenever we mention him, we speak only of our love. After all he came to teach us a better life through his suffering, a difficult role, so the least we can do is to forgive him.*

Forgiveness frees us to live our life in love and peace instead of hate. I think we keep ourselves trapped by living in the past. Let go of the past and live for the "NOW." We can choose to look deep and learn from the drama and chaos in our lives. Thank others for the lessons they bring to our lives. Do we or others control our lives?

We have the choice of how we respond and allow situations to affect us. We can choose to see them as positive or negative. We have the power to take action; no one else can do it for us.

Look deep inside yourself and light the lamp in your soul and let it lead you. Learn to listen to your inner voice, it never lies. Pay attention to everything, nothing happens without a reason.

David Hawkins, a psychiatrist, author of the book *Power vs. Force,* shows on his Scale of Consciousness the energy levels of various emotional states. Survival remains the primary focus at levels below 200. Hate/anger calibrates at 150, forgiveness at 350, and love at 500. Viola chose on her journey from abuse to empowerment to shift her consciousness, as well as her children's, from anger to love.

Dan Millman in *The Life You Were Born to Live* describes Viola's life challenges as *here to work through issues related to independence, emotional honesty, and cooperation, finally experiencing freedom through discipline and depth of experience.* He explains with these life lessons a person needs priorities to free themselves and freedom as being internal – *freedom to be themselves, the freedom from self-doubt, and the freedom from fear.*

Viola summarizes. Through my journey from abuse to empowerment, I learned a valuable way of handling unhappy memories. I would let go of unhappy memories of pain and hurt, a type of editing, and remember only all the happy times of peace and joy. This made it easier to forgive and love. Now I no longer remember the suffering, as strange as that sounds, only the good memories.

The next chapter shows two examples of assisted healing.

CHAPTER 5

HEAL OTHERS:

RECEIVE ASSISTANCE OURSELVES

OCEANNA: A SOUL KEEPER

O ceAnna, like Viola, experienced a paradigm shift – a change in mental perception, which resulted in lessening her suffering.

A soul keeper is one who consciously, or sometimes even unconsciously, gathers up lost souls and keeps them safe until they can be released back to Source.

Ken Page – *Heart & Soul Healing.*

The challenge for a Soul Keeper remains in assisting others without a drain on their physical, emotional/mental, & spiritual energy. A Soul Keeper, such as OceAnna, may also have a life purpose assisting people with physical pain such as parents.

I arrived as an accidental birth, the youngest of three. I screamed in my crib. Who would want to be part of an angry arguing family, explained OceAnna?

Left out, I became invisible, withdrew, and created my own inner world. I still withdraw to this day as a coping mechanism when I become overwhelmed.

I presently live at home taking care of my father and mother, both of whom have advanced health challenges. I had reached a level of overwhelm and, yet, I choose to stay and assist my parents. I know this as a contract I have made with them on an inner soul level.

My parents place me in a position of making all the major decisions concerning them, as well as lifting the family's despair and hopelessness as they negotiate all their daily physical ailments.

I experienced a paradigm shift around Veteran's Day 2008 and since this shift it has become easier to be around my parents. I have come into a state of Grace and experience less suffering as I no longer resist my purpose with my parents. I am here to assist them in their transition from this physical plane.

SINNET: HORSES as HEALERS and MENTORS

Sinnet Olina Tiwaz, a horse whisperer, begins a description of her life before the grace of horses assisted her healing.

Horses changed my life and helped me become aware and balanced. They came when I desperately needed to grow on a personal level.

Life has challenged me and as a young teenager I developed a severe eating disorder in the desire to control my life. I learned early in my life that being a highly sensitive empath was unappreciated. On the contrary, my family suppressed all feeling. In short, I grew up in callous surroundings with emotional and psychological abuse.

Therefore, during my childhood I developed many chronic illnesses such as asthmatic bronchitis and diffuse stomachaches, which I considered my way of escaping from the pressure of everyday reality.

I adapted to the world through depressing my emotions and forcing my body to cope with the stress of working out and starving at the same time. Therefore, for many years in my young adulthood I lived a life in control, so I thought. This turned out to be the worst lie until horses entered my life.

In later chapters Sinnet explains how horses acted as instruments of Divine Grace in her healing.

In previous chapters, we have seen as Eckhart Tolle, author & spiritual teacher says, *Suffering cracks open the shell of ego, and then comes a point when it has served its purpose. Suffering is necessary until you realize it is unnecessary.* Tolle also says, *As*

far as inner transformation is concerned . . . All you
can do is create a space for transformation to hap-
pen, for grace and love to enter.

These stories highlight journeys through suffering
with perseverance, the assistance of others, and in
some cases the intervention of grace.

In review, some of the ways we suffer occur by giving away our power, taking on other people's feelings,
feeling ashamed, and sexual, emotional, and mental
abuse from family members. We have also seen some
ways to lessen or even heal suffering by working with
good therapists, practicing meditation, receiving energy healings, shifting our mental perceptions, learning life lessons and empowerment, and discovering
our life purpose through our experiences of suffering.

In the next chapter, we examine the challenge of
fear and what we can do when our minds start blowing fear out of proportion, creating more pain and suffering.

CHAPTER 6

HOW to FACE YOUR FEARS?

People have a hard time letting go of their suffering. Out of a fear of the unknown, they prefer suffering that is familiar.

Thich Nhat Hanh, Zen Master

We can empower ourselves even more by simply letting go. Fear is clinging onto something, holding on, and not letting go.

Ian Cameron, *Heal Thyself*

Fear began as an instinct for survival. Today our mind magnifies fear through the memory of past pain and through imagining what might happen in the future, which could cause pain. As we pay attention to the fears our minds manufacture, the fear gains power for *energy follows thought* – The Law of Attraction.

Fears involve our terror of the dark and the unknown, to the loss of loved ones, our health, jobs, and money. Then we have fear of failure, doubt, fear of death, and finally fear of complete annihilation.

In 2009, the breakdown of the economic system through fear, greed, and corruption created mass fear, pain, and suffering for people around the world. What can we do to face our fears and overcome their challenges? What can we do when our minds start blowing fear out of proportion, creating more pain and suffering? The following experiences show how ordinary people dealt with their fears for positive learning and change.

MICHAEL: DREAD of the UNKNOWN and DOUBT

The psychological condition of fear is divorced from any concrete and true immediate danger. It comes in many forms: unease, worry, anxiety, nervousness, tension, dread, phobia, and so on. This kind of psychological fear is always of something that might happen, not of something that is happening now.

Eckhart Tolle, *The Power of Now*

Major challenges in my life have given me the choice of facing my fears, trusting, and taking a courageous leap into the unknown for a new phase of personal growth. Challenges have manifested through outer events and people, as well as my own inner fears.

My first major fear arose after working for three years with teens. In 1978, I got excited about working as a team counselor with other professionals. My psychologist friend Bob and I travelled from Edmonton,

Alberta where we lived to Los Angeles to receive training.

First, we had to go through our own therapy. After two weeks, Bob got scared and ran away. No longer did I have a partner for future work in Alberta.

A major decision loomed before me after finishing two months of therapy. Should I go back to my old life in Alberta or continue the emotional growth in Los Angeles? A bolt of fear struck, penetrating deep into my whole being. In Los Angeles, I had no job and little money. Already thousands of dollars in debt for the therapy, my greatest fear involved ending up as an alien on the streets of a foreign country, homeless.

The most primitive fear of basic survival ran deep within me. I imagined myself in the heart of downtown Los Angeles among the other homeless. Penniless, I would find myself living under a makeshift cardboard shelter propped up against a metal wire fence in an abandoned lot. Fear of being robbed or beaten would be on my mind all the time. Once a day lining up for a meal a local salvation mission, I would be another insignificant figure in a long string of broken-down hopeless men.

Fear is a belief that something awful might happen, while faith is belief that something good will happen.

Anodea Judith, *Eastern Body, Western Mind*

As you can see, my own mistrust tapped into a fear of lack and loss, which became my greatest obstacle. I decided to leave L.A. and before I left I imagined and wrote out the worst scenario if I returned. In addition, I wrote a positive outline of expected events such as having a place to live, a job, and community support. In spite of the fear of stepping out into the total unknown, I knew intuitively my emotional growth depended on returning to Los Angeles.

In March 1979, Voyager curved around Jupiter revealing a different composition and appearance of Jupiter and its moons than previously known. The biggest discovery showed a ring of boulder-sized debris surrounding the Jovian planet. The next fifteen years would involve the challenge of facing the boulders of fear, which surrounded me every day as a salesperson.

The second day after my return to Los Angeles, in January of 1979, I found a job, a sure sign of grace. At the time, my sales experience involved one day selling door to door and three months estimating roofing materials for a building supplies department store. My knowledge in my new job of selling printing amounted to zero. On top of that, I remained shy, reserved, and dreadfully afraid of speaking. Speaking meant revealing myself, feeling unsafe and vulnerable.

When your heart races, your chest tightens, the adrenaline pumps, and the butterflies flutter in your stomach, be with all of these sensations. Observe the

*unpleasant sensations caused by fear, go deeply into
them, and they will dissolve.*

Ian Cameron, *Heal Thyself*

At this time, I had no training in being present and
allowing my fear to dissolve. Therefore, I lived with it
as I went door to door in High-Rise office buildings
each day.

The memories remain so clear; I enter the main
floor elevator of an office building I have never been
in before. As the elevator rises to the first floor, so
does my anxiety level. The doors slowly open and with
reluctance, I drag myself into the hallway. There half a
dozen or more doors to unknown businesses loom.
The closer I get to an office the more leaden my feet
feel. With a sweaty hand, I grasp an unfamiliar door-
knob and dread washes over me for I know rejection
faces me on the other side. With trepidation, I open
the door and walk toward the receptionist.

With each rejection, office after office, I feel more
depressed and lower in spirit. I believed salespeople
belonged on the lowest rung of the employment lad-
der.

In the first year, I would do about ten of the above
calls. Then I retreated to the lobby to sit down, center
myself, and gain courage to continue the ordeal. After
15 years, cold calling became a little easier, even

though the specter of fear always walked with me as I roamed corridors of unfamiliar offices.

Although I had no opportunity to use my creative gifts in sales it developed certain qualities of character such as persistence, patience, integrity, and service to others. These qualities assisted me later as a seminar leader and teacher of energetic healing.

As a teacher of energetic healing, I met two more major challenges. They both involved overcoming fear by facing it and trusting my intuition. It is interesting that one of the challenges presented itself through a meditation teacher in Los Angeles, Sathya, which in Hindu means "truth."

The first challenge occurred about a year after I had been teaching people energetic hands-on healing. Sathya would throw the gauntlet of fear directly in my face. It would be a challenge of my courage to go beyond the fear into standing firmly upon the bedrock of my inner truth and trust.

Some of the group had gone with Sathya to start a spiritual community in a remote location in New Mexico. The Los Angeles group, including myself, continued to meet in the evenings to sit in meditation.

One day, after about a year, a written manifesto arrived from New Mexico. As I examined the document disbelief flooded me. In Sathya's words it stated, *It has been given me by authority of God to have eventually one hundred and eight wives.* Further along he said, *It is no longer necessary to have one committed sexual relationship for the members of the group.* Before, he had stressed the importance of commitment. Intuitively, I knew this teaching as unsuitable for me.

No longer could I associate with Sathya while remaining true to myself. My whole being, however, trembled at the thought of opposing him.

Summoning my courage, I went to the next group meeting in Los Angeles. The group included my girlfriend Beth and my friend Walter who felt the same way I did. The other dozen members unquestionably followed Sathya's word as law. My throat constricted and I felt a sinking, weakening sensation in my stomach as I declared to the group my decision to leave. I explained that I felt uncomfortable about the changes in sexual behavior and my top priority remained teaching healing.

The backlash of the group's anger floored me. The group strongly opposed my decision. In the ensuing discussion, they verbally attacked me. It felt like physical blows upon my body. Vulnerable and quivering inside, I wanted to rush from the room.

A few days later a verbal ultimatum arrived, delivered third hand to me from Sathya. It dictated, *Attend a group meeting on Friday or else the healing energy will no longer work for you.* At this point my familiar

friend, fear, arose. Fear's accomplice, doubt, also upset my trust in the healing power continuing to come
through me. What if Sathya could really it cut off?

In spite of my fear, I knew instinctually I had to
stand on my own and follow what felt right in the
deepest part of my Being. If I remained one hundred
percent dedicated to teaching the healing, as I claimed
to be, then I had to stand in my truth, regardless of
the consequences.

On the particular day the healing energy supposed-
ly discontinued, I had wonderful results with a group
of AIDS patients. The healing energy continued growing stronger from that time forward. To remain empowered in my own creative gift of teaching and healing, I had to face the fear of being disconnected from
the Divine Source and trust my own inner teacher, intuition.

The other challenge over one year later involved
four members on a board of directors for a healing institute. We all had spent two years of dedicated work
building this institute.

In bringing the healing energy into the world, I
believed I needed the other board members. After two
months of intensified personal healing involving a
combination of breath work and hands-on healing, I
became more empowered. This empowerment per-
mitted me to discard the last bonds of codependency

with this group just as a fledging bird swoops away from the nest, never to return.

Other institute members expressed interest for more active involvement in board meetings. My intuition shouted, "Spirit wants expansion of the healing energy." Could the energy lift beyond the bounds of the board's confinement?

Feeling their power threatened, the board members turned on me with the viciousness of hyenas. Banding together, they wrote a discrediting letter describing me operating as an independent satellite of the institute, yet still accountable to them. Furthermore, two of the members wanted to take over my teaching role. Outraged, I felt like fighting them tooth and claw. After getting over my initial anger at their betrayal, I realized that instead of resisting, I needed to let go and surrender into the hands of Spirit.

The next two months found me adrift on a sea of uncertainty and upset as constant thoughts of doubt assailed my mind. Distraught, I turned inside and asked Spirit, "What am I to do?" Confused, bewildered, and alone in this challenge, I entered into the *dark night of the soul* where I had the choice of surrendering everything. This surrender included even the agonizing possibility of giving up my life purpose of teaching healing. The sunlight of clarity slowly emerged out of black chaos as I continued meditation and asking Spirit for direction.

Although friends gathered around and supported me, I felt alone in my soul. Transformation occurred from the inside out. The dark night engulfed me like a protective cocoon until I emerged like a butterfly into the beauty of a new world.

Because I chose to face my fear, loneliness, and doubt, staying present with it rather than resisting, and surrendering my ego role of healer and spiritual teacher, Divine Grace opened a higher expression of healing and the doorway to teach in another country.

We all have the challenge of facing our fears like Brooks Crown, an elderly woman who now has passed on. She said, *In my journey of discovery I have moved through fears by facing them, by trusting my intuition and taking action. Then the fear dissolves. I love the wonder of doing something new and exciting. Facing fears and walking through them I learned to stand empowered in the truth as I knew it at the time.*

Besides the above examples, I have had other challenges facing my fears and doubts in career, emotional situations, relationships, and with other spiritual teachers. Trusting my intuition rather than looking outside myself for knowledge and being secure in the wisdom of my heart rather than my head has been a major life challenge for me.

Every person on the planet wrestles with some core fear.

Without identifying your core fear and understanding how you tend to react when your fear button gets pushed, your relationships will suffer.

Gary Smalley, *The DNA of Relationships*

CHAPTER 7

WHAT FACING OUR FEARS CAN TEACH US

JULIANNE: FEAR of BEING POWERLESS and VULNERABLE

I *must succeed in everything I do. I must be loved. I must be in control. I feel inadequate.* From our earliest years, Stephen Wolinsky in *Quantum Psychology* teaches that we create a false self that can trap us in our fears.

Julianne, a therapist, describes at the age of 46 her second memory of sexual abuse at the age of two. *I did extensive personal therapy with Stephen Wolinsky. He dismantled my identities by having me write answers my inner child pretended to know. This method took me beyond my rational left brain. It came out that my uncle had molested me.*

The EMDR - Eye Movement Desensitization and Reprocessing - Technique does two very important things. First, it "unlocks" the negative memories and emotions stored in the nervous system, and second, it helps the brain successfully process the experience, says Carol Boulware Ph. D.

Julianne also used EMDR to heal her fear and abuse. Psychotherapists use EMDR for trauma. Usually a therapist guides the client to recall past trauma and gain new understanding of body feelings, emotions, thoughts and the associated images. The client moves their eyes back and forth while recalling the events.

Julianne explains her experience with EMDR. *I used a photo of myself with the uncle who abused me. In the past whenever I looked at that type of picture, I noticed that the little girl looked miserable and I felt miserable in my body. I shrunk up inside. With EMDR, it took one hour for my defenses to break down. I first noticed a slight shift in my mouth and then I made contact with myself as a two-year-old baby. I curled up into a fetal position and holding onto a teddy bear, cried. I felt vulnerable for weeks afterwards.*

Julianne feels gratitude and knows herself as more than her body sensations, feelings, or thoughts. She would agree with the following statement from the spiritual psychology known as Psychosynthesis, *I have a body and I am more than my body. I am I, a center of pure self-consciousness.*

Julianne spent years healing the fears locked into her nervous system by using therapy, EMDR, journaling, and MAP, a program designed to connect you with the inner medical unit of the White Brotherhood where a team of physicians assists improving your health on the needed levels. The book, *MAP: The Co-Creative White Brotherhood Medical Assistance Program,* by Maechelle Small Wright explains the program.

Julianne continues. *I have done a lot of inner work including journaling, receiving assistance from inner masters, and working with a MAP – Medical Assistance Team, - for ten years. When I saw my uncle a couple of times I had no feeling about the past anymore.*

My life experience now helps me as a therapist to assist healing abused women and teenage girls. I have felt the fear of men, the vulnerability, and the giving away of my power.

SHIVANI: FEAR and SUFFERING and FEAR of LOSING CONTROL

When fear comes, watch it.
Be face to face with it.
Encounter it.
Look deep into it.

Osho, a spiritual teacher

Shivani spent years suffering because of the fear that if she grieved her son's death, she would lose herself in the pain.

I never shed a tear for my son's death for years. I never took a deep breath for years feeling that my heart would explode for I avoided the pain my son experienced drowning. My former husband and others blamed me for Luke's death. The dam of my grief would burst forth later, says Shivani, a nurse and healer.

Three hundred people gathered in a New York hotel with twenty therapists present. They encouraged us to go up to someone and be honest. I chose the head therapist and said, "You make me want to puke." Then I went back into the midst of the group.

Another therapist slung a comment back to me, "You must be the drama queen with the dead kid."

I burst a primal scream and went hysterical crying. Before, I had cried for my friends' suffering. Now I cried for the first time after my son's death. I had suffered in survival mode, for if I admitted the false belief that I had killed Luke, I would die.

Later through rebirthing, I experienced another breakthrough. During a session of Radiance Breath work developed by psychologist Gay Hendricks, I began to breathe comfortably. For five years whenever I came to the point of taking a deep breath, I stopped. I refused to experience the suffering my son had gone through. This time I let go of control and chose to continue breathing. Then I felt ecstasy. I saw Luke never suffered. He had taken a deep breath and moved into the Light.

As my spiritual teacher, Osho, said, "When you watch suffering suddenly you are not the sufferer, and you start enjoying. Through suffering, you become aware of the opposite pole, the blissful inner being."

I am an Army-trained RN and physician's assistant. At twenty-eight years old, I gave up nursing, put on a backpack, and gave up everything. My personal experience, however, developed a compassion for others' suffering, which has assisted me in helping three girlfriends through their suffering when their children committed suicide.

Rebirthing allowed the breath – spiritus – to enter Shivani's body as grace. She looked deep into her fear and felt the opposite of suffering, the bliss of her inner self. *"It is not possible for the dark cloud of fear to permanently obscure the sun, which is the joy and love within you,"* Ian Cameron, *Heal Thyself.*

JACQUELINE: FEAR of POWER

Jacqueline Stone, Author & Spiritual Coach, eBook, *Rising from Ashes*

Our deepest fear is not that we are inadequate. Our deepest fear is that we are powerful beyond measure. It is our Light, not our Darkness, that most frightens us.

Marianne Williamson, motivational speaker

Jacqueline says, *I realized a while back I had an unconscious fear of power. Just the word power made me feel uncomfortable. I used EFT and meditation to find the root cause.*

God is powerful; I am part of God. I have all the qualities of God; therefore, I must be powerful too. If I fear power then I have rejected that aspect of myself. I am resisting my full potential. It follows that I am still afraid to reveal my whole true self, which equals a lingering fear of judgment, which goes back to feeling "not good enough." I harbored an underlying core belief,

"I am less than everyone else." I needed to hide that fact while working hard to make up for this lack from my birth.

Shame as the root emotion made it difficult to receive praise. It felt like people praised me for something I was not. I therefore hid the "truth" lest they found out how small, weak, and stupid I really was.

True power is within, and it is available to you now. So anyone who is identified with their mind and, therefore, disconnected from their true power, their deeper self rooted in Being, will have fear as their constant companion.

Eckhart Tolle, *The Power of Now*

Jacqueline continues. *I knew the untruth of my faulty thinking; yet, my unconscious had a different belief. I still based my actions and reactions on these underlying false beliefs. How could I fix it? Now with awareness of the truth I could change my beliefs by turning my attention to the truth that contradicted them. I had to focus intentionally on the truth of my being and consciously choose my new beliefs, and then repeat them continuously until they ingrain themselves in my consciousness. Then my unconscious accepted them as true. Now I could express and experience more of my potential.*

In meditation, I asked the question, What is holding me back? How am I limiting myself? Why do I fear power?

I sat in silence with my focus on my heart. The answers would come as memories of past events showing me my disempowering behaviors. I would write out the experience, how I felt at the time, and look at how disproportionate those feelings were for the situation. That led to searches into my childhood to find the early experiences when I first remember those feelings. I found my reactionary patterns and subconscious fears based on the reactions of a child to things she failed to understand.

JACQUELINE: HEALING the FEAR of POWER

My parents used shame and guilt to control our behavior. When still very young I learned my par-

ents wanted to abort me. The way they treated me confirmed they did not want me. In the mind of a child, this translated into a clear message, "I was not good enough from the moment of conception." My parents' tactic proved effective and it instilled the concept of power as negative, only to be used to ma- nipulate and hurt others. Their use of parental power destroyed any sense of self-worth for my siblings and me.

EFT, the Emotional Freedom Technique created by Gary Craig, a non-invasive physical method re- leases emotions from our cellular memory. An inten- tional statement begins the process followed by tap- ping on pressure points while repeating a brief statement of the issue. When I first learned of EFT, I remained skeptical, yet I desperately wanted to heal. I had a great deal of physical pain as well as emo- tional pain, both supported by unnamed fears.

With EFT, I addressed my fear of power as one of the issues. I used the intentional statement, "Even though I have this fear of power, I completely love and accept myself." While tapping on the pressure points I repeated, "My fear of power." It took only a few sessions to relieve the sense of anxiety surround- ing the word "power."

Have you ever thought about how the concept of power makes you feel? We exist, in fact, as powerful beings with the capacity to create incredible good or *unspeakable harm. Would you like to start embracing the truth of your powerful nature and consciously using it to heal and uplift?*

As we are liberated from our fear, our presence automatically liberates others.

Marianne Williamson.

I knew on the surface that I am just as wonderful and capable as anyone else, yet my unconscious had a different belief and it ran the show. I still based my actions and reactions on these underlying false beliefs. How could I fix it? I changed my beliefs by turning my attention to the truth that contradicts them. I had to focus intentionally on the truth of my being, consciously choose new beliefs, and then repeat them until they ingrained in my consciousness. Whenever the old beliefs surfaced in my thoughts, words, or actions, I consciously said, "No, that's untrue." Then I reaffirmed my value and qualities. Eventually, my unconscious accepted them as true.

Jacqueline changed her fear beliefs through self-inquiry in meditation.

Now the words of the Buddha make more sense when he said, "At the root of all suffering lies wrong identification." We are all far more than the false thoughts that underlie our fears and give us tunnel vision about who we are and what we can do.

Eric Christopher, therapist

In addition, with EFT, Jacqueline cleared and healed cellular memories which she may have received while in the womb about not being good enough.

JACQUELINE: TRYING FINANCIAL TIMES: FEAR of LOSS and SURVIVAL

Trying times, as many experienced in 2008, can bring up old fears even after we have done a lot to heal them. This is true especially of financial struggles because we have felt unsupported by love, life, and other people in our past. This situation, however, creates an opportunity for us to make great strides in our personal growth.

In the past, physical and emotional abuse may have damaged our self-esteem and self-worth. We feel undeserving of love or any good in life. Our bruises and bones heal much more quickly and easily than our hearts, spirits, and beliefs. Thus, developing self-love remains crucial. When we learn to love ourselves, we again regain feeling worthy of the good in our life. Then our feelings and beliefs reflect back this good.

Financial struggles show we feel undeserving of support; we have yet to trust Life. I've been given the opportunity to experience this personally so I could see the fear lingering in my consciousness and chose to change it.

We can also ask for more than just enough. We can ask for an abundance of every good thing in our lives: money, health, love, creativity, and success. An important point to remember, our subconscious must believe the same as our conscious mind or else it will sabotage our efforts.

Carolyn Ball, M.A, has written an excellent book, *Claiming Your Self-Esteem,* which I use to teach teen-age girls to improve their self-esteem, recognize and reprogram critical thoughts, and recover from code-pendence. The reprogramming technique, also known as thought records in cognitive behavior therapy, assists us to become more aware of and change our critical thought patterns, which sabotage our efforts to create positive change.

Did you know that the energy of fear can be used as excitement to propel us forward into action rather than remaining petrified and powerless? Kathryne-Alexis, a life path consultant, uses excitement to transform her emotional suffering.

KATHRYNE-ALEXIS: CHOICE: FEAR or EXCITEMENT

Love is what we are born with. Fear is what we learn. The spiritual journey is the unlearning of fear and prejudice and the acceptance of love back into our hearts.

Marianne Williamson, author & spiritual teacher

Kathryne-Alexis, a life path consultant talks about her own perception or mental method of transforming her emotional suffering. *We can look at fear as the food that feeds separation or redefine and direct it into a feeling of excitement to be, do or experience something better, more loving. I learned to shift the energy I had labeled fear into fuel and courage to make new choices.*

One perception drives us to avoid the fear and the other moves us towards it. David Hawkins M.D., *Power vs. Force,* has formulated a consciousness scale to calibrate levels of emotion. Fear has a score of 100 while excitement, the other side of fear, rates at a higher level of energy of possibly 310. Courage attunes to 200 on the scale while love calibrates at 500. The average level of human consciousness according to Hawkins scale functions below 200.

Which way do we choose to use the energy of fear? Would we choose the lower level of energy and be caught in the fear – false evidence appearing real - or consciously choose the excitement which can be used to drive us forward into positive change.

Just as we can choose to upgrade our thoughts previously referred to as conscious languaging, we can also upgrade our emotions into a higher level of con-sciousness. Can we be ready to look at our beliefs and emotions and see if they still serve us in the highest truth? Do we have the courage? Can we feel excited in the face of fear? Can we make the conscious choice for the higher level of consciousness, which involves change?

Kathryne-Alexis says, *Yes, If I reach for feeling excited and ready then the pain and resistance ceases. Conscious choices can be made, understandings come readily. Change can happen quickly. Then truth moves from fear into love. Grace becomes a natural flow towards excitement and joy based on love. We then shift from suffering into love.*

In this chapter, we have learned how to face our fears, trust our intuition, and take action. Psychotherapy and EMDR unlock and heal fear and abuse. Breath work and surrendering control can take us from fear into the bliss of our inner self. EFT and self-inquiry in meditation has released fear from the cellular memory related to power. Increasing trust, choosing to have a positive attitude about repaying our debts, and reprogramming – changing our critical attitudes – assists in dealing with fears of financial loss and suffering.

In the next chapter, we will look at how people used meditation in calming and stabilizing their minds. Some simple forms of meditation can be used in everyday life to lessen emotional turmoil. Also identifying and changing our beliefs and critical self-talk eases suffering.

CHAPTER 8

STABILIZING OUR MINDS

*By means of meditation, a man finds freedom from
the delusion of the senses . . . he finds his own positive
center of energy . . . he becomes, therefore, aware of
his real Self.*

Alice Bailey, *A Treatise on Cosmic Fire*

What we hold in our minds/emotions affects us, in our bodies. Meditation can train our minds, which will assist us to rise above the suffering we create while trapped in *the delusions of the senses* - our emotional glamour's. Through the constant practice of meditation we develop a strong inner center of being or bridge with our *real Self* – our Souls.

TRAINING OUR MINDS

We all have minds – the concrete mind, which we develop to think more clearly. We also have an abstract mind by which we understand symbols and the patterns behind physical forms. Finally, we have the capacity to develop our intuition at the level of our souls. We use our abstract minds and intuition to receive direct information from our souls, the Divine, and to gain a glimmer of the Divine Plan.

To develop our abstract minds and intuition requires perseverance and the discipline of concentration, meditation, and contemplation. Concentration builds a focus, lifting our lower minds to the higher. With regular meditation, we learn to hold our minds steady in the light and connect with our intuitions. In contemplation, we enter the silence to tap into our souls and the Divine Mind.

Alice Bailey says in *Discipleship in the New Age – Vol. 1,* "*Glamour must give place to reality, and the pure light of the mind must pour into all the dark places of the lower nature.* These dark places hold much unconscious pain and suffering which, when brought into the light, can heal.

Tiara Kumara, founder of Children of the Sun Foundation, which focuses on world transformation of consciousness, gives us more understanding in the following passages about shifting from the lower to higher mind, liberation from false beliefs, the use of our intuition to reflect truth, and how to develop our higher minds.

TIARA KUMARA - SHIFT FROM LOWER INTO HIGHER MIND

The great transfiguration of the human personality is upon us, preparing our body for Soul union and as a conscious outward expression of the Christ principle. As we undertake intensified spiritual initiation, the sacred fires meet with the liquidity of emotion. Within the resultant steam, the self reflects. Many deeply held and disguised illusions emerge from the deep recesses of consciousness of our personality vehicle.

The natural course of initiation progresses towards an eventual fusion of the human personality with that of the Soul. This process of synthesis can also symbolically be described as an elevation of consciousness into the higher Mental Plane or into the illumined realm of Divine Wisdom.

For those of us choosing to express our Christ Self, we inspire for concentrated group focus upon the complete disassociation from the human personality self. This involves a withdrawal from all attachment to the individualized identity. This also involves a letting go of our held visions, our adored truths, our loved ideals, and all outer form to which we keep ourselves emotionally identified.

TIARA KUMARA - LIBERATION FROM the MATERIAL WORLD

Illusions, often deeply held as age long conditions, have become inherent in the human nature attracted to us by ancient rhythms and old controls. Emotional attachment to material form and its appearances sustain them. We all know the story, yet many of us well on the spiritual path continue discovering some of these locked energies still lurking in the shadows of unconsciousness.

Maya or mental illusion constitutes a belief that the physical and mental worlds we live in are the only reality. In the sci-fi movie, *The Matrix,* everyone believed in the reality of their world until the main character Neo "woke up" to discover he lived in a dream world. Is your world of mental beliefs real? Are you ready to "wake up?"

TIARA KUMARA - ILLUMINATION of the MIND

Many effective practices and disciplines dispel false formations of consciousness, which hinder us. Many of the classic texts including the Bhagavad-Gita, the New Testament, and the Yoga Sutras, for example, give a complete path of the Soul and its unfoldment. The lives of the great living Avatars who helped to lay ascension's golden brick road, including Jesus, Buddha, and Krishna, clearly demonstrated what it means to develop the powers of the Soul and to attain self-liberation.

All of the great teachings unanimously express the absolute necessity of letting go of human desire and identity to form while also illuminating the brain/mind functions.

In this light, many more of us choose to develop the mind powers through disciplined meditation and concentration. The power of concentration remains the key to the expansion of consciousness in both the human and super human field. Certain yogic meditative practices assist in gaining control over the apparatus of thought. For example, the science of Raja Yoga develops the right use of the mind as an instrument of the Soul. Today many teachers of wisdom offer Advaita, the teachings of non-duality.

Many light workers focus upon light body activation which potentially expands the mental capacities while naturally clearing out distorted perception. Many engage in the emerging healing modalities which use advanced techniques in light, sound, and color to stabilize the body's new incoming energy system. These also assist to clear out automatic conditioned patterns.

Light workers also have a growing focus upon the building of the consciousness bridge or the column of Light referred to as the "Antahkarana," which synthesizes the human personality with the Soul and the Soul with the supreme light of the Monad ~ for super human expression. The Antahkarana Bridge remains crucial for the restructuring of our new divine-human blueprint.

Note: *Building the Antahkarana and creating that which will bridge the gap, is in truth the planned* *and conscious effort to project the focused thought of the spiritual man from the lower mental plane into areas of awareness which have been sensed but not contacted – the higher mind and soul.* Alice Bailey, *Discipleship in the New Age – Volume II.*

See more information to invoke the Soul Star for purification of our physical, emotional, and mental bodies at
http://soul1.org/invocation_of_the_soul.htm

Building our bridge or Antahkarana when we become ready requires conscious effort. We begin to connect with our higher intuitive mind and also the compassionate heart. Once completed the light of our Soul floods our everyday mind with expanded wisdom. The following invocation repeated daily begins the construction of the bridge to our Soul.

Soul Invocation, *Rainbow Bridge II*

I am the Soul.

I am the Light Divine.

I am Love.

I am Will.

I am Fixed Design.

See <u>Rainbow Bridge: First and Second Phases Link With the Soul Purification</u> by Two Disciples for instructions in building the Antahkarana.

Meditation brings our purified lower mind and emotions into receptivity for impressions from our souls. For this to occur, a bridge must be built consciously between our personality and soul. I had been involved in emotional and spiritual development for thirty years before I realized the importance of building the Antahkarana consciously, which I completed over a few years.

TIARA KUMARA - STRENGTH of WILL

Our desires, always wanting more, bind us in the material world. This remains a challenge to transcend. It requires strength of will, steadfast determination, self-discipline, and a constant reorientation of the mind until the personality self holds steady and true in the light of the Soul.

The doors have finally opened to us, as a collective, to enter into the higher Mental Plane which provides clear and pure access to Divine Knowledge. We now have the opportunity for complete Soul union and the resultant emergence of the Christ Self in outer world expression.

This vast subject can only briefly be touched upon here.

TIARA KUMARA - IN CLOSING

*During self-actualization we can better under-
stand the true state of world condition which is heavily clothed in a facade of illusion and glamour resulting in serious mass scale suffering. The ultimate synthesis of the human personality into the Christ Soul
exists as the only real way to effectively serve the
Plan for Earth in collaboration with universal light
intelligence.*

*The true spiritual leaders and teachers of wisdom
emerge today in greater numbers to help guide humanity across the bridge and into the new consciousness reality. These common people from every
race, religion, nation, and culture have liberated the
Self from identity, from desire. With divine indifference and deep inner peace, these light bearers stand
humbly at the center of their being radiating love
and selfless aspiration to simply serve as an extension of the Whole, without self-reference, without
needless chattering. They neither covet nor claim
ownership to their creative presentations of truth.
They only emanate love and great wisdom as a result
of the realization that all comes from Universal Mind
and the field of One.*

*We gather in this field of One and within the
crystalline grid matrix of Christ Consciousness. We
connect Soul to Soul with unified intention towards
our collective liberation from the material world of*

form. *We shine our Christ Light upon each other and radiate this force of love to the hearts and minds of all Humanity.*

GOING DEEPER INTO SELF-INQUIRY: WHO AM I?

That which arises in this body, as 'I,' is the mind. When the subtle mind emerges through the brain and the senses, the gross names and forms are cognized. When it remains in the Heart, names and forms disappear. If the mind remains in the Heart, the 'I' or the ego which is the source of all thoughts will go, and the Self, the Real, Eternal 'I' alone will shine.

Teachings of Ramana Maharshi

Ramana Maharshi, one of the greatest spiritual teachers of modern-day India, stated the sole cause of all human suffering is a false belief about what we are. For Ramana, there is no "True Self" from which you separate from, there is only you, just as you are.

Tiara Kumara comments of the teachings of Rama Maharshi. *In truth, all we really know: we are here, now. All the rest is story. Self-inquiry assists us to see the truth of who we are now in present moment awareness. It places conscious attention on simple, single knowing of our "hereness" for no other purpose than to see and experience it directly for ourselves.*

*In the absolute sense, we really need to do noth-
ing. We are already "self-realized." Layers of maya
prevent us from this simple understanding. We mask
our Greater Self through attachment and identification with the dualistic world of who we think we are
on this plane of illusion.*

*Nothing external brings us into Self-Realization.
No practice we undertake will help rid us of our false
beliefs, apart from directly seeing the truth of our
true nature directly for ourselves. No teaching,
teacher, activation, transmission, class or book can
give us or show us the truth of who we really are.
Teachers and other means of support serve to simply
guide and inspire. The bottom line remains; we each
must do the direct "realizing" for ourselves.*

*Self-inquiry is one of the most important activities
during these accelerating cycles of purification and
dissolution. We can greatly benefit from constant
and rhythmic focus placed upon deeper self-
reflection, self-examination, and self-contemplation,
as we continually call forth the divine understanding
of the true nature of the Greater Self.*

*In our transcendence from the dual plane, the
mind is being retrained to serve as a follower rather
than the leader. When the mind stays in the heart, the
names, the forms, the stories, and even the personality begins to disappear. With the mind naturally rest-*

ing in the heart, the "I" dissolves and the Greater Self emerges. The "I AM that I AM."

See more teachings at http://www.sriramanamaharshi.org/bhagvan.html

Ramana Maharshi recommended self-inquiry as a practice of meditation. The following two spiritual teachers in the United States also teach self-inquiry as a method of awakening to our True Self.

OTHER SOURCES for HIGHER MIND SHIFTS

Byron Katie, Spiritual Teacher & author – She calls her method of self-inquiry, *The Work*. She has authored a number of books including, *Loving What Is – Four Questions That Can Change Your Life.* http://www.thework.com/index.php

I discovered that when I believed my thoughts, I suffered, but that when I didn't believe them, I didn't suffer, and that this is true for every human being.

Byron Katie, *The Work*

Gangaji, a spiritual teacher & author, *The Diamond in Your Pocket* – Her spiritual connection originates from Ramana Maharshi. Gangaji teaches about giving up our personal story and mind activity to experience the eternal presence of our being. www.gangaji.org

To be here and to know that you are here: what grat-
itude that can be.

Gangaji

CHAPTER 9

WAYS to STABILIZE OUR MINDS

JOANNA: BEYOND MEDITATION: WITNESS-ING WITHOUT EFFORT

All meditations ... hundreds of techniques are available, but the essence of all those techniques is the same, just their forms differ. And the essence is contained in the meditation Vipassana.

Osho, East Indian mystic, *Three ways of doing Vipassana meditation*

I got introduced to meditation at the age of 48, says Joanna, a retired CEO. *The spiritual retreat I studied at developed many methods of meditation, which included dynamic techniques involving breathing, movement, emotional expression, and dance.*

Vipassana meditation, which focuses on breathing, immediately attracted me. The 21 day Vipassana retreat resulted in the most powerful experience of my life. All my emotional "stuff" emerged, much of which had been suppressed all my life.

After the retreat, meditation became a part of my life and unlike many meditators I had no set discipline of meditating. It came naturally as the years went by. I no longer sat doing Vipassana or Gourasana meditation. I sat and allowed whatever emotion or insight needed to come. I went beyond a specific meditation method.

Gourasana meditation involves opening, releasing emotion, sitting in silence, and using the insights gained in meditation to make changes. Practicing this meditation regularly can lead to more harmony and a better sense of well-being in your material and spiritual life. It can also help you in solving the many day-to-day problems that arise.

Does meditation involve effort? According to Buddhists, the art of meditation, mindfulness, involves watching, witnessing without any effort or interference on our part. We witness our breath coming in and our breath going out. We witness our thoughts. When we become aware we have drifted off into the past or future, we gently bring ourselves back to witness our breath again. Buddhists call this practice stabilizing the mind.

RESISTANCE and MEDITATION

For Joanna her first Vipassana meditation resulted in a powerful experience, bringing suppressed emotions to the surface. Unlike Joanna, our first meditations can be agony because of resistance and trapped emotions in our physical body.

When I first started practicing disciplined meditation, Surat Shabd Yoga, using mantras and focusing on the middle of my forehead, I experienced intense physical and mental distress sitting still. Pain gripped parts of my body. I focused on escaping the physical torture rather than focusing my mind, which whirled with an influx of thoughts, more than usual. Neither my body nor mind desired immobility.

In spite of the distress, I remained sitting for a specific time each day. Persevering for two weeks, for two hours per day, the torture lessened. Had I known how to use the breath, it would have eased some of my discomfort. Persisting in the meditation established a new habit.

The following illustrates massage therapist Julia Marie's experience with the breath and meditation without struggle.

While taking a yoga class, I paid close attention to my breath. By focusing all my attention on the sensation of breathing, I watched my thoughts like channel surfing on TV. For me this simple activity was miraculous.

Now I consciously choose the activity of thinking. I decide what to think and when. Of course, I am not always successful, as this requires practice. Howev-

er, I no longer believe everything my mind conjures as absolute truth. Through meditation, I discovered that my mind is uninterested in me. Its concern is about preserving what is familiar not what is good for my Higher Self. I got close to wanting to be dead before I developed the stamina to quiet my thoughts and know that I am not my mind.

MEDITATION: THE INWARD JOURNEY

HOW SHAKTIPAT CHANGED JULIANNE'S LIFE

Shaktipat or the transference of spiritual power by a spiritual teacher, an act of Divine Grace, can begin an awakening to the connection of our Real Self. An awakened spiritual teacher can transmit shaktipat by a sacred word, a look, or a touch.

Julianne's first experience of shaktipat changed her life. The bliss, if experienced, may be for a short time while in the presence of the spiritual teacher or for longer periods afterwards.

In spite of the initial grace given, with meditation we need to make a concentrated effort to focus and hold steady with our minds on a daily basis, even if for only a few minutes. Then we will continue dissolving the hidden seeds of our emotional suffering and strengthen the connection to our Real Self.

Meditation happens through the grace of a Siddha Master; it is our birth-right. All we must do is to shift our focus from the outside to the inner Self.

Muktananda – Founder of Siddha Yoga

A therapist told me Muktananda would take away my suffering, states Julianne, a therapist. *At the age of 28, I felt a welling up inside me when I found out Muktananda would be in the Catskills in New York State. I emotionally/intuitively knew I had to see him. I had no previous experience with meditation or a spiritual teacher. I had no money. My boyfriend of two months lent me the money.*

Muktananda gave shaktipat to the people gathered in the room, touching them on the tops of their heads or their third eyes in the middle their foreheads.

Chaos reigned. People yelled in anger, laughed, or assumed yoga postures. Muktananda stuck a finger in my third eye and slapped me on the back. My heart opened like in a Divine love affair and for the next year, I experienced utter bliss.

Two years later spending five weeks in India, I began serious meditation practice. Uncooked seeds of fear intermixed with bliss arose. I began my sadhana, spiritual discipline of self-effort, with meditation and chanting as part of my life.

MICHAEL: MEDITATION CHANGED MY LIFE

Like Julianne, meditation assisted in changing my life. With Transcendental Meditation, TM, I experienced deep physical relaxation and release of daily work stress, as well as a feeling of peace at the end of the meditation.

After four years of daily practice of a Hindu meditation, my psychological addiction to alcohol had dissolved. I could now take a drink or leave it.

Finally, over the last fourteen years my connection to my Higher Self has strengthened as I receive direct knowing or insights beyond my regular mind.

It is for us to find what meditation practices work best at any particular time in our lives. As we change, so will our practice.

40 years of meditation has led me to numerous practices including TM, Hindu, Tantric, Nature of the Soul, Kriya Yoga, and Buddhist. I have gone from very easy relaxation, to disciplined focus on the third eye, to developing a higher focus beyond the crown chakra, and back to following the breath and returning my focus to the present moment.

I undertook the TM initiation ceremony to receive a mantra, a sacred word, to aid focusing my mind during meditation. Morning and evening, I sat for twenty minutes in a chair repeating the mantra in silence. After a few minutes, I slipped away into a deep state, emerging twenty minutes later physically relaxed in a high state of peace.

TM, as a deep form of relaxation, assisted passing beyond the barriers of my mind. It helped me contact higher forms of Light. The colors of Light I received included violet and sometimes deep blue like the midnight sky. At times, I progressed into the Golden Light. For six months, I daily persevered in the practice of this meditation.

After TM I launched into the practice of Surat Shabd Yoga, a Hindu meditation involving the repetition of mantras and holding a focus at the third eye. I continued this meditation of Inner Light and Sound for a minimum of two hours per day for over nine years. Because I had so much mental chatter, mantras served as a necessary aid for me to focus.

Developing the ability to concentrate moves us into higher levels of Light. The moment our mind quiets, we can hear "the still small voice" within: our Higher Self. We may be unable to hear the "voice" as an actual voice; however, the communication can arrive in flashes of inspiration or intuition.

After almost forty years of practicing different types of meditation, I have learned to hold steady when emotional reactions occur and stay present with the emotion and discomfort. I sense in my body the emotion clearing. As the emotion transforms over time, peace or bliss fills the previous places of discomfort.

We usually picture meditation as sitting still in silence. Meditation can also be active, which helps bring repressed emotions to the surface of our awareness. Shivani, an energy healer and artist, describes her experiences with two types of Active Meditations.

ENHAUSTING the MIND and EXPRESSING REPRESSED EMOTIONS

Many meditative techniques require one to sit still with a silent mind. For most of us, stress in body and mind makes this difficult. Before we can access the stillness within, we need to let go of our tensions. Ten Active Meditations scientifically designed by Osho enable us to consciously express and experience repressed emotions and learn to watch our habitual patterns. Osho, also known as Bhagwan Shree Rajneesh, an India mystic, lived in the US in the 80's.

Shivani, a healer and artist, talks about her experiences with meditation.

We may have experienced meditation. We may never have meditated. If meditation attracts us, it can be one tool to ease our suffering.

I have practiced many forms of meditation over my thirty years upon a spiritual path of inner growth. Meditation assisted me to go deeper into the suffering created by my mind. I realized my mind never stops. My spiritual teacher, Osho, uses methods of meditation exhausting the mind. Once the mind becomes tired, we can tap the pool of deep silence.

I practiced Gibberish meditation allowing nonsense sounds and movement to release whatever came up. This meditation took me to a state receptive to silence.

Osho explains Gibberish meditation. *Gibberish is to get rid of the active mind, silence to get rid of the inactive mind, and let go is to enter into the transcendental. Remember, the first step of the meditation is Gibberish. Gibberish simply means throwing out your craziness, which is already there in the mind.*

Shivani continues. *Dynamic meditation, another release technique, assisted me to clear emotions and thoughts to tap into silence. Meditation has allowed me to became aware of my suffering and detach from it.*

Dynamic meditation includes three stages of release to prepare to tap into the inner silence. *This witnessing has to be carried in all the three steps. When everything stops in the fourth step you have become completely inactive, frozen, then this alertness will come to its peak,* says Osho.

Meditation helps letting go. In meditation, we observe everything, which comes to us without reacting or judging. We learn to accept the itching sensation on our body, the bubble of anger or craving arising in our mind. We note the rising and falling of our feelings and thoughts without clinging to or avoiding them. We then reach a state where we start seeing or feeling our true inner nature of peace and silence.

VIOLA: A PRESENCE of MINDFULNESS

Previously I talked about the art of meditation, mindfulness – observing and acting in a state of self-awareness in our everyday activities. Viola, an abuse survivor, shares her states of mindfulness.

My spiritual outlets came in all forms such as alone time. I also looked at work as "my time" to learn and grow, to interact with others, and to expand my skills to get on my own. I looked for every opportunity at work to grow further within the company. I taught myself skills so I could move forward.

I joined a gym and went every day. While working out I put my full focus into it and blocked out everyone around me and went within myself like a sort of meditation. I spent hours at the gym giving back to myself.

I meditated while driving alone. I slowed down and drove less hurried. Why all the hurry anyway?

*Increasingly bring Presence (self-aware conscious-
ness) into normal everyday life. This is what the
Teaching is all about, and it directly breaks Human
conditioning. This means Honor this moment, and
every form that this moment takes – this can be done
by giving clear Still Awareness to the "little doings"
of life.*

Eckhart Tolle, Spiritual Practices

*I went to the park and sat to watch the trees,
which I love. I watched the small animals go about
their everyday life. How could I do the same in my
own life? I watched the clouds in the sky and noticed
how they go with the flow of the wind, never fighting.
Watching people going about their lives, I wondered
if they saw what I saw. Did they feel what I felt within what surrounds us every day? I am amazed how
nature can calm us, if we allow it. Spirit will come to
us and speak if we open,* says Viola.

*I remember one time going to the park upset.
While sitting in my little chair with my radio and
book, three ducks waddled up next to me. As an ani-
mal lover, I welcomed them and said hello. All three
of them looked up to me with such love in their eyes,
toddled to the edge of my feet, and sat down as if to
encircle me in comfort. They stayed for at least an
hour.*

*People in the park remarked on my new-found
friends and exclaimed in amazement how the ducks
came up and sat with me. It calmed me. I even took*

pictures to remind me how spirit can come in the form of nature to bring us peace when we need it the most. We have only to open and allow.

As Viola shows, we can practice meditation throughout our daily lives by being mindful while we exercise, work, drive, or enjoy nature.

MINDFULNESS: FULL ATTENTION to the PRESENT MOMENT

The concept of mindfulness practiced by Viola comes from Buddhism. Our minds, like a pendulum, constantly swing back and forth between the past and future. How often do you stay focused in the present moment?

When our minds calm, insights come. Insight - Vipassana – means learning to see clearly. We can learn to pay attention to our physical and emotional sensations and thoughts – internal dialogue - as they arise in the moment.

Eugene Gendlin in his book *Focusing* teaches us how to become aware of our *felt sense* – our body awareness, which when allowed opening, flows into the next deeper moment of increasing clarity and healing. Gendlin's six steps teach us how to be mindful through paying attention to our body awareness. See more at www.focusing.org

I mentioned internal dialogue above. Mindfulness assists in cognitive behavioral methods like thought records, a method of becoming aware in the moment and reprogramming our critical internal dialogue.

Reprogramming begins with becoming aware of our emotions when an event or person triggers an emotional reaction in us. We stay present with the emotion and become aware of the critical thoughts circulating in our head. If we write the thoughts down, we become aware of even more. Take one of the main thoughts and look at what percentage of it represents truth.

A thought may be, *I am not good enough.* Is it true that you are not good enough all the time or some percentage less than that? Usually it is less. Write a statement of positive self-worth to replace the old. The statement represents something where you are good enough in an aspect of work, relationships, communication, etc.

Whenever you get emotionally triggered again and the old critical thought resurfaces, after feeling the emotion and letting the critical thoughts run for a little while, then repeat the new statement in your head a few times.

Our critical thoughts have kept us company for years so it takes some time using the reprogramming method before we notice change, as the new belief slowly replaces the old critical thought that has kept us locked in suffering.

You will have a number of new reprogramming statements for different critical thoughts.

In ongoing three-month self-esteem groups I teach teenage girls, most of them see results when they use reprogramming on a consistent basis. We have used Carolyn Ball's, *Claiming Your Self-Esteem*.

I have the teens also practice a method of a mirror exercise. The mirror exercise again allows them to be mindful of critical thoughts and trains them to begin to rise above their old thoughts, which keep them locked in suffering. The teens like it once they start to experience changes in their perceptions of themselves.

Stand in front of the mirror and look at yourself in the eye while you say out loud, *I love myself.* Do it every day for a minimum of twenty-one consecutive days after you get up and before you go to bed. If you miss a day, start over.

Be aware of the first thought that enters your mind. At the beginning your subconscious critical thoughts will emerge. This is good and the purpose of the exercise. Later on your thoughts will change to more positive.

The next meditation from Kathryne-Alexis, like the mirror exercise, is about feeling love within ourselves.

Kathryne-Alexis, an energy healer explains, a Heartseed meditation. *I begin the day by loving the seed within my heart, imagining it growing to fill my body. Then going within my heart, I unconditionally love all myself, radiating out as far as possible. I feel a unity and knowing of the love that is everywhere for all to connect with and remember. It is different each time and for each person I share this meditation. It is truly a gift beyond measure that I am grateful for receiving.*

As we have seen in this chapter we can meditate in many different ways, both formal and informal. Concentration or developing a focus purifies our false beliefs. We can learn through practice to become more neutral rather than staying caught in our emotional reactions and false ideas of reality.

Actual meditation means developing the ability to hold our minds steady once we have focused through concentration. Then we can contain our emotions and stay present with them. Then they will transform without effort.

The third part of meditation, contemplation, develops our ability to bridge to higher states of consciousness. Then we receive clearer information, less colored by our emotional states and wrong perceptions, through our intuitions. Intuition can be a higher direct knowing, a clear inner vision, or a feeling sense in our bodies of rightness.

Meditation assists us to lessen the suffering in our lives.

Many of us have no idea of our codependency or the degree of its power over us. In **Part 2**, we will look at how our codependent behaviors create suffering, how to recover, and thereby increase joy in our relationships. We will also find how psychological understanding and energy healing combine in healing our wounded inner child and our unconscious Shadow aspects, which run our lives and create unhappiness when we remain unaware. We also examine whether suffering is really optional

PART TWO

- Empowerment versus codependency
  - Caring for ourselves
  - Healing physical pain
- Causes behind physical pain
  - Healing self-sabotage

CHAPTER 10

THE REAL TRUTH ABOUT CODE- PENDENCE and EMPOWERMENT

Relationships do not cause pain and unhappiness. They bring out the pain and unhappiness that is already in you.

Eckhart Tolle, *The Power of Now*

This chapter illustrates letting go of victimhood and recovery from codependency. As codependents we give away our power and the truth of who we truly are.

Codependency creates much suffering in relationships. I believe from teaching about codependency to groups for a number of years that over 90 % of American families have some degree of codependency, from mild to severe. Are you or have you been codependent? Can you recognize the behaviors of codependency?

This chapter also mentions briefly how the *Dark Night of the Soul* presents an opportunity for us to connect to a greater truth of our souls and the Divine. To go through this most intense suffering of separation requires courage to take a leap into the unknown and also our willingness to sacrifice our stance of victimhood.

Lastly, the chapter talks about the *still small voice* of intuition, which all of us can develop to receive greater clarity of truth.

A baby screams red-faced in rage. He bangs his head against the brown metal bars of a crib. He feels constricted within the prison of his body. He wants out. He wants to return to the free-floating bliss he instinctively remembers within his mother's womb. After a while, exhausted, his screams turn into a whimper.

I am this baby at the age of about two years. The cries called for attention, recognition, and love. My mother gave the best she knew how and I wanted more. By the age of five I had learned my family could never give me what I needed so I withdrew quietly inside.

I continued retreating inside myself in my early teens as I experienced my father venting his anger during his drunkenness towards my mother. Feeling vulnerable in such volatile situations, I choose to retreat into myself and kept my mouth shut. It fell unsafe to say what I felt and thought so I adopted a stone faced expression as if nothing affected me.

My mother, as an unaware codependent, continued in a twenty-year cycle of victimization as she ena-
bled my father's cycles of drinking. In later personal
relationships with women, I too acted like a powerless
codependent victim.

Adulthood found me reserved, non-expressive,
and emotionally distant in any kind of male/female
relationship. I had learned, as a survival mode from
the emotional abuse of childhood that in relationships
I needed to hide my feelings to stay safe. Fearing any
kind of expression I had no awareness of what I felt
except numbness. I also repressed any anger unless
provoked to an extreme.

ANGELIQUE: FROZEN FEELINGS

*Feelings elicited in a child during abuse are so over-
whelming and miserable that the child shuts down or
'freezes' the feelings in order to survive.*

Pia Melody, *Facing Codependency*

Entering into my first major relationship with Angelique, at the age of thirty, I had little practice in
knowing what I felt since I kept my feelings frozen.
Expressing feelings, which had been mostly anger in
my family, meant experiencing pain.

I had learned the basics of communication skills
in college psychology, yet I remained unskilled and
unwilling to express any feelings for fear of rejection.

Angelique had initiated our relationship and I felt the magnetic pull of our attraction.

Within our first month of dating one night at her second story apartment Angelique said, *I want you to live with me.*

I hesitated, as fear welled up reminding me of my parent's emotional living hell. I ignored the fear when Angelique gave me an ultimatum that our relationship would end if I refused to move in with her and her two year old son, Mason.

In our attraction to each other, Angelique and I out of ignorance of how to develop a healthy relationship created three years of emotional and mental anguish for each other. I wanted to avoid the misery of my childhood with all my will power and, yet ended up creating the same hell as my in the family I grow up in.

The Sanskrit meaning of hell implies a joyless state. The Tibetan equivalent describes a state difficult to escape. Hell, then, exists as a tormented mental state with a lack of joy in which one feels trapped.

I felt joyless and trapped in my birth family and now again I felt trapped in my relationship with Angelique. As Rahasya in the article *Counseling* says, *It seems that suffering patterns repeat themselves. If we look at a family, the suffering pattern gets inher-*

*ited, gets transferred from grandparents to parents
to children.*

Charlotte Kasl in her book, *If the Buddha Married*
expresses the suffering that occurs in relationships.
*Understanding our attachments, how our expecta-
tions, fears, and demands lie at the root of our individual suffering, including our suffering in relationships . . . . We discover how we can use our highly
charged flashes of emotion to help us wake up rather
than retreat from our relationships. We learn to stay
present to ourselves and acknowledge our anger,
fear, or hurt, so we cease hiding from ourselves and
those we love.*

As Kasl describes, Angelique's demands on me to
express my feelings created intense suffering for both
of us until I left after three years – packed up my belongings and left after Angelique had gone to work.

We argued on a constant basis to the point of
emotional exhaustion. I would retreat as if into a suit
of medieval armor for either of us knew how to stay
present with our feelings and express them.

*The main obstacle in love is fear, the fear of turn-
ing vulnerable, of surrendering and, ultimately, of
suffering. Affective dependence makes you vulnerable especially to suffering. What we should not forget
is that pain is normal in a relationship. By shutting
down your affective flow, you block both pain and*

love from reaching you. Pain is inevitable, but suffering is optional, says Stefan Anitei, science editor.

Because of past suffering, I believed in ignorance that more feelings meant more suffering so I remained in a permanent state of emotional numbness, afraid to feel. Locked inside my body, without expression, the pain never had a chance of releasing so I suffered. In addition, Angelique and I both blocked our expression of love for each other.

I recognized Angelique's and my inability to express love after moving to Los Angeles from Canada and going through about a year of therapy learning to express my feelings. I invited Angelique to visit. During our week together, she alternated between being open, sweet, and loving to cold and emotionally withdrawn. She reflected two sides of my own personality. One morning I awoke feeling open and loving with no sense of fear. Sitting together on the east living room sofa, basking in the warm sunlight of balmy southern California, I gazed straight into Angelique's blue eyes and said for the first time in our involvement, *I love you.*

Angelique vanished as if only a ghost of her emotional presence remained. The realization struck me, *she feels unworthy of receiving love.* Either one of us had felt worthy in our relationship. We both had stayed locked, like gun-shy deer, behind private inner fences too terrified to show and talk about our individual pain.

Robert Burney, codependence counselor in the article *Letting Go of Unavailable People* says, *We need to focus on healing our self, on understanding and healing the emotional wounds that have driven us to pick people who could not give us what we want emotionally.*

Have you picked partners out of your own unrecognized and thus unhealed trauma that remained unemotionally capable of nurturing you?

GINA: VICTIMHOOD

My next major codependent relationship, after Angelique, occurred six years later after I came back from a three week trip to Egypt and Greece. Gina and I had met a few months earlier at the healing center where I studied. A strong past life connection, including Egypt, existed between us. As an attractive redhead, she emanated femininity although I felt no particular sexual draw to her.

This became the first of a pattern of another two relationships. Over a period of about ten years, I would allow myself to fall into sexual relationships where I really had little desire. Although I told Gina after six months I no longer wanted to continue a sexual involvement, she stayed living with me for another two and a half years as she had no way of supporting herself.

Through my relationship with Gina, I discovered she carried tremendous suppressed emotional pain from an unhappy childhood, a car accident that resulted in constant physical pain for years, and a lost once flourishing business. She lacked money, a job, a car, or family or friends to turn to. Her clothes crammed the closet of my small bachelor apartment. In addition, boxes of her belongings stacked from the floor to the top of the nine foot ceiling of the inside entranceway.

I lacked the heart to throw her out on the street when our relationship turned cold after six months. After two years together it would take a year of weekly hypnosis before I would trust my own feelings, build the strength to stand up for myself, and tell her she had to move out. To tell her, I needed to go beyond guilt and codependency that she would be unable to function without my help.

Gina wallowing in the addiction of her emotional pain became like a black cloud hanging around me, of allowing myself to be victimized.

Most of the time around Gina, I felt as if I had fallen into a black funk, which included depression and feeling bad about myself. Gina's feelings ran my life, a classic symptom of a codependent.

Guilt and fear of expressing my feelings allowed Gina to take advantage of me. One day after six months, jobless and penniless, she saddled up to me as I stood in the narrow kitchen of the apartment. *A yearly payment for my time share condo comes up soon. I lack the money. I am going to lose it,* she pleaded.

Okay, I will lend you the thousand dollars. I flinched inside shrinking away from her, as the heavy load of obligation settled upon my shoulders.

A few months later Gina cornered me again in the confines of the kitchen with another problem that I as a good codependent could rescue her. I lacked the awareness that I had the right to say no. *I need a car so I can get back working in real estate,* she said.

I don't have that kind of money, I gulped backing away from her. *I'd have to get a loan from my bank.*

Melody Beattie, *Codependent No More,* says, *Codependents often find themselves saying yes to requests when they would prefer to say no . . . they try to please others instead of themselves.*

Coasting around in a ten-year-old 1975 green Plymouth, which I had brought for her, Gina excused her lack of sales, month after month, by assuring me that the big sale lurked just around the corner.

As time went on, I become more irritated with her belongings piled up in my apartment. My emotional states became subject to her manipulation. The pattern of being a victim and lack of responsibility for knowing and expressing how I felt, I knew well as a child. On top of this, I lacked the ability to know how to ask or receive for myself.

Gina became my worst nightmare come to life. At about the age of eight a comic book described a young man attracted to a beautiful woman. He married her. After the marriage, the woman revealed herself as an old witch. Now married, she had the man under her power forever. This story terrified me as a child.

Did Gina take my power? No, I gave it away to her.

Most of the time, I suppressed my anger. Gina would bluster and rant on and on about some behavior of mine she disliked, as I got more depressed and sunk into feeling bad. The five-year-old boy inside me believed in his badness.

During my time with Angelique, I still saw unclearly how I came to the rescue of women in pain or how I allowed myself to be the victim. Gina magnified my codependent pattern more clearly. She reflected how I let her emotions run me rather than responding to feeling and expressing my own. She reflected to me how I gave my power away and allowed myself to be a victim.

SHARON: JOURNEY out of CODEPENDENCY

Codependent people can be obsessed with the pain and suffering of the other person. That allows them to sacrifice themselves, Carol Cannon, counselor, in an article *Signs of a Codependent Relationship*

As a codependent, I learned to repress my feelings. I choose to repress expressing myself for fear of a physical beating by my father. I later realized this as an adult. I felt emotionally abandoned by my father because of his physical absence a great deal of the time and even when physically present he remained emotionally absence. I had little sense of self in relationships and looked to women provide this for me because of being afraid to show my real self. I found my identity through being a caretaker and helping. Caretaking rates as one of the four roles in codependent behavior as a way to feel better or in other words receive a temporary boost to one's self-esteem.

With Gina, I learned how to stand up and fight harder for myself then I had with Angelique. No longer, however, did I want to fight for it only brought more pain. During my time with Angelique, I remained in ignorance of how I rescued women in pain and how I allowed myself to be the victim and suffer. Gina magnified my codependent pattern more clearly. She reflected how I let her emotions run me rather than expressing my own feelings. I avoided expressing my feelings for fear of rejection.

Without knowing, we create a cycle of conflict, a cycle of hurting, attacking, and withdrawing from each other. This cycle then goes on and on without either person ever noticing his or her role in it. It's this cycle of conflict that creates the suffering in relationships, says Bill Ferguson, author, and relationship workshop leader in an article *Learn How to End Conflict in any Relationship*.

Like most people growing up, I received no education on the dynamics of a healthy family, proper communication skills, or awareness and expression of feelings without blame. I resolved no longer to continue the misery of my parents in my relationships before I ever entered relationships and yet, I ended up out of ignorance repeating the same patterns of conflict. *We all seek the relationship pattern that we're familiar with, however unhappy it might make us,* says Carol Cannon, counselor.

Because of my fear of expressing my true thoughts and feelings, my partners would get angry, criticize me, and feel hurt at my lack of response. Then I withdrew even further. Then they withdrew and the cycle of conflict would repeat in endless loops.

A few months after I asked Gina to leave, Sharon, a sweet, loving, seductive, attractive, dark haired woman came into my life. She, like me, kept her emotional pain wrapped up deep inside. As a child, her grandfather had sexually abused her for years. In her unconscious, she carried a deep anger towards men just as I carried repressed anger about women abandoning me.

Sharon now describes her experience of me. *Michael appeared as a handsome, soft-spoken, spiritual, wise, quiet, gentle, and caring man, unlike my mentally abusive former husband. I felt safe being in his presence and inviting him into my life for I never sensed an ounce of meanness in Michael.*

Throughout our four-year relationship, including marriage, we each stood separate from each other resisting our individual pain. In spite of our efforts, our separate stances made it difficult to see and touch each other at a heart level. Beneath our anger, we hurt. We both felt unlovable and I wanted to avoid feeling that pain.

Sharon speaks again this time now about her personal pain, critical thoughts, and feelings. *I knew none of this at the time. I knew in my heart I loved Michael; however, I remained ignorant of how to express it verbally or intimately. My rape as a child ripped me apart. I lost confidence and respect for myself. I felt filthy, betrayed, helpless, and ashamed. I blamed myself and hated my body. Confusion, frustration, anger, resentment, fear, depression, and hatred silently filled the pores of my being.*

Then I allowed the verbal abuse from my former husband with words such as; you are ugly, fat, stu-

pid, and will never amount to anything to penetrate my spirit. I hit rock bottom where I became anorexia and attempted to commit suicide twice. Suicide seemed the only way to end my pain and suffering. On an inner level I got the message, 'It is not your time to die. Get yourself into the hospital and when you return you will become a healer, teach around the world, and write books.' None of this made sense to me at the time.

I learned about my inner child and codependency through months and months of therapy, workshops, and working with my mentor, Linda. When I met Michael, all I had learned still needed to connect to the core of my Being. So when Michael came into my life my past pain reactivated.

I warred within. Part of me wanted to open up to Michael. Yet, another part of me, my wounded inner child, battled with me whenever I desired to speak my truth and become close and intimate. I still needed more healing of the deep seeded wounds from my sexual abuse as a child and the mental abuse from my former husband. How could I give the nurturing to another which I lacked for myself?

The pattern that kept repeating in my relationship with Sharon involved lacking feeling good enough about myself. I had to do something to change. In my family, my father dumped emotional and verbal abuse upon my mother. In her unhappiness, my mother criticized and nagged at my father to change, to quit drinking. Caught in between I learned to stay quiet hoping to minimize the conflict. Consequently, I felt invalidated and invisible. Many of my childhood dreams involved being invisible to my pursuer. I felt unsafe.

When you don't trust, life becomes very difficult. You fight, resist, hang on, and withdraw, says Bill Ferguson in the article *Learn How To Let Go*. I lacked the trust to express the truth of what I felt. I resisted feeling my pain and even though in the depths of my being I wanted to heal, I remained ignorant of how as shown in my reactions to Sharon.

As Sharon described she suffered emotional abuse in a brief previous marriage to the point of giving up eating, becoming anorexic, and losing the will to go on living. Both of us had a major issue of trusting the opposite sex. Throughout our relationship, snuggling up to me she queried, *What is going on with you.*

Fearing to voice my real feelings, I cringe from her touch. *Nothing,* I reply as I withdraw into the safety of silence.

Sharon sensing my withdrawal slams the door of her heart closed as her three-year-old inner child suffers forlorn, hurt, and unlovable. Consequently, the five-year-old boy within me now retreats feeling abandoned.

Icy silence reigns in our household as neither of us talk. In pain, we both seek refuge in isolation.

Sharon continues. *When Michael and I resisted speaking our truth, our souls suffered. In some cases, I no longer felt empowered or lively. I disconnected because I stifled the expression of my spirit. I lacked integrity with my truth so I experienced pain, suffering, and separation.*

I encouraged Michael to share his feelings with me and like me he remained afraid to say the wrong thing because of being judged, so at times it remained easier be quiet and stay in isolation. He enjoyed his quiet times in and out of meditation and I gave up the joyous music and laughter between my daughter and me to make sure I pleased Michael. After all, I remained a people pleaser.

Later after two, three days, or sometimes up to one week finally breaking the quiet Sharon would come to me saying, *We need to talk.* Drawing close to me, she began opening her heart about her feelings. Feeling safer my five-year-old inner boy sidles a little closer to her, allowing me to share how I have been feeling.

This pattern of withdrawal and brief open communication seesawed throughout our time together. In the end, we both learned we could climb out of isolation, open our hearts, communicate, and feel the tentative touch of a finger of love.

We caught a glimpse of a different truth where we could share our real nature and the pain. Opening our hearts and sharing ourselves created a truth sweet like roses firmly rooted in rich moist black loam.

Sharon continues. *When Michael and I connected and spoke our truth I experienced an oneness between us I had never felt before. A place within me felt peace, love, and harmony. Previous unspoken words allowed us to catch a glimpse of our truth for one another, as well as for ourselves.*

Like in my relationship with Angelique and Gina, I rode the roller coaster of codependency with Sharon. If someone had called me codependent, I would have strongly denied it. With my fear, I had become a loner, self-sufficient, and dependent upon no one. In spite of my illusion of separateness, I had felt responsible for Angelique's son, Gina's finances, and Sharon's health; they needed my help. I said yes to requests for help when I really wanted to say no. Feeling like a victim, unworthy, and believing I lacked the capacity for giving or receiving love all contributed to my codependency.

I suffered in the ignorance until Sharon introduced me to the idea of codependency. When I read the book, *Codependent No More,* by Melody Beattie I began to see my full-blown codependency. As Sharon became happy, I felt happy. When Sharon got depressed, I became depressed. All my life I allowed women's moods to determine my feelings as I rode the roller coaster of codependency.

Yes, I tried to figure out what women wanted to hear. Yes, I had difficulty expressing emotions and knowing my needs. Yes, I found it safer to feel other people's feelings rather than expose my own.

Sharon continues. *Like Michael I too wanted to please people, especially those closest to me. I felt unimportant unless people needed me. I found it difficult to make even small decisions such as what movie to see or where to go for dinner. I valued other people's opinions more than my own.*

Codependency went hand-in-hand with my low self-esteem. When I first heard about co-dependency from Linda, my mentor, I refused to believe she meant me. After all, I wanted to please everyone, everyone except myself.

I thought I showed love by all I did. In reality, I showed no love. I demonstrated selfishness and never allowed people to be themselves, live their lives, or allow myself to embrace my life. I refused to consider what could have been important to me for it never mattered. Others mattered.

Someone stated, "Codependency is any and all actions, thoughts, feelings from the perspective of the false self rather than the True Self."

Sharon assisted me in recognizing my codependency. Also with Sharon, I started to become aware of, speaking to, and healing my inner five-year-old boy. Sharon balanced her health, diet, and spirituality through my influence, while I integrated my inner feminine energy and emotions with her help. All this helped my standing firmer in the truth of my True Self, which allowed me, at times, to experience the present moment in a state of peace. Maybe there could be more to relationships then separation surrounded by pain.

After my relationship ended with Sharon, it took another two experiences before I grew out of codependency. Part of my helping people and allowing them to use me included giving them money and never receiving payment back. In a previous sales job, I never collected seven thousand dollars in commissions owed me. With Gina, I had lent her a total of about seven thousand dollars. After she moved out from my apartment I called to tell her I released her from the debt as I knew she would never be able to repay me.

Michael has been a blessing in my life. I learned to trust men again. He educated and assisted me with my health and walked hand in hand with me as I awakened to a new reality about spirituality. As a rescuer, I saw the potential Michael had as a healer and teacher, yet he lacked faith in himself to follow his dreams. How two people like Michael and I see

the potential in one another yet never within our-
selves.

After Michael and I ended our marriage, I con-
tinued to study with my mentor to heal my past, em-
brace my truth, and express my True Self. I learned
to stop caring about other people's thoughts and op-
tions. They belonged to them rather than me. My on-
ly obligation remained to be true to my Spirit.

I remained out of relationship until nearly ten
years after Michael and I left one another. During
those ten years, with love and passion, I started liv-
ing my life purpose as a healer, writer, and traveling
the world teaching. In 2000, I committed to a loving
relationship with Hector and my heart now opens to
receive and give the immense love, compassion, inti-
macy and devotion my spirit longed to express. I
have awakened all aspects of myself. I found my
journey out of codependency led to my happiness and
peace of mind.

BETH: EMPOWERMENT

Codependence is about giving away power over our self-esteem.

When we look outside for self-definition and self-worth, we are giving power away and setting ourselves up to be victims.

Robert Burney, codependence counselor, in the article *Codependence vs. Interdependence*

I fell into my next codependent relationship where my personal life and my life purpose became hopelessly entangled. I falsely believed I needed a female partner to assist in carrying out my life purpose. With this relationship, the most challenging, I finally broke free of the yoke of disempowerment.

The breaking free required looking inside myself rather than outside for connection. It required the choice to face and go through a *Dark Night of the Soul* where I surrendered everything including the healing institute, being the principal healing teacher and the willingness to give up my life purpose. It required following the truth of my *still small voice* of intuition.

I met Beth while attending a meditation group at her beach apartment overlooking the bright Pacific waters of Southern California. Through a series of events, we would wind up working together establishing an institute for a new frequency of energy healing in the world.

Beth and I both came from highly dysfunctional families. Her mother who felt unloved addicted to food and casual sex with strangers. In her jealous self-hatred, Beth's mother viewed Beth as a female rival.

Like Beth's mother, my father's out of control self-destructive drinking stemmed from a man full of self-loathing, self-pity, and a sense of being a total failure. Lost in the pit of his sorrow my father refused to acknowledge my existence.

Both Beth and I had at the core of our unconscious a deep sense of being unlovable, of being unworthy. Consequently, I believed I lacked the strength to bring the new energy healing into the world on my own. The lack of confidence in myself convinced me I needed a female partner to assist in holding the concentrated focus for the healing to be established.

Using Beth as a clutch, I leaned on her hoping she would empower me. Our relationship teetered back and forth between her being in the depth of despair and being calm. Her feelings also became my feelings. It became complicated because the personal and business relationship intermixed.

As Pia Melody, *Facing Codependency* says, *The heart and soul of codependence lies in the difficulty codependents have knowing what their feelings are and how to share them.*

Beth saw herself as a workhorse dedicating much of her spare time assisting me in organizing to build a healing institute. She often said about herself, *I feel unappreciated.* She meant she felt unloved by me. She did the work because she believed that would gain my love. I loved her as a confidant, as a spiritual companion never a romantic lover.

In our relationship, I also gave my power away to Beth. Her control became clearer in the last two months of my association with her. No longer, however, did I remain quiet. I began expressing. Whenever I acted following my intuitive clarity Beth would berate me, burst forth into an ugly rage, or attempt to manipulate me.

I realized I could blame her and expect her to make up and give me what I missed as a child. On the other hand, her reactions of rage and manipulation could be used as opportunities for me to go beyond the emotional pain of childhood rather than being caught up in the reactions. She gave me a chance to go: beyond feeling unloved, into a place of clarity, into a state of courage where I spoke the truth, as I knew it which empowered me.

When I choose to speak truth, the whole universe supported me. The universe sent two gifted healers, Mary and Pat, to assist me. For two and one half months, I received a weekly one-hour concentrated combination of hands-on energy healing and breath work.

Emotionally and energetically in ten sessions I let go of past childhood pain, which included lack of trust, fear of standing up to women, and fear of speaking my truth. The frightened child within me released the control.

In the healing two aspects of me, the inner child and a higher aspect of me came together bringing realizations, *I am loving, worthy, and empowered.* This change included expressing appropriate anger, making mistakes, learning and gathering wisdom from those mistakes.

CHAPTER 11

WHAT EVERYONE OUGHT to KNOW ABOUT SPEAKING OUR TRUTH

For some people the material world – solid objects - makes up their truth or perception of reality. Yet the physicist knows reality as material, light, and energy – E=MC2.

We all suffer from limited perception of the bigger picture or reality. Personality truth comes from limited perceptions, the left brain only, our attachments and aversions, and our illusions of what we believe to be real. Adding another element, our inner child wounding distorts our reality, particularly in relationships.

What we know and experience consciously makes up the truth for us at that particular moment. On a hopeful note, truth has many interpretations and develops as we gain more clarity as our inner child heals and our consciousness expands and we also develop the ability to know the intuitive truth from the level of our souls.

Intuitive truth comes from our Higher Self/soul as a more expanded vision. Intuitive truth makes no logical sense to the rational ego yet in our heart, we know it as fact. In the astronomer Galileo's time, the established authorities proclaimed the sun revolved around the earth. Galileo's expanded view showed the reality of the earth circling the sun.

Most of the time in my codependent relationships with women, I stood upon the false ground of personality truth based on fear and pain rather than a solid foundation of intuition from my soul.

In relationships teetering on fear and anger, I often plummeted into a pit of depression to wallow in despair. Seldom did I stand with both feet planted upon a foundation of intuitive truth as Galileo had. Seldom did I stir beyond the claw of fear clutched around my heart to enter into a garden of truth, a garden with sweet scent of the flowers of shared open communication intimacy, and trust with a female partner. In terms of codependence, I lacked the ability to say no and to set limits, as well as knowing and having the courage to speak up about what I felt and needed.

I froze rigid with fear in my relationship with Angelique as we both tumbled into a pit of despair, misery, and emotional pain. Trapped, we endured the hell of hopelessness and unhappiness, which seemed unending. On rare occasions, when I felt more emotionally open, relaxed, and comfortable with myself, I reached out a hand inviting Angelique into the sunlit garden of truth. Angelique, like a deer, bolted from the invitation of basking in the warmth of shared intimacy.

Angelique harbored a subconscious fear I might harm her physically or emotionally, which I had no idea of at the time. Thus, she either hid too terrified to enter into intimacy.

Although we never talked about it, we both unconsciously recognized each other's pain and fear. Perhaps in our hidden thoughts we hoped being in relationship would ease our individual pain. Instead, the pain magnified like the white head of a boil swollen to bursting.

Our relationship brought up the issue of abandonment for Angelique. Too terrified, as my father had been, to be emotionally present I remained blinded to really seeing Angelique as she did to me. Frozen in my own pain and unable to ease Angelique's agony she became more angry and hurt. Unable to feel me along side of her, she felt forsaken. Long before I left physically, I emotionally abandoned Angelique like my father.

In my relationship with Angelique, I learned how immobilized in fear and pain I had become.

In my next relationship, I continued to flee from the truth of my suffering and to Gina there seemed no escape from the bondage of her unhappiness.

Often, I allowed Gina to drag me into a pit of hope-lessness where I got mired in the mud of self-pity and victimization. When Gina verbally attacked me for being emotionally unavailable I would say to myself, Why am I being attacked, I don't deserve this. My self-esteem nose-dived to the bottom of the emotional barometer.

With arms flung heavenward Gina begged me to bail her out of her hopeless situations when she de-pended upon my financial ability to rescue her.

Gina's lack of movement in any area of her life smoldered as slow burning resentment within me. Sometimes the other side of victimhood, resentment, ignited and I stood in red-hot anger. This action only increased Gina's own anger.

Throughout our relationship, Gina strove with needling poker probes of verbal assaults to pierce my emotional armor. With me being as far distant as Mars, she sank deeper into frustration and sorrow.

Finally, in my last year being with Gina, individu-al weekly professional hypnosis sessions helped me to gain clarity, which assisted me to drag myself out of my pattern of victimization and powerlessness

Hypnosis helped me glimpse some awareness of my emotional patterns. Hypnosis also assisted a nat-ural release through dreams of anger, anxiety, and conflicts. Within the safety of the dream arena, I could express without fear.

In spite of my personal growth, I would refrain from recommending hypnosis. In hypnosis, instead of developing my own will as I did for instance in meditation, I handed my subconscious over to the will of the hypnotist. Hypnosis made me aware of some of my basic patterns and developed my courage to stand up to Gina. It, however, ceased going deep enough to release and heal the core emotional issues. Hypnosis could be compared to hiring a cleaning service to clean the house while, meanwhile, a lifetime of hoarded dysfunctions lay buried in the depths of the musty basement.

Although in my relationship with Gina I remained in my emotional pain, I did begin to see deeper into the truth of who I was. Some of my basic psychological patterns emerged, which I would be confronted with in future relationships. These characteristics would need releasing and healing before I stepped into standing up for myself and confidently speaking my truth. The patterns that affected me and those around me included repressing who I was; being inexpressive; and anxiety and mistrust interacting with people. They also included being nonassertive and refusing to set limits with women; looking for outside approval; fear of being vulnerable; and lack of self-love and trust in myself.

As I terminated my relationship with Gina, I desired going beyond the emotional patterns of the past that kept me trapped in pain. In my next relationship, with Sharon, I caught a fleeting glimpse of strolling in a garden of expressed truth, hand in intimate hand.

 Sharon offered a big step forward as she abstained from dragging me into her pit of despair.

Both Sharon and I stood in personality truth at the beginning of our relationship. We, however, went through much self-growth together. In the end of our relationship, we still stood separated by anger towards the opposite sex, mistrust, and unworthiness. Occasionally, we wandered into the garden of truth yet, without a solid core of trust we left quickly.

With Sharon, I learned to look more deeply at my patterns of codependency and victimization. To move through these patterns would require a merging of my heart and mind, of my inner male and female energies. It would require me standing alone in my own truth and power.

I see all my relationships as opportunities for healing my inner child wounds, as well as developing greater clarity of the truth of myself, and strengthening my connection with the intuitive truth of my soul. This includes my relationship with Beth who helped teach me to stand firmly upon a foundation of intuitional truth rather than in pain and separateness. No longer did I want to step into a pit of unhappiness with someone else, even if this meant remaining alone for the rest of my life.

Over the next nine months, after the relationship with Beth, I remained alone. After six months of aloneness, a strong longing for female companionship threatened to pull me into another relationship. Unconsciously I recognized the sorrow, anger, and core lack of self-love the woman carried that I felt pulled towards.

On an intuitive level, I knew getting involved with this woman would be repeating an old pattern of unhappiness. Later, I became aware this woman had been a test to see if I would fall back into a previous form of relationship or whether I had grown enough to enter an entirely different kind of relationship.

Through my inner knowing, I realized I needed to stay with my feelings of aloneness. The last three months of solitude became crucial for integrating the male energy to stand alone in truth with my inner feminine energy, nurturing, and loving myself. This could be considered a marriage of aspects of my own male and female energies. This trial of solitude, during the Dark Night of the Soul, prepared me for my next and final relationship with my wife of today, Lyn.

Before meeting Lyn, I had accepted being alone for the rest of my life. One of thirty people at an evening talk and demonstration I gave about energy healing in Toronto, Canada, Lyn sat anonymous within the group. She told me a few months later, I instantly recognized you as soon as you turned on the healing energy and began speaking. I felt, as I had known you all my life, like we had always been together.

We never spoke to each other during or after the lecture. Afterwards she announced to her rational minded father who had been absence from the lecture, I have met the man I am going to marry.

Lyn continued to keep me in the dark about her interest in me. She decided if the universe meant our relationship to be I had to recognize it on my own.

On the afternoon of the second healing seminar I taught in Toronto, as it wound down I began saying good-bye and hugging the participants. Unsuspecting, I approached Lyn. As we come together in our first embrace, I felt something different from anything I had ever experienced before. My sense of the twenty other participants in that once dark basement, which through the weekend transformed into an environment of healing and light, vanished. I found on an inner level, amongst an expanse of stars glittering against the dark background of space, a feeling of unity engulfing me.

Lyn whispered, "What do you feel?"

I have come home, I answered in an embrace I never wanted to leave.

In the summary of my learning's in relationships with women, I spoke a little about the garden of truth. With Lyn, we both entered a garden of truth together. Before we could enter into the garden, however, we both had to break down barriers to go beyond our fears with each other. This occurred in the first two years of marriage.

In our unconscious we each feared physical and emotional harm from the other because of past hurts. Therefore, we played an emotional seesaw for a while before showing more of our true selves when we discovered no attacks came from the other person. As the love grew between us, we learned to trust and stand solid ground without fear. Sometimes one of us would step into the garden of truth inviting the other to join them.

The flower blossoms within our garden consist of love, respect, trust, and intimacy. These allow us to open up communication knowing that neither of us will harm the other if they speak their truth, as they know it at that particular moment. Without judgment, we unconditionally accept each other.

Our joining in the garden nourishes us. It allows our individual creative gifts to grow, which includes Lyn's gift of healing and mine of healing, spiritual teaching and writing.

Our relationship grows as a gift to each other. It gives us an opportunity to merge our individual masculine and feminine strengths to be the truth of who we are at a core level.

It has taken me many years of learning how to develop my inner masculine strength to stand in the truth of who I am while in relationship with women. My pattern, until my relationship with Lyn, has been a fear of judgment and being hurt for revealing my thoughts and feelings. My fear kept me prisoner to codependency. When my partner felt good, I felt good. When she expressed unhappiness, I fell into a pit of misery. Sometimes the woman became the persecutor berating me for lack of communication and I went into feeling victimized. My mate, however, became just as victimized by the persecution of my icy unloving silence.

It has taken seeing my emotional patterns and a great deal of inner work to release these subconscious archetypes of past emotional pain. It has taken listening to my intuition; letting go of control and trusting. It has taken courage to go beyond my childhood experiences of feeling unloved. It has taken Lyn courage to step through the pain of her family splitting up because of her mother's alcoholism. It has also taken her even more courage to let go of taking responsibility and taking on the emotional pain of others close to her.

It takes courage for both of us to stand in our truth and explain how we feel to each other. This involves neither of us judging the other nor having expectations that the other person change. Judging, verbal attacking, or emotional defending stops the communication.

My speaking from a nonjudgmental place gives Lyn a chance to see how she feels. The unconditional love of accepting each other exactly as we are gives both of us the opportunity for emotional nourishment and growth.

Are you ready to learn greater clarity of truth, to stand empowered, and speaking the truth of your higher intuition? It's never too late.

In her late sixties Brooks Crown, a Hospice caregiver represented a living example of it never being too late. *In my changes I am learning to stand empowered and speak my truth with love. One of the lessons I discovered; I want to stand in my power. I want to speak my truth with love. As a woman, I have given away power over and over in this lifetime. Seeking to look from a higher perspective I keep surrendering my little will to the greater Will of God more and more each day.*

CHAPTER 12

WHAT CODEPENDENCY CAN TEACH US ABOUT CARING for OURSELVES.

I am going to share a few examples from other people's lives of their experience and learning's from being in codependent relationships.

JACQUELINE STONE: CODEPENDENCE to INDEPENDENCE

Jacqueline, an abuse survivor, adopted some codependent behaviors; she gave her power away for survival. Through her experience she became whatever she thought people wanted her to be to ward off the fear of rejection. She entered into further abusive relationships with needy people so she could feel needed.

Jacqueline begins by saying, *Although I failed to see it at the time, I needed to feel needed and valued because I had no sense of value for myself. I felt I had to 'earn my keep' in each relationship*

One husband and one boyfriend abused me for many years. Although my first husband never abused me in anyway, he kept an emotional distance and slept with another woman. I left him six years before I married the abusive husband.

I avoided intimate relationships. I found it diffi-cult to trust men. In addition, I lacked trust in myself. I feared disappointing my partners, of being not good enough. It took a long time before I began heal-ing from the events of my childhood.

Bartending became a perfect career for it pro-vided a physical barrier between me and the custom-ers. Even with friends, I withdrew from opportuni-ties to build relationships and connect. At times, I re-fused to answer my phone, even if my best friend called because I felt vulnerable.

Many of us go through life with walls around our hearts to protect us from being hurt. Those walls pre-vent us from loving fully or receiving the love of oth-ers. My work on the 'Recovering from Abuse blog' centers on healing the heart of the victim, yet, abusers need to heal too.

Pia Mellody in her book, Facing Codependency, talks about different types of boundaries – energy fields around us to keep people from coming into our personal space. *People who have been abused may use walls instead of healthy boundaries, walls of fear, anger, silence, or words for a feeling of safety and they can switch from one type of wall to another to remain invulnerable. They (walls) do not allow for intimacy . . . . A wall can be appropriate, however,* when a person needs protection from someone who is abusing them, says Pia.

Jacqueline continues. *Pain in the heart drives people to be abusive. Pain in the heart makes others think they deserve abuse. The cycle of abuse passes on through generations. It can be stopped.*

I wanted most to love and be loved; yet, my fear of the consequences far outweighed my desires. All my experiences of love included fear, pain, rejection, judgment, and/or abandonment.

I remained unaware of the damaging conditioning created by my molestation until after I left my second abusive relationship many years later. After my husband nearly killed me, I thought I would never allow myself to be abused again. It did happen again. The unconscious beliefs in my own mind allowing abusive treatment needed healing. I now know to change my life I had to change my state of mind.

On the road from victim to victory, I met a wonderful man. He sent me cards, flowers, and little gifts for no reason. He called me every day and told me how wonderful I was. The day we got married, all that changed.

I came crashing off my pedestal to become a piece of property. The abuse began slowly. My husband started eroding my self-esteem with degrading comments. He never allowed me to wear anything attractive. He isolated me from my family and friends. He took all my paychecks. He showed insane jealousy of the men at work. To top it off, he drank.

Regardless of what I said or did, I got beaten. He threw things and shoved me around, only a little at first. After the first incident, I enjoyed a break of several months before the next incident. Then the abuse became increasingly frequent.

When my husband lost his job, he began drinking heavily and gambling daily in Las Vegas where we lived. We had saved $20,000 to buy a house. He gambled that away and more.

I suffered verbal abuse daily and physical abuse two to three times a week. We had no children, thank God. I went to work with bruises and cuts even make-up couldn't conceal.

With eyes always red and swollen from crying, everyone knew about the abuse. No one said a word. Twice, my husband pointed a loaded gun at my face and many times threatened to kill me.

My husband had everything in his name. I had no property, no car, and no money. He never allowed me to have friends, so I had no one to turn to. He never let me go anywhere without him. If he wanted sex when he came home from the casino, he raped me. If I dared to say no, he beat me first and then raped me. *I felt completely helpless, trapped, and alone.*

How do we recognize predators? Dr. Heyward Ewart Ph.D., The Lies That Bind: The Permanence of Child Abuse says, *The very first indication is that a predator wants to own you, you become property, and you are treated as property. Possession is the opposite of love. Jacqueline's husband wanted to possess her.*

Jacqueline continues. *Possession showed up first as jealousy disguised as deep love. My husband refused to be apart from me or share me with others. I thought this meant he loved me completely. He kept me by his side everywhere and made it clear to other men through holding me close and other public displays of affection our connection as a couple.*

Naive when I met my husband, he made sure I stayed that way. He controlled every aspect of my life. Why did I find myself in the same position I had criticized other women for a few years earlier?

Jacqueline's husband denied her reading books on prayer to gain strength in dealing with him. When he forbid her to read them she says, I felt a rush of power, strength, and resolve foreign to me. All love or concern for my husband died at that moment. I became numb to his insults. My body felt nothing when he beat me that night. Next day she filed for divorce.

When Jacqueline told her husband she had just filed for divorce, The tough angry man shrank back down into his chair. He became the most pathetic little boy of a man I had ever seen.

The road of healing has been long. I am a happy, confident, capable person now. I have five children and a husband who never raises a hand to me. I am going to college, starting a business, and have written a book. It's been seventeen years since I started my life over. I have forgiven my former husband. I am no longer angry or afraid.

So many people have suffered some kind of abuse in their lives. It can be difficult to heal the wounds of the past, yet, I have. We may be caught up in victimhood and only we can make the choice for change and empowerment.

Jacqueline dug deep into the heart of life to face and overcome her fears. Freedom for her means independence and being herself, as well as being spiritually liberated. She has found her life purpose of personal coaching and teaching by example through her experience and also writing. Dan Millman, *The Life You Were Born to Live*, would verify Jacqueline's life purpose by saying, *Those on this life path are here to work through issues related to independence, emotional honesty, and cooperation, finally experiencing freedom through discipline and depth of experience.*

Jacqueline ends by saying, *The life work I do now has grown out of the experiences I've had and the personal discovery that comes from examining them.*

Recovering from codependency means learning to care for ourselves as shown by the next example.

JULIANNE: RECOVERY FROM CODEPEND-ENCY: LEARNING SELF-CARE

Boundaries are about knowing where you end and someone else begins. It means having a good solid sense of self and a working understanding of the working personality of the other person, all the while knowing the other person has full responsibility for self-care.

Pat Wyman, author, *Three Keys to Self-Understanding*

Julianne, a therapist, begins by saying, *Like many girls in the Western world; my family raised me to be codependent.*

When I married I wanted my husband, Chris, to pay attention to me all the time like my father. Over twenty-five years, Chris acted just like my father with intermittent adoration and withdrawal. My self-esteem depended upon Chris loving me.

In the last five years of our marriage, I began to take care of myself. I had my own friends and spiritual practice. I recognized us as two separate souls pursuing our own paths. I felt the deep pain and if I held myself back from my self-growth for Chris, I would be keeping myself small.

I choose to move forward, even if it meant losing Chris. I realized my job did not involve pulling him along with me.

Although we believed we came together as soul mates, we had different life paths.

I moved beyond wanting to change him. He had his path, which I could support even though different from mine. We separated as good friends.

Does a woman's task involve shouldering her man's emotional needs? Does she need to be the sole one who experiences and expresses the emotions in the relationship?

JOANNA: MEETING OUR OWN EMOTIONAL NEEDS

Codependency is about having a dysfunctional relationship with self.

Robert Burney, Codependence Counselor
www.joy2meu.com

Joanna, a retired CEO, lived through decades of codependent relationships. She says, Codependency dominated all four of my marriages, to varying degrees, yet I had never heard of this creator of suffer-

ing. My marriages consisted of unhappiness, manip-
ulation, and discord from the emotional baggage of
both partners and my childhood background.

At a point, I realized all the blame no longer lay
with my partners. I needed to heal the suffering from
my own childhood. Since the age of 24, I have been
driven and have persevered to heal myself. My jour-
ney involves continuous self-growth and inner heal-
ing.

Codependence counselor, Robert Burney says,
Codependency . . . to be emotionally anorexic. Not
having our emotional needs met in childhood sets us
up for the behavior patterns that cause our adult
emotional needs to go unmet . . . reflections of our
Spiritual wound . . . that deep empty longing can on-
ly be filled spiritually, by reconnecting with our
Source.

The still small voice I have referred to on occasion
remains an important concept to consider in regards
to our understanding of truth. How do we learn to
recognize our own still small voice? See the following.

THE STILL SMALL VOICE

The still small voice embodies our personal inner
voice of truth. We may have heard it called the sixth
sense or the intuition. This inner voice goes beyond
our personality, intellectual mind, and our emotions,

which can keep us locked in limitations of false truth through fear.

We, like Kathryne-Alexis, a life path consultant, may have learned as a child to keep our intuition to ourselves.

Kathryne-Alexis talks about her childhood. *I knew when my intuition felt right. Yet, every fear of being different, called crazy, or shushed by older relatives in front of company lead me to be silent. On the other hand, now, as an adult we may only listen to our sixth sense when it suits our rational mind. Again Kathryne-Alexis comments, I have always heard or felt my intuition; sixth sense . . . . I ignored, ran, or listened to my guidance only when it pleased me.*

We all have access to the truth of the still small voice within. It may come through a hunch, an intuitive feeling. All of a sudden, awareness flashes through our mind, which feels perfectly right. We remain unable to explain to our friends where the intuition came from. In rational terms, we remain unable to justify it either. Yet, we know within the fiber of our being, it is truth for us.

Brooks Crown, a Hospice caregiver, explains how her intuition operated for her. *Intuition, which gives a greater perspective, has always been my strongest extra-sensory skill. I have not always trusted my intuition and gradually over the years, I have learned to pay more attention to it. My intuition often oper-*

*ates as a nudge to take a 'leap of faith' with no logic
backing it up. The decision to sell the bookstore represents one such intuitive nudge. I had reached a
place in my spiritual growth where my Higher Self
knew the time had come for me to move on. This occurred before consciously being aware of stagnation
happening in my life.*

We all perceive information differently. Neurolin-
guistic programming explains people predominantly
either feel, see, or hear information coming to them.
In receiving truth from our still small voice, some of
us get words or thoughts coming through, which involves a type of seeing or hearing. We hear inner
sounds or higher pitched vibrations. Like Socrates,
we may even hear the voice of a higher aspect of ourselves, our Higher Self speaking directly to us. Others
of us get intuitive feelings. Sometimes a rush of energy shoots through our body, or up our spine, or we get
a strong sensation in our gut. Body feeling occurs for
Kathryne-Alexis. *I get 'God bumps' or 'skin
knowledge' when I am to join in some gathering in
person. When skin knowledge comes, when I feel a
wave of love envelop me, I realize all life supports my
participation.*

It has been my experience, as well as other people,
to feel my whole body vibrating like a tuning fork with
the speaking of truth in our presence. We tend to en-
vy, myself included, those people who have a natural
gift of clairvoyance, which allows them to see colored

light or images. Yet, this is only one of four ways of receiving intuitional truth. Last of all, we may receive truth through a direct knowing. Each way is unique; our specific access to the truth of our inner voice.

On occasions I receive a sense of an image. Now more often than years ago I will see images when I am asked a question and I tap into my knowing sense. My natural ability involves an inner knowing. Also when involved in channeling energy for a client in healings, I feel in my body the emotions and pain releasing from their body.

My inner voice also communicates through thoughts or words coming into my mind sometimes. At these times, I have refrained from figuring anything out whenever the information suddenly appears.

The most common way I receive communication with my inner voice thus comes through direct knowing. An insight will suddenly flash before me. In clarity, I realize that to act upon the insight would be for my highest good. The action involves going beyond the limitations of my mind and the "truth" of the personality. This used to bring up fears of trusting the truth of my still small voice. Now I have learned to trust.

How do we develop our intuition, our still small voice? Go inside yourself and listen in the stillness. Pete Sanders, a MIT graduate, *You Are Psychic*, explains how to develop your intuition.

Also through a daily practice of meditation, our intuition develops. Yogananda, a spiritual teacher, explains this in his commentary on, *The Bhagavad Gita, No devotee should be satisfied until he has sufficiently developed his intuition . . . by impartial introspection and deep meditation . . . He will know the interiorized state of communion in which his soul 'talks' to God and receives His responses, not with the utterances of any human language, but through wordless intuitional exchanges.*

In summary, speaking our truth and standing empowered includes recovering from codependency where we give our power away to others. It means the willingness to accept and express the truth of what we feel and need as individuals. Then we can begin to heal to become more whole emotionally and spiritually.

The truth of who we are expands as we learn to choose to overcome our suffering in relationships. Pain may be inevitable, yet suffering remains optional. In other words we have a choice to continue in our cycles of suffering or learn how to shift from victim to empowerment and to heal our low self-esteem and the wounds of our inner child.

Most important, we can continue to look outside ourselves or go inside and make a higher connection to truth, power, and self-worth.

CHAPTER 13

PHYSICAL PAIN/ENERGY HEALING: GET RID of YOUR PAIN ONCE and for ALL

E ckhart Tolle, a writer and spiritual teacher, describes his experience of enlightenment at the age of twenty-nine in *The Power of Now* after suffering long periods of depression, dissolving his old identity, and radically changing his life.

Tolle describes two levels of pain, present and past. He says, *There are two levels to your pain: the pain that you create now, and the pain from the past that still lives on in your mind and body. He explains certain emotions as also aspects of pain; Resentment, hatred, self-pity, guilt, anger, depression, jealousy, and so on, even the slightest irritation, are all forms of pain.*

As you will also see, emotional causes lie behind much physical pain. Heal the emotions and the pain dissolves.

Gary Craig, developer of EFT – Emotional Freedom Technique, has clients and healers use his technique around the world to release the emotions be-hind physical ailments. Gary says, To me, fibromyal-gia and most other physical ailments are merely bodi-ly manifestations or symptoms of unresolved fear, trauma, rejection, anger, guilt and other emotional causes. Take care of the emotional causes and the physical symptoms tend to fade.

Pat Gurnick tells of her long journey rebuilding her health after suffering for years with Chronic Fa-tigue Syndrome and Fibromyalgia pain. In some cas-es, like Pat's, emotions may not be the core cause of the physical pain. The cause may be environmental like pesticides or molds. In Pat's recovery her body needed to be flushed of toxins and the emotional component involved the regulation of her emotions.

You may be lucky to be free of Chronic Fatigue and Fibromyalgia pain. Read Pat's story because you may know someone who does suffer with these condi-tions who you can help. Also at the end, Pat lists re-sources, beneficial to all of us, for improving our phys-ical and emotional health.

PAT GURNICK, PSYCHOTHERAPIST and CERTIFIED LIFESTYLE COUNSELOR

HOW I SURVIVED CHRONIC ILLNESS – ONE WOMAN'S STORY of RESILIENCE
www.caringcounselor.com

Pat built her health, after years of debilitation from Chronic Fatigue Syndrome, CFS, and Fibromyalgia pain, with a relentless pursuit of insights from leading specialists and her own personal tenacity.

I will never forget the month and year I came down with an illness of unknown origin, January, 1990 in Los Angeles, California. My life would never be the same, explained Pat.

What caused my sickness, perhaps, an environmental toxin? My car had an exhaust problem so I naively drove with the windows open to blow the exhaust back out again. One night coming home from my night job, unbeknown to me, I drove through an aerial pesticide spraying for fruit with my car windows open. This spraying continued for a total of 12 times over the next five months because of a pandemic Mediterranean fruit fly – Med Fly infestation in fruit crops.

Subsequent to this chemical assault, my immune system became dysregulated. I developed debilitating fatigue, flu-like symptoms, swollen lymph nodes, fever, aches and pains, bladder and stomach problems, difficulty concentrating, and major depression, to name a few.

Dysregulation means the nervous system retains some energy without complete discharge as would be normal. Over time the person handles stress less well.

THE SEARCH for DIAGNOSIS and UNDERSTANDING

The main symptom of CFS is an unrelenting tiredness not relieved by rest and greatly exaggerated through even the smallest amounts of exertion. One often feels like one is walking through molasses with weights tied to every part of one's body. Maria Mann, author, *Verity Red's Diary: A Story of Surviving M. E., and CFS sufferer*

If you feel tired, you are not alone – in United States and European Union 1 out of 4 persons suffers from tiredness says Peter Novak, author, End Tiredness Program.

Pat continues her story. *This began the revolving door of doctor visits. I was lucky enough to find* Dr. Hyla Cass, MD, *a specialist in nutritional medicine and now an expert in chronic fatigue syndrome - CFS. She speculated I might have CFS and Fibromyalgia, and consequently referred me to* Dr. Murray Susser, MD, *- eventually listed in the Alternative Doctors Hall of Fame and wrote the book, "*Solving the Puzzle of Chronic Fatigue Syndrome*." He concurred I had CFS and Fibromyalgia and confirmed the diagnosis of CFS by a blood test called "Chronic Fatigue Syndrome Panel 2" through* Immunosciences Lab.

Dr. Michael Goldberg, MD, FAAP, a member of the Neuro Immune Dysfunction Syndromes (NIDS) Medical Advisory Board, *also confirmed my diagnosis* *through a <u>brain SPECT imaging scan</u> - helpful documentation if you seek disability benefits.*

Two years after being diagnosed, I moved to a new apartment. I worked as a Drug and Alcohol Counselor for Chronic Mentally Ill Substance Abusers at Brotman Hospital in Culver City, California - my health rapidly deteriorated while I struggled to find a way to remain functional on the job. Six months later, I became bedridden. I continued different medical and holistic protocols to no avail.

I had no idea the inner layer of my apartment ceiling was filled with stachybotrys mold – <u>www.mold-help.org</u> , also known as the "black mold" - one of the most dangerous indoor toxic molds, as well as other saprophytic fungi mold which produce deathly mycotoxins.

At that time, a member of my support group and "mold survivor"

Diana Meier entered my home and exclaimed she could not breathe. She stated my home was infested with mold spores. She was correct. I will be forever grateful to her for recognizing the toxic situation I was living in, and advising I move immediately. Diana Meier www.moldgoddess com.

According to Dr. Gary Ordog, a neurotoxicologist in Los Angeles, and <u>Dr. Gunnar Heuser, MD, PhD</u>, an Environmental Illness specialist, I subsequently de-

veloped *Cushings Disease/Pituitary Tumor from the mold injury, which I had removed December, 2003. (See my Cushings Disease Story at* www.cushings-help.com/patg.htm.*)*

Dr. David Bell, MD, author of the new book *Cellular Hypoxia and Neuro-Immune Fatigue*, states that toxins can initiate CFS: *Yes, mold and environmental toxins can definitely cause or initiate ME/CFS. Somehow toxins affect the cytokines in a way similar to the classic mononucleosis infection to set off the illness,* he explained in a recent ImmuneSupport.com Q&A.

Pat continues. *As a result of the Chronic Fatigue Syndrome intensified by the mold, I became sicker and unable to read, write, drive, or balance well enough to stand up to even bathe myself or make my food. I was debilitated from neurally-mediated hypotension. My blood pressure became erratic. It dropped when I stood up and I became light-headed and unstable on my feet. Weak and in continual pain, I could not even move my arm to brush my hair. For two and a half years I needed outside assistance. So disturbed with my body and mind unable to function in harmony, I wanted to end my life.*

CFIDS ASSOCIATION OFFERS a VITAL CONNECTION

In order to thrive, anyone living with CFS must repeatedly rejuvenate the will to live and to find joy in living, even while chronically ill. It can be done! No one and no disease can take away the freedom to choose how to respond to a difficult situation.

Lucinda Bateman, MD, Fatigue Consultation Clinic

Pat continues her story. *A shell of my former self, I struggled to stay alive. I knew I needed to find a reason to live. I needed to connect to people who understood what I struggled with. I also knew "being of service" to the community and being productive would make my life have value. So I contacted the Chronic Fatigue Immune Dysfunction Syndrome Association of America (www.//CFIDS.org) and decided to become a hotline contact.*

It gave me something to focus on and a reason to believe in living. Being a hotline contact was not an easy task. For a CFS patient, it's like climbing Mt. Everest. I had to monitor my time and activities. Talking 30 minutes on the phone exhausted me. I had to watch my energy expenditure closely or else I could be bedridden for days.

I had to learn to live within "the energy envelope." I developed ways to settle my neurological system and give my body an opportunity to heal. I found ways to make my home environment user friendly and to decrease my stress levels through self-nurturing behavior: meditating, listening to soothing music, taking a relaxing bath, receiving a massage, watching videos, eating pleasurable food, etc. I needed to be careful to stay out of any dramas.

My body already fought a war with illness and I wanted to learn how to turn this off; to give a new message to my body – you're safe. I started monitoring people, places, and things in my life to maintain my energy. At first, it felt selfish, and then this new form of self-love and empowerment helped me feel emotionally stronger. By learning how to be friends with my body, I started transforming into a new person.

I knew I wanted to create a safe environment where other people with Chronic Fatigue Syndrome and Fibromyalgia could feel accepted and share their minds, receive support, resources, and referrals to health care providers. So I started the CEFCA Support Group at a local church. CEFCA stands for "Chronic Fatigue Syndrome, Environmental Illness, Fibromyalgia, Candida, and Allergies." At first, because of my condition, unable to sit in a chair, I lay on the floor to facilitate the group. For information about Environmental Illness/Multiple Chemical Sensitivities, see the Rocky Mountain Environmental Health Association website.

ST. AMAND PROTOCOL: A TURNING POINT for the FIBROMYALGIA

Pat continues. *Dr. St. Amand believes that both Chronic Fatigue Syndrome and Fibromyalgia are re-*

lated to each other. He believes that both are caused by a buildup of phosphate in the body, creating significant pain throughout the body. Chronic Fatigue Syndrome and guaifenesin treatment are a successful match because the guaifenesin flushes out the toxins in your body, allowing you to recover from your symptoms . . . many common household items can completely block the effectiveness of the guaifenesin treatment. www.chronicfatiguerelapse.com

At that time, unable to even walk one block because of pain and weakness, my body felt like it had just been in a car accident every day. Nine months after I began the group, September of 1993, I saw Dr. R. Paul St. Amand, MD, Director of the Fibromyalgia Treatment Center *in Marina Del Rey, CA, for help. He confirmed my diagnosis of Fibromyalgia and prescribed a substance called guaifenesin, which helps CFS in some patients. Within six months, my level of health shifted for the better. After two years, finally pain free, I could jog again.*

During that time, out of necessity, I moved my support group to Kaiser Permanente's hospital conference room. Due to the tremendous need for support among CFS patients, more than 100 members came to each meeting to hear top specialists in the field lecture, including renowned doctors such as Dr. Jay Goldstein, MD, *now retired, Dr. Jacob Teitlebaum, author of* "From Fatigued to Fantastic," *and others I have mentioned above.*

I ran this group from 1993 to 2003. My commitment to serve the community gained me an Honorary Recognition Award from the CFIDS Association.

CONTROLLING the REMISSION to RELAPSE SEESAW

Pat continues her story. To this day, I rarely have pain from Fibromyalgia. As for Chronic Fatigue Syndrome, I had a slow, gradual increase in vitality. I learned how to "live within the energy envelope" <u>using a simple energy level rating scale of 1 to 10</u> and pacing myself to attain a better level of functioning.

Initially, I went back and forth from remission to relapse, until I changed my lifestyle. No cure exists, the cause remains uncertain, yet I have found once I adapted my lifestyle, I achieved greater health. I am well now.

Today, I have my life back. As a psychotherapist, and "survivor" of Chronic Fatigue Syndrome and Fibromyalgia, I help others develop and adopt strategies like energy level management and self-pacing to function better on a daily basis and have a better quality of life.

Pat through perseverance learned to overcome the challenges of CFS and fibromyalgia. Through her power of choice she discovered over time positive ways to manage her energy levels. She also chose to use her life experience and learning in service for the easing of pain and suffering in others with similar conditions. Pat learned a valuable lesson of loving her body and herself.

Do you give yourself permission to nourish and love yourself, to be aware of your needs and feelings and give expression to these for your well-being?

CHAPTER 14

COULD OUR PHYSICAL PAIN be an OPPORTUNITY for HEALING?

L ana explains an energy healing experience where she discovered her physical pain in her hip, heart, and head had a direct relationship with the emotional pain in her family, which she had carried throughout her life even though she had resisted feeling the agony consciously.

LANA: EMOTIONS UNDERLYING PHYSICAL PAIN

The only way out is through. You have to feel it, to heal it.

Dr. Barry Weinberg, *A Clear Path to Healing*

Lana, a core energetic healer, received a Bowen therapy healing session for physical discomfort above her left hip in the lower back. The pain subjectively registered eight out of ten in severity.

Lana said, *I realized I needed to experience and hold steady with the pain rather than going back and forth avoiding it.*

Of course we resist pain. It hurts. Then, however, we inflict our pain on others through anger or we repress the pain and take it out on ourselves through self-loathing, anger turned inward, or physical disease.

If you have physical pain and have no access to a professional healer, have a person sit with you and hold the energy while you go directly into the core of the pain. Your support person needs to sit with a compassionate heart with no emotional reaction or desire to "fix" anything. Breathing into the pain and releasing it on the out breathe also helps.

If the support person gets trigger emotionally, they need to contain their emotions. This means resisting the urge to reach out to fix the other person because they feel their own discomfort. The support person contains the discomfort and sits with it in the moment with sustained attention as they also continue to hold the energy for the other person.

I chose to experience the pain and go through it, said Lana. *I recognized the pain of being separate from God. I relived my childhood and witnessed the pain in my family I had resisted. As a child, I shut down for I could not live with the unbearable pain. Now as I entered into the core of the pain, it energetically traveled from my sciatica, through my heart chakra. Once all the pain dissolved in the heart, it traveled into my head. I have had agonizing migraines for over thirty-five years.*

Oh, my God, Lana cried out in agony, *It is all my families' pain. I am experiencing every pain I have ever resisted.*

Later Lana looked up into the heights as if from a great cavern in her head. *I am totally empty in my body. The pain no longer hurts.* Lana realized, *I can experience others pain without encountering the resistance of my own pain.*

Unlike Lana we may only experience our own physical pains. Lana also felt the emotional pain behind her physical agony. In my experience as an energy healer, usually emotional causes underlie physical pain. Are you aware of the emotions behind your pain?

Lana demonstrated that emotions can lie behind our physical ailments. In the next story, Shannon Nelson tells how energy medicine – changes in the "life force" in the body promote health - healed her chronic pain as well as depression. Have you or someone you known ever been told, Just learn to live with your physical pain?

SHANNON NELSON: ENERGY MEDICINE –
HYPE or REAL?

In early 2007, Shannon Nelson, a quadriplegic, had a friend who introduced her to energy medicine and energy psychology after the medical profession told her, "Learn to live with your pain."

Shannon comments, I would love to say energy medicine and psychology came as an answer to my prayers. It sounds so poetic, however, feeling hopeless; I never prayed much at the time.

My best friend started looking into alternative medicine out of desperation. She spent countless hours doing thorough research on every promising option. At the time we harbored skepticism towards anything unless it could be proven scientifically.

After a few weeks of intense research, she decided to order a book, *The Biology of Belief* by Dr. Bruce H. Lipton. She read the author's background and found him to be a world-renowned cellular biologist rather than just a wishful thinker. Reading Dr. Lipton's book, I came to understand our thoughts create our feelings and our feelings create our health.

Our thoughts and emotions have an energy frequency like everything around us. For example, even though we may be unaware of these frequencies on a conscious level we know when someone feels 'heavy' or 'lighthearted.' Dr. Bruce Lipton has found, *Your thoughts are creating not just the environment inside you; your thoughts are activating the resonant structures in your environment and will bring things to you. Essentially, we create our world by our thoughts and beliefs.*

The Universal Law of Attraction states in another way what Bruce Lipton has scientifically proven at Stanford University's School of Medicine. The Law of Attraction says energy makes up the Universe. This even includes all physical matter, which Einstein proved in his equation $E=mc2$. Lastly, and most important, energy follows thought. In other words, we create our inner worlds and attract things to us in our outer worlds though our thoughts and feelings, conscious and unconscious, which we can choose to change.

So if feelings affect our health, what if feelings also affect our DNA? Greg Braden, scientist and author, The Spontaneous Healing of Belief, has shown through scientific study that DNA changed its shape according to the emotions created by the researchers. With love DNA relaxed and the strands unwound. With anger DNA tightened and switched off many of its codes. Have you ever felt shut down by a negative emotion?

Shannon continues. *Even though it shook me to the core and despite all the scientific evidence presented in Bruce Lipton's book, I remained skeptic.*

How could I become hopeful overnight after a decade of misery? I chose, however, to clasp to the new found hope. Then I received an introduction into energy medicine and put some of the techniques to the test with the help of my friend. Astonished, I wondered how something so simple could be effective.

Next we read "The Promise of Energy Psychology" by David Feinstein, Donna Eden, and Gary Craig. We found it enlightening! We ended up ordering additional information about energy medicine, especially EFT - emotional freedom techniques, which we put to the test. The technique amazed us.

Energy Psychology as an emerging paradigm uses physical interventions to change thoughts and feelings, usually in less time than talk therapies. Albert Szent-Gyorgyi, Nobel Laureate in Medicine says this about healing and the physical body, *The cell is a machine driven by energy. It can thus be approached by studying matter or by studying energy. In every culture and in every medical tradition before ours, healing was accomplished by moving energy.*

EFT founded by Gary Craig, an engineer, uses energy medicine by tapping acupressure points to release emotional issues or physical pain held in the body. Gary offers at his website www.emofree.com free EFT manuals, tutorials, and videos so anyone can learn to do the technique for themselves. Bruce Lipton, PhD comments, EFT is a simple, powerful process that can profoundly influence gene activity, health, and behavior.

Thousands of people around the world use EFT every day. Silvia Hartman, PhD reports, Up to 85% of people who have tried it have rated it from 'helpful' to 'very helpful.'

Shannon continues her experience with energy medicine. *Energy medicine like every healing technique takes time to release physical or emotional pain. It, however, has helped me.*

Before energy medicine and energy psychology, I took a powerful prescription pain medication three times a day, which provided only partial and temporary relief. After a few weeks of applying EFT I began feeling a lot better and with other forms of energy medicine such as Reiki on a regular basis, I gradually stopped taking pain medications and antidepressants altogether. I also began to understand our thoughts create our feelings and our feelings create our health. Amazingly, I got up in my wheelchair for longer and longer periods of time without the aid of prescription medications.

I am happy to report I am no longer in constant pain; neither bedridden nor depressed. In fact, I am taking adult education classes to prepare myself to join the work-force once again. My plans for next year also include mentoring children. I am happy to report I am currently able to stay up in my wheel-chair all day.

In no way am I suggesting you replace your med-ications and/or medical treatments with energy medicine or energy psychology. I owe my life to modern medicine. I would not have survived break-ing my neck in a country without cutting-edge treatment for spinal cord related injuries. I suggest keeping up hope when traditional medicine no longer helps. Every form of healing has its place.

I am still integrating becoming healthy again. The fact I can be pain and depression free without the aid of prescription medications strikes me as miraculous. My mental attitude, also, has dramatically changed. While I still have "breakthrough pain" every once in a while I no longer feel like a victim. I now know most physical ailments result from unresolved emotional trauma. I currently work on my own list of unre-solved emotional issues, one at a time. The more clo-sure I bring to an old issue, the better I feel. I strong-ly believe forgiveness played a crucial role in my re-covery.

Breakthrough pain comes hard and fast. It can be an instantaneous intensifying of all-over dull pain, or it may come as a localized sharp stab or fiery sensa-tion says Dr. Scott Fishman, *Q and A on Break-through Pain.*

Shannon continues. *I came to realize the reason I experienced so much physical pain; I carried guilt for a long time. When I first began using EFT I made a list of the things I felt guilty about starting with my accident. I used to blame myself for it. When I truly forgave myself, the pain began to subside.*

I recently began working with an EFT professional. While I do give myself credit for overcoming chronic pain and severe depression, I have to admit I had no idea how much emotional baggage I still carried until I began working with the EFT therapist. I am finally beginning to make peace with the various traumatic events from my childhood.

In 2005 while going through a particularly dark time, I joined a chronic pain support group seeking answers. I posted a message about my condition on one of their message boards and got several replies from caring people, some going or had gone through similar situations. I also read what I can only describe as horror stories of people suffering indescribable physical and emotional pain. Like me, most of them had already tried a variety of prescription pain medications and anti-depressants; and like me, some of them had sunk into hopeless. I will forever be grateful to those compassionate individuals who reached out in spite of their own pain.

To this day I feel heart-broken whenever I remember some of the postings by people in so much agony. They just wanted a way out. I knew if I ever found any relief for my pain or a glimpse of hope, I would make it my mission to spread the word and reach out to people experiencing physical and/or emotional pain.

My mission involves reaching out to people experiencing despair due to health problems, especially chronic pain and depression. Whether you suffer from physical or emotional pain or know someone suffering, I would like to invite you to contact me for help, inspiration, and support.

I finally found meaning to my years of suffering; I am embracing my new mission wholeheartedly.

I believe the accident made me more empathetic towards others. I've always considered myself to be a compassionate person, yet before my accident I was more self-centered. When it comes to other people I am a very forgiving person and I've always had a challenge accepting and forgiving myself.

Do you believe you have incarnated on this earth to learn lessons about choices, empowerment, or abundance, etc.? If you believe our experience on earth holds the opportunity for spiritual growth and expansion of consciousness then at some point in our development we also have the ability to share our spiritual gifts in service to ease the suffering of others and to assist them in their growth.

Shannon Nelson has had more than her share of life challenges to learn from. Maybe Shannon experienced the breaking of her neck to break the connection with her former life. This gave her a new choice to follow the path of her soul and finally to share the abundance of her inner discoveries in a vision of assisting others who suffer physical and/or emotional pain. She overcame depression and powerlessness to reclaim her power and her life and in so doing found her mission/service.

THE EMOTION CODE: HEALING CHRONIC PHYSICAL PAIN

The Emotion Code method of energy healing developed by Dr. Bradley Nelson, for healing emotional trauma, also assists in releasing chronic physical pain. The following testimonial by Peggy Goodman describes this method.

I am a physical therapist in Rupert, Idaho. I do the chronic pain management for the physical therapy department at the hospital where I work. When I have patients with chronic illness or chronic pain, what I have found is that there is almost always an emotional aspect that is tied to their pain or illness especially if they were not improving. Your Emotion Code information was very helpful for me as a therapist to help patients identify the emotions, which caused a "charge" or elicited a response as they went down the list from your Emotion Chart. I would have them mark the ones that stood out for them and have them give me a number from (1-10) to list the intensity of the emotion for them. I would then muscle test and see how many heart walls and/or hidden walls were present, how thick, what type of material they were made of to help me understand and get a better handle on the heart walls so they could be cleared. They could always relate these emotions and heart walls to particular instances in the past that had brought them. I would use Nikken's magcreator to roll over their back as I had them breathe deeply and give permission to release them by blessing these emotions, making them sacred and sending them up to God. When I would re-muscle test, the intensity of the emotions would be less or cleared as would the heart walls. I also found that I could clear many emotions at the same time as well as more than one heart wall at a time if there were more than one, if I could identify them first and the emotions that went with them.

One of my patients was a lady that was diagnosed with A.L.S. (Amyotrophic Lateral Sclerosis). She came in with numerous neurological symptoms that would be consistent with that diagnosis. As I had her read your information on heart walls, identified emotions that were bothering her, and had her work on her home exercise program, her neurological symptoms faded and she is doing well, much to the surprise of her neurologist.

Often physical pain is associated with emotional barriers and so I use your information to help decrease chronic pain and it is very effective.

CHAPTER 15

REVEALED: WHY OUR PAIN CAN HAVE an UNDERLYING EMOTIONAL CAUSE

MICHAEL: FROM SUFFERING INTO HEALING

In my journey from suffering into healing, I have undergone discomforts in various parts of my physical body. The most persistent over the years have been headaches and eye tension, emotional heart tension, and fatigue. Through experience, I discovered that a body pain hints at an emotional conflict emerging from my subconscious. Bodily aches and pains, symptoms of deeper underlying emotional causes, signal the continuing need for physical and emotional purification.

Over thirty-five years of personal energy healing has taught me two things. Our body tissues trap unexpressed emotions in increasingly deeper levels like the layers of an onion. Once we discover the central core of the issue and release it than subsequent layers tied into it can also clear. Secondly, an emotional issue will release usually only when I become aware and get the lesson behind the emotional or physical pain.

I have also found when I trust and surrender to the Grace of the Divine then the healing occurs the most easily.

Some form of energy healing has been the most effective in my releases and the furthering my personal transformation each time.

The following tells stories of people who have experienced physical and emotional pain upon their journey, how they coped, and the changes they underwent.

PAUL DAVIS: CHRONIC FATIQUE SYNDROME

Paul Davis, an acupuncturist, says, *As my spiritual journey progressed, I went through changes in my energy levels. In my early twenties symptoms of chronic fatigue started. For about ten years, I lived with an uneasy balance of chronic fatigue. I suffered a major collapse at thirty in which I could not work for several months. This started me on a study of alternative health leading to certification as an acupuncturist.*

In 1994, when I opened up my physical, emotional, and sexual nature, my energy improved. I maintained a good diet and did a lot more exercise over the next few years. In addition, a regime of radionic remedies removed miasmas, low-grade viral infections, parasites, and heavy metals. Several healers, including hands-on healer's, assisted me in releasing a heavy load of trapped emotion, old agreements, implants, entities, and fear based beliefs.

The following demonstrates an episode of Paul's experience of accelerated healing. *When in India in 1996 I visited Sai Baba. Spending twelve days receiving his darshan – blessing - twice a day I went through days of deep meditative states, flu like symptoms, fear, feelings of rejection and unworthiness, and physical pain; I rebroke my thumb from a previous injury. It was if Sai Baba had me on an operating table the whole time working on me very precisely. Two months later, I still felt a lot of clearing.*

I equate my sustained energy, stamina, lighter emotional state, and greater joy to energy healing and initiations of Light. Also I see my health improvement as a result of taking charge of my life and expanding my consciousness.

LANA: HEADACHES and EMOTIONAL HEART PAIN

Lana's story of discomfort is like many women experiencing severe headaches as the menstrual cycle occurs. *My head felt as if seized in a vise grip,* says Lana.

Being on a spiritual path Lana realized the shutting down of the crown chakra at the top of her head contributed in a major way to the headaches. *Often my crown shut down. At these times, I would often be going through rapid emotional changes, which brought up fears. Once I understood the root of the fear and released it, the pain lifted.*

Lana also had sharp discomfort, for several years, in the area of the heart chakra in her back. *The area between my shoulder blades ached, whenever my heart chakra expanded, indicating trapped emotions. For example, when I received Shiatsu, a type of acupressure massage, and the therapist ran healing energy through the sore spot in my back memories arose. These included childhood sorrows. At other times, scenes of old tortures and wounds from past lifetimes sprang before my eyes. I breathed with the energy releasing the pain.*

As a core energy healer, Lana knows she needs energy healing for her own personal emotional issues. She also uses other methods. *I release the fear and pain behind my physical discomforts through hands-on healing including Bowen Therapy, meditation, exercise such as walking and yoga, and breathe work such as breathing through my heart. My lifelong depression and wishing to die have been replaced by a love of life, trust, and joy.*

Discomforts hound us whether or not we journey on a spiritual path. However, like Paul Davis or Daniella Frasson whom I discuss next, we may need a physical or emotional crisis to precipitate our looking inward and choosing a spiritual path. Desire for self-discovery motivates us to understand the emotional issues underlying our discomforts as well as to find tools to cope and heal.

Our discomforts signal some imbalance. We can ignore the signal as Lana did for a number of years with her heart pain. Her anguish unknown to her at the time involved the accumulated sorrow of the loss of many loved ones. She denied the memories, avoided the pain, and closed down her heart. The pain remained until she allowed, *Wounds from past lifetimes to spring before my eyes.* Did she have to relive the original trauma? No, she needed to face it, receive the message to release the hurt, and allow her consciousness to expand.

Physical pain may be an imbalance or the denial of trauma. It also occurs when on a path of self-discovery. Our consciousness in expanding meets with our emotional limitations such as fear or anger. Lana illustrates this concerning her headaches. *I would often be going through rapid emotional changes, which brought up fears.*

Paul also told about his multitude of discomforts while in the magnified Light field of Sai Baba, an East Indian spiritual teacher. *It was as if Sai Baba had me on an operating table the whole time.* Paul's brief stay in India prompted a deep physical and emotional cleansing, which lead to an expansion of consciousness.

DANIELLA FRASSON: MIGRAINES and DEPRESSION

Daniella Frasson, a Shiatsu therapist since 1996, did she know how to cope with migraine headaches or varying stages of depression. It took her life falling apart before she chose to wake up. Within a short time she lost her job, her lover left, her father died of cancer, her brother withdrew his support, and her mother refused to take her in.

The following illustrates Daniella's state of mind; *As if in a vortex spinning out of control into oblivion did anybody really care? Who am I? What do I want? Where do I go from here? Sheer terror, confusion, and anger accompanied me as my only companions. Asking for death, I wished to disintegrate into nothing.* At a crossroad, Daniella chose meditation and a path of self-healing and discovery.

In regards to her headaches Daniella states, *My migraines over the years worsened until I remained migraine free only one week out of the month. I took stronger medication, which alleviated the pain only marginally.*

After studying craniosacral therapy Daniella realized, *One of the reasons I feel these headaches came on so strong is because the inside of my head as well as the actual cranium shifted and expanded, invisible to the naked eye.*

Through various forms of energy healing Daniella now remains migraine free up to two months at a time.

In reference to depression Daniella comments, *I was clinically depressed or in varying stages of depression from as early as age five. After one year of intensive psychological and spiritual therapy with a gifted therapist and major life changes, I made a conscious shift to my life path. That significant October 1992 I came out of depression forever. Now the not so good days remain fewer and further in-between. At times feelings rush in, strong as a wave with overwhelming emotions racking havoc. Then they quickly disperse. I am myself again. When my mood lowers I realize another layer of learning surfacing for me to recognize, which leads to a healing.*

As I mentioned earlier physical discomfort also occurs in spiritual growth. Daniella comments that she experienced, *Whole body aches and pains similar to the flu sometimes. These periods included spiritual awakenings and messages, which made me think of them as milder versions of the native American Indian vision quests.*

Daniella coped with her migraines, emotional lows, and other physical changes with the help of acupuncture, Shiatsu, craniosacral therapy, and energy healing. She also used nutrition, regular exercise, and meditation.

Because of Daniella's personal emotional healing and growing spiritual awareness, she is better able to facilitate the healing of her clients. *My clients notice the healing energy being more powerful. I am able to assist them to have clarity with deeper emotional issues. My clients mention how soothing and healing my hands feel. My hands get hotter faster with a more intense heat now.*

Daniella explains the cause of physical discomfort. *When emotional trauma occurs it is like a foreign bubble of energy that gets trapped. It puts up a fierce or sometimes subtle fight to free itself creating varying degrees of discomfort in the body. When people feel nothing, I have noticed in my practice they appear out of touch with their body. In other words, they create barriers upon barriers of a protective shield to avoid their trapped emotions. Anger, frustration, resentment, bitterness, or fear of being unworthy or abandoned always surround the energy bubbles. These emotions flag us of an energy bubble to deal with. I follow the path to the source of the bubble and assist the client to realize and incorporate the lesson they need to learn. Then the bubble releases into the Light, which allows the freeing of their mind and spirit. It is important to align the physical body, as the release affects it as well.*

KATHRYNE-ALEXIS: OVERATING and MIGRAINES

Speaking of barriers Kathryne-Alexis a transformational counselor mastered creating protective shields to avoid emotional discomfort. *In 1989, the beginning of my awakening to my spiritual path, I became conscious of energy flowing into my big toes and up my body. You laugh. I had shut down before. You could call it emotional stuffing in that every time an emotion raised its head I ate for comfort. Burying my emotions, weight fluctuations became a part of my life. My intestines slowed to a crawl. Unresolved issues of starvation, rape, grief, anger, rage, and self-worth compacted my colon. My menstrual cycles descended cramped and heavy. A protective armor of fearful angry emotions also manifested as tight, pinched, inflamed back muscles. In addition, in the past, headaches, migraines, and weakened vision plagued me. By college, I gulped Advil all day and finally a muscle relaxant as well. At acute times, I also utilized a shot of cortisone. These migraines thundered on in times of challenges with male authorities. Forcing myself to exercise I induced pain in muscles and joints, as well as a shortness of breath. Minor injuries also occurred.*

By my thirties, I ingested spirulina and other food supplements to detox the Advil and pharmaceutical buildup since childhood. Holistic nutritional counseling added to my understanding of the nutri-

ents my body needed to assimilate and balance the energies of living on a spiritual path.

In 1992, I asked God for wholeness and knowing. I prayed with the intent to be a clear pure perfect channel of my highest expression. I choose to integrate, incorporate, release, and reveal all of my selves - conscious, unconscious, and Higher. As a result, I understood physical weight as a resistance to let go of emotions.

In the last few years, I am more conscious of what I put in my mouth. Listening to body cravings I ask what is in my best and highest interest to eat by muscle testing. I also get mental pictures and use my intuition to guide me. One time I got a picture and word message about green beans. Green beans persisted in my thoughts for days. Finally, buying some I overcame my judgment about eating them raw and began to munch. My body rejoiced. Later looking up their usefulness a holistic book described exactly what my body needed at the time.

For almost two years I received massage therapy and hands-on energy healing to relax and release compacted tension and blocked emotions and memories within my body.

I no longer have headaches as I once did. Now twinges here and there indicate an energy opening.

Yoga and dance teachers supported me in accepting a graceful, gentle balance of exercise. Brisk walking at a steady pace proved to be a simple technique to move energy. As each level of my spiritual growth required more oxygen for expansion, I used more breathing techniques.

Overall, the release of my protective shields of emotions has made my body softer, more agile, and strong. Sleep is more restful. People sense a glow and peace around me. My energy level remains higher and when my energy drops it signals an emotional issue.

In summary, Paul, Lana, Daniella, and Kathryne-Alexis all used various forms of energy healers, exercise, meditation, and nutrition to release their physical pain and the underlying emotional causes, as well as take charge of their life and chart their spiritual path.

CHAPTER 16

WHAT BEING DISABLED CAN TEACH US ABOUT EMPOWERMENT

Jacqueline tells a remarkable story of physical healing. As the result of an accident, she lived on medications and her doctor condemned her to a possible wheelchair. With a determined attitude to heal she started using essential oils and herbs to release herself from being a prisoner to prescription drugs.

JACQUELINE STONE, AWAKENING CONSCIOUSNESS: FROM DISABLED TO EMPOWERMENT

The natural healing force within each of us is the greatest force in getting well.

Hippocrates

Healing and empowerment rests near and dear to my heart because of my own experiences. I know what it feels like to go from being strong, healthy, and vital to nearly helpless at a relatively young age. Until a car hit me, I always worked out and could do about anything I set my mind to. It devastated me to lose this. Healing has been tremendous, says Jacqueline.

In early 2008, I walked slowly and painfully with a cane. My doctor recommended no driving, going up and down stairs, or any unnecessary walking. He said I should get a walker and consider a wheelchair. I lived on medications day and night at the age of only 46.

A year later, I walked without a cane without a limp! I walked and used the stairs; I even exercised. I no longer take medication for anything.

My doctor wanted to do another surgery on both of my knees and have me living in rapidly increasing disability. I refused to accept his diagnosis or prognosis. I am so grateful that I did. Life is so good now and I feel "able" in all things. I owe my healing and rejuvenating to herbs and essential oils, as well as attitude. That's why I love sharing about them with others. They've given me back my life.

I've found a wonderful way to heal my body, help others, and make some money, although I started out differently. I used to live on prescription medications that did more harm than good. I had been hit by a car on my bike and then went through 13 surgeries in only four years. When my surgeon wanted to do another, I refused. I decided to do something else.

A friend told me about <u>Holy Tea</u> and how it cleans the toxins out of the body and got rid of built up chemicals. Then I discovered the benefits of herbs and <u>essential oils</u>. After a little research, I decided to give them a try.

I used chamomile, catnip, and nettle to make a tea before bed to help me sleep without chemical assistance. The nettle and catnip also helped with nerve inflammation. I still have a broken bone in my neck with spurs that grow into the spinal cord.

Before the herbs I used Neurontin for my neck and Celebrex for arthritis, which brought relief for pain and they also damage to the liver. That's where Holy Tea came in. Holy Tea has an herbal combination that cleans the liver and supports proper liver function. It also cleans the entire digestive tract, as well as the colon, unlike other cleansers. My digestive tract grew sluggish from medications I took to protect it from the other medications I took.

Pain medication also created problems for my liver and stomach. Getting off pain medication suddenly can cause hypersensitivity in the nerves because the brain no longer produces its own serotonin. Essential oils help. Arnica relieved pain in my neck and joints. Peppermint and eucalyptus helped with pain in the muscles and tendons and rosemary and lemon oil restored mental clarity, which I lacked on pain medication or because I missed sleep because of pain. Lavender oil helped with skin issues that arose from a weakened immune system.

I had lived with constant fatigue for several years due to all the physical stress on my body. To regain energy and vitality, I rubbed lemon or orange oil on my palms and feet, alternated with clove and cinnamon.

After a complete hysterectomy, I entered menopause early, with full force. This called for another medication. I began using St. John's Wort herb in a tea with Black Willow Bark, or I diffused a little lavender, jasmine, or peppermint oil to relieve hot flashes, night sweats, or mood swings.

I no longer have any symptoms of menopause. It only took four months to be completely free of all medications and also the symptoms.

I would be remiss if I omitted stressing the importance of my attitude through my physical ordeal. I refused to give up. I remained determined to become healthy and strong again. I developed a deeper sense of self-love, self-respect, and a commitment to my spiritual fitness. Otherwise, I would still be a prisoner to prescription drugs.

Talk about one of the best decisions I ever made, my health, vitality, and emotional wellbeing has improved tremendously and I get to help others receive the same benefits. Now I turn to nature for relief

from pain, swelling, congestion, arthritis, meno-
pause, emotional issues, fatigue, and for overall
wellbeing. I feel much better.

Thomas A Edison remarks that, *The doctor of the*
future will give no medication, but will interest his
patients in the care of the human frame, diet, and in
the cause and prevention of disease.

Next Rob Gonzalez describes his unusual, yet effective method of easing suffering for others, as well
as his use of music for his own pain relief.

ROB GONZALEZ: MUSICIAN-SONGWRITER-POET

PHYSICAL SUFFERING: SERVICE

Is suffering really necessary? Yes and no. If you had
not suffered as you have, there would be no depth to
you, no humility, and no compassion.

Eckhart Tolle, *Stillness Speaks*

Rob Gonzalez says, *In 2006 a doctor diagnosed*
me with something called psoriatic arthritis, similar
to rheumatoid arthritis without the extensive defor-
mation of joints. Psoriatic arthritis does, however,
destroy the joints of the hands, feet and lower back.

I am currently on a chemotherapy drug, in low
dosage, to arrest the joint damage. Of course, with

the arthritis comes joint pain, extreme fatigue, and muscle pain.

I struggle on a daily basis and I have found out some important things about chronic illness. First and foremost, it has been a blessing to "that which I AM." I have greater compassion and understanding for others who suffer chronic illness. I am deeply moved by the stories of others who have somehow managed to work through their suffering through service to others. This has brought me to this place in my life.

I often question my service to others as a healing modality until someone writes and tells me how much I have helped them understand themselves. I find that funny. I often don't understand my own path. Do we really know how much we touch others lives?

I've had complete strangers start talking to me about their troubles right in the middle of a shopping mall! I hug, listen and say very little and later I tear up over the blessing bestowed upon me. There is no greater blessing than to be in service of others.

So now though I have trouble walking or being active, I have found another avenue of service. I think we can all find some way to serve even though it may seem insignificant. I find myself judging whether my contributions make a difference until I hear from someone thanking me for something I said or did that I had forgotten.

I also find relief from pain by playing musical instruments. I played guitar for over 40 years and about five years ago the Native American plains flute (Siyotanka) drew me. The arthritis has slowed my hands down considerably yet playing guitar or flute takes me to a place of pure spirit where the body becomes insignificant.

While in that special zone all accomplished musicians attain when playing, I experience no pain. Music fills my soul with beauty and light. Traditionally considered a love instrument, young men courting their favorite lady played the Siyotanka. I understand how this instrument brings love to all who play it and hear it.

I hope my experience helps others understand why suffering can become a part of our personal path to God. Though I didn't consciously choose this illness, I believe my soul chose it for a good reason.

Compassion can be a difficult lesson when we fail to see the depth of suffering in others. We just tend to look at the outer and often miss the inner. Our soul knows this and then chooses the path of suffering to allow us the opportunity to grow into a compassionate loving being. It took me a long time to come to this knowledge. At first I felt betrayed. Why would a God of love allow suffering?

I realized over time, I rather than God had chosen.

I have found the best reliever of pain and suffering is in loving others on this difficult earth path. We have all chosen this path for various reasons.

I would call Rob a true listener. Tolle calls this, the arising of alert attention, a space of presence in which the words are being received . . . the space of conscious presence that arises as you listen. In this space we meet the other person without any barriers of separation. *In this space, we come together as one awareness,* says Tolle.

I have experience this "one awareness" on a number of occasions as a coach with teenage girls as they talk about their suffering.

Next Rob Gonzalez shares a poem of his.

My Heart is Thawing
Rob Gonzalez

Winter has passed
My heart is thawing
In the warmth of the Light

Whispers from above
Something is calling
To those who will Love

Love is our Being
Nothing less, nothing more
The soul's expressive singing
All that is necessary
Is a simple state of Being
Realizing all things fall into place

Forgiveness follows Love
Unnecessary in Its Light
The graceful flight of a dove

Living in Grace
Released from earthly bonds
Spirit shines upon our face.

SUMMARY: HEALING PHYSICAL PAIN

Pain remains trapped in our physical bodies until we become ready to look at and heal the emotional causes behind much of the pain. According to Eckhart Tolle, *The Power of Now, pain will continue to occur as long as we remain unaware.* He considers emotional pain, *The main cause of physical pain and physical disease.*

Tolle continues to explain that the intensity of pain we create depends on our unconscious resistance to experiencing the pain in the present moment. He also says that the resistance, *On the emotional level, it is some form of negativity.*

Tolle continues. *If you keep your attention in the body as much as possible, you will be anchored in the "Now".* Remember, I mentioned Eugene Gendlin's focusing method earlier. This develops awareness of our "felt senses" in our body, moment by moment.

When we learn to surrender to the present moment and feel our pain fully at its inner core we experience according to Tolle, An unfathomable sense of peace. And within that peace, there is great joy. And within that joy, there is love.

Robert Stevens, *Consciousness Language*, has discovered also in transforming our unconscious language into conscious language, love lies at the other side of transformed physical pain, contraction. Robert says, *By changing one word within ourselves, we expand, contract or alter our consciousness.*

In the *Diamond in your Pocket*, spiritual teacher Gangaji talks about the difference between pain and suffering. She says, *We feel pain in our physical bodies. Suffering is spread over time and must be accompanied by some story about the pain. Suffering results from contraction around pain. When we choose to open our minds, meet and feel the pain in the moment, rather than resisting, then we discover in the heart of the pain, love which heals.*

Tolle, Stevens, and Gangaji all confirm once we fully experience our physical pain in the present moment, it opens and transforms into love. I will clarify that holding a focus and containing our pain has to be developed as a skill over time. A professional healer with experience with this method can teach us how to hold and contain our pain. Most important, the healer will remind us when we have lost our focus, usually unconsciously, and give us the choice to come back to the present moment and contain our pain again.

I will also remind you that just because we have learned how to experience our pain fully in the present moment doesn't mean it transforms in an instant.

We have learned some of many ways to transform physical pain in this chapter such as methods of energy healing involving acupuncture, craniosacral therapy, EFT (Emotional Freedom Technique), the Emotion Code, and Shiatsu. People also used breath work, detoxification of the body, exercise including yoga and walking, meditation, and nutritional supplements and herbs as well as essential oils.

In the next chapter, Energy Healing/Energy Medicine, we explore further benefits of energy healing to lessen emotional trauma and stress as well as the importance at all times to include healing the inner child. We will also discover how to bring to light the unconscious parts of ourselves and turn them into strengths as well as retrieving parts of our soul, which have split off because of trauma.

CHAPTER 17

ENERGY HEALING/ENERGY MEDICINE: DISSOLVE the CAUSES BEHIND MOST PHYSICAL PAIN

Doctors are beginning to understand that we possess unique energy systems that help to maintain health.

Richard Gerber M.D., *Vibrational Medicine*

Healing can involve physical, psychological, or soul healing. Physical healing cures disease and builds vitality in the body. These types include allopathic or regular medicine, which uses drugs and surgery, and alternative systems such as acupuncture, anthroposophic medicine, ayurvedic, chiropractic, homeopathy, naturopathy, and osteopathy.

The next type of healing, psychological, uses various systems of psychotherapy to improve the client's emotional and mental wellbeing through focusing on relationships, behavioral change, or self-growth.

The third type of healing uses a connection to the energy of the soul, which flows through the healer and into the client to release energy congestions on the mental or emotional level, which then vitalizes the mental, emotional, or physical bodies. This energy healing can heal emotional stress and dissolve the emotional causes behind most physical pain.

Eric Robins, M.D. says, Someday the medical profession will wake up and realize that unresolved emotional issues are the main cause of 85% of all illnesses.

In this chapter, we will see how psychological understanding and energy healing combine in healing our wounded inner child and our unconscious Shadow aspects. Soul retrieval gathers back lost parts of our inner child who has split off because of trauma. In addition, soul retrieval brings back Shadow parts ready to enter the light of awareness. We will also gain some understanding of the spiritual experience known as the "Dark Night of the Soul," which about 25% of spiritual seekers encounter on their journey from suffering into healing.

Energy healing, which I mentioned, involves connecting with our soul. Our soul, according to those who have explored the hidden nature of man like Alice Bailey, defines an aspect of our essential nature. It makes a rose a rose, a diamond a diamond, and each of us unique. Bailey describes the soul like an immense searchlight, the beams of which can be turned in many directions. One of these directions can be assisting others to heal.

Connecting to our souls as healers means higher beings such as angels, archangels, spiritual masters, and the energy of Divine Source can come through. As a conductor of these energies, we work in the client's energy field to assist in the dissolving of mental, emotional, and physical congestion and pain.

Alice Bailey in Esoteric Healing describes two types of healers, magnetic and radiatory. Some healers, like my wife Lyn, have the ability to use either type of healing, depending on the needs of the client. The magnetic healer links to their soul, heart, brain, and hands. They bring more life force or prana into the client. The radiatory healer links to their soul, heart, brain, and then radiates their soul presence drawn down into their bodies into the energy center or chakra that the client needs. The client's soul takes charge of the degree of stimulation of their chakras.

Therefore, the magnetic healer increases life force in the client, while the radiatory healer increases soul energy. Training and practice teaches both healers on how much energy to transmit safely.

Alice Bailey in *Esoteric Healing* says this about healing from our souls, *The true and the future healing is brought about when the life of the soul can flow without impediment . . . .* She also says, *Any man or woman – given real interest and prompted by the incentive to serve – who thinks, and loves, can be a healer.*

THE WOUNDED HEALER

What is a wounded healer? The doctor is effective only when he himself is affected. *Only the wounded physician heals*, says Carl Jung, *Wounded Healer of the Soul*. An article, *The Wounded Healer on Crystalinks* also says, *It is the wounded healer who has gone through suffering, sometimes great, and as a result of that process has become a source of great wisdom, healing power, and inspiration for others.*

Chiron, the wounded healer in Greek mythology represented as half human and half horse as a master healer who failed to heal himself. He shows us, however, the necessary of recognizing our own wounds and that they can be healed. In my experience, we as healers have an obligation to ourselves as well as our clients to be continuously healing ourselves and seeking assistance from others.

Thus, when we accept healing as necessary for ourselves as well as service to others, we share our creative gifts and fulfill our purpose. We also become mentors encouraging our clients. *The mentoring relationship is interdependent with the acts of giving and receiving, teaching and learning, flowing both ways*, says counselor Pam Howard in the article, *Chiron: The Wounded Healer as Mentor*.

We usually experience healing of our suffering through our own efforts and the assistance of other healers. Can horses, however, be our mentors and heal us as well?

Sinnet Olina Tiwaz, a horse whisperer and artist in Denmark, has experienced horses as mentors and teachers in her own healing and personal growth.

Bonnie Treece in her article, *Heart Connections and the Healing Power of Horses* says, *Openhearted communication between horse and human has the potential to promote self-healing by enhancing one's ability to recognize emotional congruence . . . From this place-in-the-heart, we can experience a sense of love, gratitude and finally, the willingness to give up what doesn't work in our lives.*

HORSES as HEALERS

Horses enable people to make contact with feelings they'd buried deep inside their Shadow.

Chris Irwin – Clinician and Author, *Horses Don't Lie*

Sinnet Tiwaz, a horse whisperer says, *I had to go through three major levels in order to become my personal best and feel the freedom of a soaring spirit. Through the way of the horse back to Greek mythology embraces the horse as an archetype. The horse as a metaphor bridges the world of our consciousness with the subconscious.*

Horses as prey animals remain hyper alert. They need to be able to be fully aware of any possible danger in order for them to survive as herd animals living in a distinct hierarchy with strong leadership. When interacting with people they mirror their feeling in a given moment, which forces us to be alert and focused – to stay in the body instead of the head, which has been our accustomed way in our world.

This approach to horses enables us to feel, see, and embrace our real selves behind the curtains of role-playing. Horses as honest, reliable animals have no ability to pretend. They remain natural giving us immediate feedback on the way we conduct ourselves.

I continued working with horses that mirrored all my weaknesses as well as strengths along my path of self-discovery.

The first level of discovery involved becoming fully aware of who I am and what has defined me as a person so far.

At the next level, I had the choice to accept the pain and release it with the goal of healing.

In the final level, I transmuted all the past regrets into the power of wisdom and light by learning how to balance duality.

Sinnet expands on her three levels of discovery in the next chapter in her Dark Night of the Soul.

OUR INNER CHILD: OUR UNLOVED SELF

HEALING OUR INNER CHILD

An eternal child lurks in every adult.

Carl Jung, *Collected Works, Volume 17*

Who is the inner child? Our inner child represents us as a child, a child who was possibly ridiculed or abused. The inner child lies trapped between the ages of birth to adolescence. The inner child's psychological nature consists of childhood negative and positive experiences, emotions, and self-worth. Besides being the result of our childhoods, this accumulation passes down through the generations of our family. Our inner child resembles a boy or girl; newborn, age three, five, eight, or ten who looks just the way we did at that age. This child can be the same sex or the opposite sex.

One aspect of our inner child feels unloved, unrecognized, and fearful: in other words, the neglected or abandoned child. This child craves nurturing and unconditional love. This child neither sees nor feels the light. Instead, it feels trapped, sad, and lonely inside of a dark, non-nurturing world. This feeling of lack of love passes down through our family bloodline. The next generation no longer inherits the lack of love once we heal it in ourselves. Healing our inner child heals the inner child of our children and our children's children.

If ignored our child hides in a corner of our psyche until something triggers his or her pain. Their emotional reaction can sabotage our success if the child's intent differs from our conscious intent.

Our inner child has a whole body of emotions. Wounded and powerless our inner child searches outside ourselves for love and esteem. When we experience an emotional reaction or have our "buttons" pushed by a situation or person, this is the inner child's response to old unhealed emotional wounds.

Our inner child feels the rage, anger, hurt, sadness, or hopelessness. Sometimes it just wants to give up and die.

The first three energy centers – chakras - below our abdomen carry a great deal of the pain of the inner child. These chakras carry our fears, anxieties, and sorrow, which make up the life of an unloved child. An inner child in pain can only reach out for the love they yearn for with conditions attached to that love. Our top three chakras above our heart deal with our ability of giving truth, insight, wisdom, and purpose. Our heart intermediates between our top and bottom chakras and as the inner child heals, our heart opens more reaching out to others with loving arms.

Our inner child yearns for us, as the adult, to hear, love, and heal them. It we choose to continue to ignore that undeveloped emotional part of our self, than our inner child will continue to run our life without us being conscious of this.

So now, we have a choice. We can continue to react and keep doing the same thing over and over and expect different results or we can choose growth and healing for our inner child and emotions.

A great deal of healing goes on for the inner child in the first three lower chakras. Our inner child also requires unconditional love in fostering life and growth. In our healing towards wholeness, we can desire for our inner child to mature into a fully-grown adult.

In our healing, seek an environment of unconditional love. When we walk through the door of a healer, we should feel an air of unconditional love and nurturing. Our inner children want to feel safe as if wrapped in the arms of a loving mother.

We can be a loving mother or father to our inner child. We can visualize our inner child at a particular age and feel or see them in our arms. Look into its eyes, stroke it, and speak to it for this child is us. The child will than feel safe to come out of hiding into our arms. We can imagine holding our child against our chest. We speak to it and allow it to speak to us about its needs.

When our inner child feels safe, she or he can move into higher levels of joy as fears lift. Fears separate us. Until we fully heal, a part of us will feel like an unloved child. Releasing all the issues of hurt, the inner child grows closer. This adult opens in childlike wonderment to all life. Do you want a happy healthy inner child?

One good tool to begin the healing is John Bradshaw's *Homecoming: Reclaiming and Championing Your Inner Child* in audio or paperback.

CHILD of the RAINBOW

The following tells a symbolic story of healing my inner child over a period of years. Perhaps all our inner children can relate in some way.

Once a very sad child existed who spent most of its time uncontrollably sobbing. Most of the time the child hid away, in fear, in the darkness of its little fortress like room. The child's agony flowed like molten metal outward where it hardened into the walls of the fortress. This fortress of impenetrable steel constructed layer upon layer by the child kept at bay all the pain, violence, and anger of the outside world.

Some of the child's agony differed from the molten metal and frigid as Arctic ice lay buried in the depths of the pit of its navel. Emerging from the depths of this pit, twisting tendrils clenched their icy fingers around the child's heart. The tendrils went even farther into the child's jaw. The tendrils grew stronger each time the child clenched its teeth in anger to cover up hurt. This anger also reinforced the strength of the steel walls.

One day a Golden Figure of Light arrived outside the child's fortress. Pink Light of unconditional love poured forth from the arms of the Golden figure. The pink Light filled the fortress where the child crouched in fear. As feelings of love permeated the child's pain racked body the depths of frozen pain melted. Unconditional love soothed like a relaxing hot bath, engulfing the child's whole body. The steel walls of the fortress melted layer upon layer until only a pink bubble remained. Then with a pop, the bubble evaporated.

During the melting the child found itself walking through gray liquid walls of fear and sorrow into pink and green fields of light, unconditional love, and healing. The child finally emerged into a sea of pink light.

The child cart wheeled about in uninhibited joy. It could see multi-colored fish swimming everywhere. The child looked about in wild-eyed bedazzlement enchanted by this new world of wonderment. From somewhere close by the voice of the Golden figure gently and sweetly whispered into the child's ear, Look at the fish. Breathe these into you. Receive each fish as a gift.

The child breathed deeply. With each breath the fish that were all joined in the pink light drifted closer.

Finally, all the fish and the child merged as one. A rainbow of iridescence color burst forth from the being of the child. Other children around the world saw the rainbow arc across their skies. They smiled to each other knowingly, "Another one has been freed."

CODEPENDENCY and INNER CHILD HEALING

Codependency, as an addictive behavior, involves taking responsibility for someone else's thoughts, feelings, or behavior. We learn to negate our own needs and falsely believe that whatever we do is "not enough" and therefore "we aren't good enough." We have a choice to hear the voice of our wounded inner child and to heal or to continue to live in pain and codependent patterns.

For those of us on a journey of self-discovery or spirituality, codependency and inner child healing remains a necessary part to experience greater oneness. By practicing becoming conscious of our reactive emotional behaviors, we can, over time, become a more detached neutral observer and thus not a victim of our inner child's rage, anger, and other eruptive behaviors.

Each wound healed lessens the pain and contributes to our becoming more whole. Unfortunately, many times we resist the pain, say "No" to change, and remain in reaction. Healing ,on the other hand, involves giving the inner child a voice, the willingness to be present in the moment with the pain, i.e., saying "Yes," and feeling vulnerable.

Choosing healing over just surviving with our recurring reactive emotional patterns takes us out of the victim and giving away our power and esteem to others, i.e., codependency.

Healing our emotional wounds allows our inner child to grow, which has been an important part of my healing journey.

MICHAEL: RECOGNIZING MY INNER CHILD

I remained ignorant of my own trauma of emotional wounding that my inner child carried from my birth family. My first major relationship with Angelique and her young son, Mason, mirrored back to me the wounding of my own inner five-year old child.

Reclaiming our childhood is painful because we must grieve our wounds . . . . Grief work is the legitimate suffering we've been avoiding with our neuroses . . . . Grief work, which has been called original pain work, demands that we re-experience what we could not experience when we lost . . . . our childhood . . . . The spiritual wound can be healed. But it must be done by grieving, and that is painful

John Bradshaw, *Home Coming*

One day after we had been together for about two years, Mason and I walked through stacks of toys in a department store. Mason seized upon a large red truck that he wanted.

Mason I am not buying this truck for you now, grasping it from his eager hands.

Mason hurled himself down upon the floor in the midst of other shoppers. He started screaming at the top of his lungs, his four-year old arms flailing up and down, in a full out temper tantrum. Heat rising in my face, I glanced over my shoulder for possible onlookers. I wanted to disappear.

Unlike Mason, I had squelched the voice of my inner child. My inner child, however, indirectly made himself known, through my relationships, for much of the time I felt like a powerless child. It would take over ten years before I acknowledged and began healing the rage and loss of love my inner child felt.

CHAPTER 18

BEWARE of YOUR SHADOW and HOW to SPOT IT

The Shadow a part of our unconscious, which until brought to consciousness will sabotage our success at every turn.

THE SHADOW

With the paradigm shift in the world because of increased light flooding the planet the Shadow rears its head more often. A paradigm shift signals the transition from one model of perception to another. We gain an expansion of vision by seeing through a new lens.

The Shadow, which exists in us, groups, institutional bodies, and humanity as a group, resists the new frequencies entering our planet and our bodies. This Shadow aspect as defined by the psychoanalyst Carl Jung makes up a part of the unconscious mind consisting of weaknesses and instincts.

Everyone carries a Shadow, Jung wrote, and the less it is embodied in the individual's conscious life, the blacker and denser it is.

The Shadow's face has never seen the light and fears exposure. It shows it's self through our projections unto others and our resistance to saying "Yes" to Life and the Divine Will. Many of us deny that these unacceptable or unwanted thoughts or emotions belong to us. As we increase our light quotient, everything in our Shadow aspects rises up into the light of day.

Once our physical body "rewires," we adjust from 30 - 40 – 50 % light to eventually 100%. Once our body fills with 100% quotient of light many of our previous emotional and mental patterns of pain, illusion, and resistance have dissolved through willingness, effort, and the choice to say "Yes" to Divine Will.

If we choose to increase our light quotient, we can choose to allow our Shadow aspects to rise to the surface of our awareness, recognize them, and permit the light to dissolve them. Blaming others only keeps the Shadow imprisoned within us. First contain the resistance and then through conscious breathing through our whole bodies and our heart and intent, we can allow the Light of the Divine Fire to burn through all parts of us. Intent means we release all emotions, judgments, and old paradigms into the fire to dissolve.

THE SHADOW: OUR UNKNOWN SELF

Everyone carries a Shadow, and the less it is embodied in the individual's conscious life, the blacker and denser it is.

Carl Jung, *Psychology and Religion*

As we journey through our chakras, we encounter aspects of our Shadow emerging for healing. Our Shadow consists of aspects unknown to us. These parts of ourselves we deny, discount, and resist knowing: all the unintegrated parts. The Shadow consists of both light and aspects turned from the light. Our Shadow harbors all the aspects of ourselves we fear, which includes both strengths and weaknesses. Our Shadow stands between us and our Higher Self.

Our Shadow, although a constant companion, stays hidden from us like an invisible ghost or like a stranger unable to make itself known because it speaks a different language. This stranger may be an outcast or it may become an educated scholar with many gifts for us. This stranger wears a jumbled, patchwork cloak of many colors and also ragged, dirty, and splattered with garbage, yet other parts contain bright shining jewels. Our Shadow contains some of the powers we fear because we once abused them.

It takes great courage to turn around and face this Shadow stranger. We will be looking at ourselves. We will be facing our worst fears. One of the easiest ways of confronting our Shadow consists of going into the core issues using some method of energy healing.

Self-inquiry also assists when we ask ourselves, What prevents me from giving and receiving all I can in this life? Can we give unconditionally without any thought of receiving? Can we give without thinking, What's in it for me? Allow our Shadow to be healed until we can give in a balanced state.

When our Shadow comes forward most of us draw back in fear and hide overcome by the fears, a state of imbalance. Abuse of power imbalances us as if we teetered upward on the edge of a seesaw. Far off balance we grasp outwards clutching at others in an effort to gain balance. Only when we let go of control and manipulating others do we come back to inner balance. The seesaw returns to a place of equilibrium.

Fear also accompanies us on the down end of the seesaw. Reacting in fear sends us sliding down to the ground. Someone in great fear can go over to the side of power efforting to gain it back. Does balance exist on the other side of the seesaw? No, it inhabits the center fulcrum of the seesaw. True power comes from the divine, the fulcrum of our seesaw, which lies inside us.

Facing and leading our Shadow into the light brings forward the gifts of the shining jewels – our undeveloped potentials - upon the Shadow's cloak.

HEALING: THE UNCONSCIOUS SHADOW

To confront a person with his Shadow is to show him
his own light . . . Anyone who perceives his Shadow
and his light simultaneously sees himself from two
sides and thus gets in the middle.

Carl Jung, Civilization in Transition

My experience has shown me when my Shadow
looms out of the darkness, to confront me face to face,
it seeks the light. My responsibility requires holding
steady with my Shadow. I can choose to contain its
energy, which involves holding any emotions that
arise as if I held a full glass of water steady without
spilling any. This requires feeling any emotion that
arises and staying present with it. This allows my
Shadow to begin to emerge into the light of day.

If, on the other hand, when a situation arose
where I had some emotional reaction, I allowed my
mind to run rampant with all kinds of possible scenar-
ios and let my emotions bounce around like a yo-yo
fluctuating from one extreme to the next, my Shadow
would be unable to come forward into greater awareness.

Kathryne-Alexis, a life path consultant, has this to
say about the self-saboteur or Shadow. *We live in a
world of contrast; seemingly dualistic, yin/yang,
black/white, and unconscious/conscious world.
When we allow our unconscious to flow into our*

awareness, then any memory, belief, or emotion of suffering can be remembered, understood and delabeled. In other words, the emotional charge becomes neutral energy and then can be utilized for a current desire.

Kathryne-Alexis continues. *When we struggle or resist our Shadow, more suffering results. Be ready to look at the Shadow self when it has come to consciousness. It has truly surfaced because you are ready to accept, forgive, and make a new choice.*

According to Carl Jung, the originator of analytical psychology, our Shadow contains the repressed/suppressed aspects of our conscious self, with both constructive and destructive sides. On the destructive side, our Shadow represents everything we wish to leave unacknowledged. People can be greedy or brutal and still manage to hide these truths from themselves. On the constructive side, our Shadow can contain hidden positive aspects, the "gold in the Shadow."

When our Shadow remains unintegrated, it can show itself in two different ways. We can project our Shadow onto other people through, for instance, blame that leads to conflict, or we can see ourselves as being inferior or bad in some way. Our Shadow shows itself as what we resist becoming which exists within the depths of our unconscious. Our Shadow serves like the shadows in a painting to give us life and depth.

We also have an opportunity each month to see the reflection of an aspect of our Shadow arising from the depths of our subconscious. At the time of the full moon and even more intensely during full moon lunar eclipses, we all can chose to become aware and release mental and emotional programming standing in the way of fulfilling our life purposes and moving into greater self-empowerment.

RELEASING the ILLUSION of DEATH and FEAR of the DARK

Tiara Kumara, founder of Children of the Sun - COS, describes the gift of the dark moon or lunar eclipse. *This dark moon, also known as the "dead" moon, is a phase with no solar reflection, leaving the lunar face in darkness.*

This lunar cycle symbolizes the union between the moon and the sun or the union between light and dark. A lunar eclipse also symbolizes death and re-birth. With full moons generally illuminating what's been held in the subconscious, an added lunar eclipse greatly amplifies this effect. Whatever stands in the way of embodying our true purpose reflects back to us in high intensity.

These supportive and highly potent energies serve as a catalyst for greater phases of purification, also resulting in greater levels of self-empowerment.

In this intense period of the striping away of all illusion, many in our family can experience the "dark night of the soul" in order for a rebirthing to occur. In the field of awakened consciousness, this indicates a spiritual initiation period of extreme purification. The "dark night" is a deeply personal experience often characterized by a seeming absence of light, confusion, and aloneness. Its purpose liberates and releases the chains that bind.

Initiates on the path of enlightenment may experience several "dark nights" until authentic realization of the true self.

Tiara now describes the gift of the full moon to release our fear of the Dark and the illusion of death.

During the Full Moon Grid Transmissions, we continue with unrelenting focus on releasing old mental and emotional programming. We can dissolve all attachments to individual self- identity while invoking fearlessness in all aspects of our lives.

In this fearlessness, we unify on the planetary grid with the intention of releasing the illusion and all associated fear around death; and whether we hold this energy consciously or unconsciously.

At the deepest core level, most all fears arise from the fear of death, the biggest unknown. We claim the knowing that we are eternal beings; however, much fear around this transitory process still embeds deeply within our cellular matrix. This causes fear based attitude, emotion, and behavioral reaction to persist in our lives, and again, often in unconscious manifestations.

To be afraid of anything lessens our ability to love, unconditionally, and to authentically embody our Divine Presence.

We also unify with the intention of releasing the fear of the dark. We let go of false perception surrounding the supposed external "dark forces" out to get us, to harm us, to infiltrate our work. This great illusion causes much chaos, divisive attitude, and collective separation.

From a state of expanded awareness we can realize: Any and all seeming invasive dark energy perceived by the self is an aspect of self. These perceptions as thoughts and feelings arise from the separated, individuated self. We attract to us all we hold in our perceptions.

Once we clear these separated impressions from the deepest recesses of our consciousness, we become fearless. We experience rebirth and rise from states of suffering into the great illumination.

In a state of absolute fearlessness, we naturally open into dissolution of our identities, our thoughts, and our physical attachments into the peaceful flow of Divine Presence. We can also more readily surrender into the depths of darkness and discover the fertile richness this dimension holds. By surrendering to and accepting the darkness inherent within ourselves, we can receive and consciously embody the totality of Self.

In the wholesome knowing as eternal beings unified with all energy, we can step into our true power and embody the great perfection of who we truly are.

We have a choice during full moons to allow our fears of death and the Dark, as well as aspects of our Shadow, to emerge into the light and begin to dissolve. As we clear the great illusion of separation, we begin the awakening into the Oneness of all life and the birthing of our True Self.

You can join Children of the Sun for free and participate in their monthly group Full Moon Grid Transmissions at www.childrenofthesun.tv

Next I explain soul retrieval. Soul Retrieval refers to shamanic practices that aim to reintegrate various interpretations of the soul that might have become disconnected, trapped or lost through trauma - www.wikipedia.org/wiki/Shamanism Recovering and healing parts of our inner child and Shadow may involve soul retrieval.

CHAPTER 19

LEARN HOW to DO SOUL RE-TRIEVAL

S hamanic healers perform soul retrieval as a main service. The shamans recover the person's vital life force, lost or stolen, which can create physical or emotional illness. The integration after the retrieval takes time.

If a stolen part had the quality of love, we may have grown up with a closed heart or a heart-wall as described in a previous chapter. This creates a challenge in giving and receiving love. With the missing quality returned, we can begin to learn how to love, over time.

MICHAEL'S SOUL RETRIEVAL: INNER CHILD and SHADOW

I asked for the healing of my heart-wall – the protective emotional barrier around my heart - and the giving away of my power as a victim. Both have been lifelong challenges. Lyn, an energy healer, assisted me by holding energy and asking questions, which I answered intuitively. I intended to dissolve the heart-wall.

I realized 85 % of my heart-wall connected to the victim and heart-wall, also connected to my Shadow. My child, the victim, remained hidden away in pain and agony behind the heart-wall believing the illusion that the wall protected him.

I gently held and contained the Shadow energetically as directed by Lyn.

Lyn said, *Your Shadow like a crippled child never knew love. It struggles and fights now. Your power fed the Shadow who sucked it up like a black hole.*

As a victim, I gave away my power, unconsciously, to the dark hidden part of myself, my Shadow.

Lyn explained more. *If we just hold energy the walls will never dissolve because the Shadow feasts never ending. The Shadow must also be contained at the same time as holding the energy.*

Holding means focusing a steady one pointed attention on what occurs in the present moment. Containing involves maintaining emotional control of feelings as they arise in the moment.

As we held, interplay began between my heart-wall and the Shadow, resulting in chaos.

Lyn commented, *When the stage of chaos occurs, some clients become agitated and bitchy. They want to go back to feeling comfortable. Sometimes they argue or blame.*

Keep containing and holding gently with no judgment towards your Shadow. Your Shadow like a neglected child hides stuck in darkness. It never knew what it's like to be in the light. It lives in a Garden of Death where no life exists.

I never experienced agitation only sadness or pain in areas of my body as we proceeded.

Then Lyn said, *Your Shadow has disappeared. Reconnect.*

Lyn explained to me that clients often disconnected from whatever parts they might be containing because of lack of focus or fear. She had to remind them to reconnect, sometimes many times during a session as they keep popping out – going out of body. Meditation, as a discipline, develops our ability to hold a focus in this type of healing. There, however, remains a fine balance between holding a focus and surrendering to the Divine Will.

Lyn continued guiding me. *Reconnect. Connect your heart and inner child to the Shadow, all parts of it in all times and dimensions. Contain all the sadness and agony of your inner child. Then a healing ground or womb can be created. Settle your mind and allow the child to go deeper into the past.*

In the past you have given your energies away to everyone else. Now invite your inner child to receive the healing. Once he takes in the energy, he can then disseminate it out to others.

Breath in the sweetness of the divine's breathe in- to your lungs. Divine Grace comes in as the pain and the old leave. Your heart-wall dissolves as the light and darkness of the Shadow begin to flow into one other.

I said, *It flows like the yin and yang, intermin- gling.*

Lyn said, *The more we contain then the light moves into the Shadow. The Shadow dissolves in the light. Allow. You may feel peace like in meditation; your body will relax.*

At this time I only felt occasional areas of pain in parts of my body or sadness. Lyn explained that what I felt meant the dissolving of the connections to the pain and agony.

Lyn said, *All pain has linking connections. Unless the client allows healing to occur, the emotional pain will increase. Pain needs loving like a child in pain rather than leaving the child by themselves. Then the child has to "tough it out."*

Sometimes client's fight the healing with their personal will, never allowing Divine Grace to enter.

Lyn expressed her joy as she said, *Beautiful, I see your structure of pain, the heart-wall, dissolving.*

A tear trickled down my right cheek.

At the end of this healing, I expressed to Lyn an event that occurred on my fifth birthday. I had always seen it as significant, yet had never understood it fully.

My mother asked me to tell her how old I was.

I remember my mind being a blank. So my mother told me to go outside until I told her.

We lived on a farm and I went, by myself, down near a grain storage shed. I stayed outside for most of the afternoon, crying my eyes out. I never cried.

You made some critical choices at that time, Lyn said.

I agreed. Choices including burying my feelings and staying invisible in the family. I realized I had been stuck emotionally, all my life, at the age of a five year old boy.

Lyn said, *Your little boy only wanted to be loved and nurtured on his birthday rather than do something like repeating his age.*

At this realization, I sensed my inner child coming back home to me and maturing.

Lyn exclaimed, *I see your child's gifts returning, so many of them.*

The divine had graced my healing, dissolving my heart-wall, after 58 years.

ELEKTRA: SOUL RETRIEVAL

Elektra describes her experience of discovering how to do soul retrieval on her own.

A while back I suffered from emotional and sexual problems. I remained unable to make love or get pregnant due to negative male female relationships I had experienced within my family. I also suffered trauma from a relationship breaking up at age 17 and an abusive lover at 18. I remained unable to budge the blockage. I had forgiven everyone I could think of, done my yoga, said my prayers, and worked my magic and tantric exercises, yet something still remained unmoving.

I prayed again for understanding when by chance my first love, out of nowhere, suddenly contacts me via my DJ – disc jockey website.

This stunned me for 15 years had passed without hearing from him. All of a sudden he found me and came back to apologize for the past.

The trauma had torn a bit of my soul away, left back in time where the trauma occurred.

I had met my first love, the twin brother of my close friend Charlie who I worked with. We fell in love at first glance and became inseparable and planned to marry. Suddenly and tragically, Charlie died in a car accident. He had fallen asleep at the wheel, left the road, and died when the electric pylons fell down and electrocuted him. When John, my love, lost his twin he totally switched and became a different person.

I lost both Charlie and John as John now blamed himself for the death of his brother. I grieved, pregnant, and alone with no emotional support from my family. I cried and fell into a deep depression over the loss of John more so than the death of Charlie as I could deal with that. John alive, yet dead left me without another thought. Something broke inside.

I never healed. I felt incomplete like a jigsaw puzzle with bits missing.

I realized I needed to find the lost part of my soul. After our traumatic parting I felt a pain in my chest and a great depression. I never felt like the same girl after. Part of me had fled.

So I researched Soul Retrieval and found when we experience trauma we often leave a part of our soul in time, frozen at a where the trauma happened. We become fractured.

I had left a love filled girl hopelessly waiting for my lover to return. She lived in a fantasy paradise close to his home where I had left her. She refused facing losing him, so she stayed in her illusion. I had to go and find her, comfort her, and talk her in to returning to me. When I had done this a wave of energy filled my body and a great healing occurred. So powerful, I have felt complete ever since.

ELEKTRA: HOW to DO SOUL RETRIEVAL

Elektra explains how she does soul retrieval.

Sit quietly in meditation, breathe gently and relax. Now think back to a time when something traumatic occurred or something which you feel changed your life forever in a traumatic way. Go back to that place and ask to be shown your lost "soul part."

See what comes to mind. Ask your Higher Self to reveal these lost parts to you. Sometimes they will be playing happily having created an alternate reality to shield them from the pain. Sometimes they freeze up like a statue or hide away terrified.

Talk to them, gain their trust, and convince them it's time to come back home. They may often be stuck in time and space at the point where the trauma happened.

When you have made peace with this lost part and regained its trust you can take its hand and invite it home. It will merge with your soul once more and you will have healed the rift.

Maybe you will feel a surge of energy throughout the body. Do this as often as you need to with as many different traumas you can think of. Sometimes we have many different soul fractures if we had many times of trauma.

Elektra learned how to do Soul Retrieval for herself. You may be able to also do the same for yourself.

I have experienced Soul Retrieval many times over my life. My wife Lyn, an energy healer, has assisted me for I remained unaware at the time that a part of my soul, which had split off in the past wanted to come back at that particular time. This event usually occurred while experiencing an energy healing session. The soul split always came back easily and gently.

In my experience many parts of us separate through trauma, which causes pieces of our soul to split off away from our being. These parts get stuck in time, need to be recognized, and consciously called back into the present time into ourselves. We need to hold a sustained attention as this occurs, for painful emotions from the original split can arise.

It takes practice to contain the emotions 100% or else we go out of body and the Soul Retrieval gets interrupted. Thus, we may need the assistance of someone skilled in Soul Retrieval to assist us. Also, our inner child needs to be invited into the Soul Retrieval for the healing to be complete for our inner child represents our emotional self.

Our soul splits remain in the past at the age when they separated. Sometimes, however, we may split off a part of ourselves and leave it with a person who we had a traumatic relationship with. Are parts of you still with someone from a past painful relationship?

Finally, we can pick up clues about possible lost soul parts by listening with care to our own or other people's language. I left my anger behind, my sense of security flew out the window, he stole my heart, I left my loyalty at my old job, I have lost my strength, or my childhood innocence is gone.

Next we take a look at the "dark night of the soul," the most intense confrontation with our Shadow.

CHAPTER 20

HOW to FACE the DARK NIGHT of OUR SOUL

HEALING THE SHADOW: DARK NIGHT of the SOUL

Everyone carries a Shadow, and the less it is embodied in the individual's conscious life, the blacker and denser it is. If inferiority is conscious, one always has a chance to correct it.

Carl Jung, *Psychology and Religion*

Entering into higher states of illumination and spiritual awakening requires purification of our personality self. Underhill describes this fourth stage on the mystical path as the "dark night of the soul." The Spanish mystic, St. John of the Cross, reports this phase as an inflowing of Spirit – Divine Grace - to purge personal imperfections. This state involves intense spiritual struggle including utter hopelessness and separation from Spirit.

Overcoming fear propelled me through a dark night of the soul at the age of forty-eight. Going through emotional and mental anguish and a total surrender to the will of Spirit prepared me a few months later to unify at a higher level my inner female and male energies.

The dark night involves our most intense confrontation with our personal Shadow called in spiritual terms the "Dweller on the Threshold." The Dweller looms before us when we become ready to face some of our mental illusions and emotional glamour's and come to grips with the illusion of duality between the light and darkness. The strength needed assists us to drive straight forward between these two opponents . . . and so may you enter into the Presence where the two are seen as one, states Alice Bailey author of *Glamour: A World Problem.*

We all carry within ourselves unconsciousness aspects of what the psychoanalyst, Carl Jung describes as the Shadow. As a child we would have called them monsters, beings that lurked in the dark to pounce on and harm us. In fairy tales the ogre, the big bad wolf, or the evil witch represents the Shadow part of us all.

So we create heroes to overcome these monsters of darkness. In our personal dark nights or the arising of our Shadows we have the choice to call up the courage to be our own heroes to face the unknown in our unconscious and triumph.

Jung advises if a person wants to be cured – of neurosis - it is necessary to find a way in which his conscious personality and his Shadow can live together. Curing means balancing our light and darkness or in other words allowing our Shadow parts to come to the light of our awareness, receiving their message, and accepting them. My experience has shown a jewel or gift lies hidden at the core of each major Shadow part as a germ of light. Another way to say it, within our weaknesses lays our greatest strengths and gifts of life service.

To confront a person with his Shadow is to show him his own light. Once one has experienced a few times what it is like to stand judgingly between the opposites, one begins to understand what is meant by the self. Anyone who perceives his Shadow and his light simultaneously sees himself from two sides and thus gets in the middle says Carl Jung, Good and Evil in Analytical Psychology.

Some of us may never face a dark night. Some of us may face a few dark nights. All of us have the opportunity to face, sometimes even on an ongoing basis, our Shadows. We can repress the Shadow, which will grow more persistent popping up to create emotional drama or on a global level, warfare, or we can chose to face this unconscious part and bring it into the light of our awareness.

Our Shadow mirrors back to us in our relationships and in our daily experiences of life. Do we tend to blame, harbor resentment, or be unwilling to forgive others when conflict appears or do we ask how can I become more aware of myself and thus change?

MICHAEL'S DARK NIGHT

When the soul embraces and accepts suffering, the pain reveals itself as the birth pangs of a new inner being.

Carl Jung

Throughout 80% of my life I have been emotionally codependent on others, particularly women. I suffered under the false belief of being incapable of standing in my own line of power. For example, in being instrumental in anchoring a new healing energy method, Laho-Chi, in the world in 1991, I believed I needed the support of my female partner, the president of the healing institute five of us established, for me to be successful.

After two and one half years as the sole teacher of the healing method to monthly groups in Los Angeles, I experienced a rapid change in consciousness over two months of intensified personal healing involving a combination of breath work and hands-on energy healing. Meanwhile, institute members expressed interest for more active involvement in Board meetings. Feeling more empowered I wanted to give members of the healing community a greater voice in the decisions of the healing institute. I intuitively felt this was right.

The four other institute Board members feeling their power threatened wrote a letter to all the community discrediting and demanding me to operate as an independent teacher, yet still accountable to the institute. I had anchored, evolved the teaching, and written the teaching manual.

I understood the motivation behind the letter for two Board members wanted, in secret, to take over the teaching role and push me out rather than being additional teachers. Outraged, I felt like fighting them tooth and claw. After, however, getting over my initial anger at their betrayal, I realized instead of resisting I needed to let go and surrender my connection to the institute and even the community of healers I had taught over the years. I believe, unknown to me at the time, my Higher Self guided me.

The next three months found me adrift on a sea of uncertainty as constant thoughts of doubt assailed my mind. Confused, bewildered, and alone, I entered into the dark night of the soul. I only realized years later, in retrospect, of what had occurred when I learned about the dark night.

Distraught, I turned inside and beseeched Spirit, What am I to do? At one point, after a couple of months I agonized over the possibility of giving up teaching healing all together. I believed this to be my life purpose at the time.

Although most of healing community I had taught supported me and some of them gathered around me at my birthday, I felt alone and lost in a sea of agony with no rudder for direction. Since I had no understanding of my state, my friends had no inkling of my inner state of barrenness, lack of joy, and motivation for I confided in no one with my doubts and feelings.

I hung on with no sense of what the future held, maybe because of my strength of perseverance. In addition, I had no institute or teaching to go back to. As a disciplined meditator, meditation no longer worked or brought me insights or peace.

You could say I lingered "caught between the worlds," except I had no vision of a future world. Stranded and lacking spiritual insight, I had no idea that all the fixed beliefs and feelings about my ego self required transforming. They needed dissolving so I could connect on a deeper level with my Higher Self and as a conduit for a higher frequency of healing energy.

Most of my life I believed I had to "do" or exert my personal will in an effort to make something happen. In the grip of the dark night, I had no power to make anything happen. I could have fought and railed against the dark night, which would only have increased my suffering or I could surrender without any "doing" and just "be."

Unknown to me at the time, my transformation occurred from the inside out. The dark night engulfed me like a protective covering of a cocoon before I would emerge like a butterfly into a new world.

Those who undergo the dark night say that after the midnight hour – the period of greatest intensity when all seems lost – light and peace appears. My midnight hour occurred when I resigned myself to the possibility of no longer being a teacher of healing. It took about two months before the light broke through.

I had done a taped radio program in Santa Barbara, California the previous year. A Catholic woman in her sixties, after listening to the radio program the next year by "accident" on a radio station in Toronto, Canada, trusted her intuition to fly to Los Angeles to take the hands-on healing training, sight unseen. Later back in Toronto, this woman through a set of "coincidents" set up a teaching weekend for me.

Still in the grip of the dark night, I wavered about going to Toronto. With the fortunate counsel of a friend, however, I agreed and made a critical choice to go. This had a major impact on my future life.

In Toronto a higher frequency of Laho-Chi, which I now called Creation Energy channeled through me. The trainees experienced incredible healings, inner visions, transformation, and a connection with Spirit within. On Saturday morning we assembled in a sterile hotel banquet room as twenty-five wary strangers.

By Sunday afternoon after releasing individual emotional trauma trapped in the body, we emerged joyous with the bond of a spiritual family.

The successful seminar signaled my emergence out of my dark night into a higher level of creativity and sovereignty. I moved to Toronto, started a new life, taught Creation Energy for about a year, and met my present wife, Lyn.

SHIVANI: HEALING the DARK NIGHT

The divine touches the soul to renew it and to ripen it, in order to make it divine.

St. John of the Cross – Dark Night of the Soul

I experienced a "Dark Night of the Soul" after the death of my five year old son. Along with my personal blame, my son's father blamed me for murder. I defended myself in court as well as with my mother. It took years for me to forgive myself, says Shivani, a nurse, healer, and artist. The hardest layer of pain involved realizing the anger I held for my son. He refused to listen to me. He disobeyed and died.

It took many, many years to see this deeply buried anger.

I suffered dissatisfied and in pain, complaining about myself or others. Something remained not

right in my life. When I saw I needed to forgive my
son, a light went on.

Perhaps a quarter of spiritual seekers on the road
to higher consciousness pass through the Dark Night.
We may pass through several Dark Nights in our life
lasting for months or years.

In the Dark Night, an absence of light and hope
prevails, as we feel all alone. We no longer feel comfortable in our old life and the new life has yet to
dawn. We remain unaware a different life even exists.

We plead where has all my joy gone? Nothing eases our suffering.

Then after weeks, months, or even years the holy
presence of Divine Grace fills us. Our mind may fill
with Light, our heart may feel peace, a flow of energy
may enter through our body, or for the first time in
our spiritual vacuum we sense a renewed zest for life.

Before, we existed as the Doer, which hung on for
dear life. Now our limited sense of self has dropped
away and also the old belief and emotional patterns,
which created suffering. Passing through the Dark
Night, we experience a higher state of awareness.

In the Dark Night, the Light of God's Grace shines
on us brightly to purify our egos in the fire of the soul.

Author Gregg Braden describes the Dark Night as one of the Essene Seven Mirrors of Relationship in the DVD, *Walking Between the Worlds*, allowing us a deeper understanding of our relationship with ourselves, others, and an opportunity to explore our relationship with the divine.

Shivani continues her story of healing. *I spent one year in the ashram in Poona, India, during my dark night, healing physically and emotionally. I know no one can heal us. We have to heal ourselves. The question I asked, How do we heal ourselves? I tried everything, past lives therapy, dance meditation therapy, the darkness meditation, over toning, craniosacral therapy, every meditation offered.*

Anyone can provoke us to look at ourselves, to look at our Shadow – the hidden unconscious parts of ourselves.

Let yourself really trust. Let yourself go deeply into your suffering, then the real inner you can emerge. My spiritual teacher always pointed us inward to our own inner teacher.

Next Sinnet, a horse whisperer, tells of her passage through her Dark Night and how her relationship with horses acted as a mirror, reflecting back her fears and a potential for learning, changing, and living in multiple dimensions.

SINNET'S DARK NIGHT: A RITE of PASSAGE

Sinnet describes horses as mirrors of truth. *I'd come to a period of my life some would call a life crisis and others a rite of passage. Due to my lifelong studies of Native American wisdom, I prefer to call this challenging period of life a rite of passage.*

This "dark night of the soul" forced me to look at the areas of my entire being and lifestyle, which lay in the darkness of my unconscious for me to change, develop, and grow.

The painful passage through the dark night takes a lot of energy and courage. It forced me beyond the edges of my comfort zone onto which I clung. There seemed no escape. In short, at twenty-eight, married, and having just given birth to my third child I realized to my shock, my husband revealed violent traits I had refused to see before. How had I ended up in this trap? It forced me into a wakeup call. Looking back I conclude this wakeup call - cruel and awful - in reality has been my saving grace. I started to look for change.

We can look a long time for change outside of our selves, especially in these times of transition with so many healing methods. Due, however, to my introverted and scared nature, I never thought one second of seeking help outside of myself. I had always been on my own and I had to cope with the fact at the age of twenty-five marrying a man twice my age as an act of loneliness more than love.

Since our well-being and survival depends on securing the protection of attachment figures, that relationship is our central concern throughout childhood, and its unresolved insecurities linger into adult life, including marriage.

John Bowlby, *Attachment and Loss*

Sinnet continues. *The wakeup call included abuse and violence – the same elements I'd wanted to escape from my childhood. Often as we seemingly face harsh facts and feel powerless, another door opens for us.*

During this period of my life I felt very attracted to horses, yet I had no knowledge or experience with these fine creatures. I initiated, however, a situation where I lived, breathed, and worked around horses all day long.

My first meeting with the horse, as an amazing being, occurred in Western Canada within the tribal reservation of the first nations in Lytton, British Columbia. Joe Dunstan, a native horseman, introduced me to the concept of natural horsemanship. My destiny seemed sealed.

Here I learned all about horse communication and how to develop a proper partnership, for the first time, based on core values such as mutual re-

spect, trust, and unconditional loving - simple basic values for all kind of relationships.

I encountered an uneasy road since I had so much to learn – about horses, and moreover about myself and life in general. The first issue I faced involved my tremendous fear of these energetic animals. At the same time, I felt so attracted to them. Facing them, one to one, in a round pen started a series of profound incidents leading to astonishing insights about living life in all the dimensions.

I will never forget my first session with a mare paint horse, Miss Fancy Candy. In the round pen, I realized my nervousness being so new to horses. This particular horse, highly spirited, made many nervous movements around me.

I'd worked with calm and gentle horses for a month or so practicing various techniques deprived from natural horsemanship and I felt confident with my new won skills. It had occurred to me that my inborn sensitive nature matched the most valued skill required in working with horses. This day this horse felt so different. Nothing worked, as I wanted.

I did everything by the book. The horse just whirled around me, getting more and more anxious. In the end, she reared and bucked all over the place.

When we change the way we look at things, the things we look at change.

Dr. Wayne Dyer, *Power of Intention*

Sinnet continues. *All of a sudden, I realized the one rearing and bucking most of all to be myself! It came as a huge wave of immediate understanding, which made me freeze up for a moment, long enough to watch Miss Fancy Candy mirroring me exactly the same way by freezing up herself. I looked at her for the first time; finally, becoming fully aware she literally spoke to me saying the words I have never forgotten since, "When do you finally start to listen?" From this day, I understood the proper meaning of being mindful.*

This very day I managed to reach out and to get hold of the life of the unseen dimensions. I felt the spirits and gentle souls so dear to me in my childhood whom I had abandoned as a grown up in my eagerness to adapt to mainstream society and to be in control.

As I started to listen to the precious Medicine Paint horses, I learned everything I needed to know about myself – our relatedness through the spirit of nature and the communication of the heart. First, however, I had to relearn how to listen to a silent language entirely based on gentleness, willingness and a firm yet open heart.

CHAPTER 21

HERE'S WAYS to HEAL YOUR PAT-TERNS of SELF-SABOTAGE HINDER-ING SUCCESS

Why do some areas of our lives refuse to change, given we would like to heal? Perhaps sabotage exists at the heart of this mystery. Sabotage can be on a mental or emotional level.

WHAT is the ROOT OF SELF-SABOTAGE?

When we want to improve our lives we set an intention of what we would like and then we look for results. We may have visualized the result and taken some actions. Why do our intentions fall short of our desired results? Maybe it's a little thing called "counter intention."

Counter Intention is a belief we hold in direct opposition to our conscious intention buried in our subconscious mind. We may for example have intent to weigh less. In the subconscious we may have a belief if we look good and attract more partners than we will have to be more intimate, yet we fear intimacy.

So which intent will win? Our subconscious or counter intention always wins because it has the greater power.

The conflict sets up an energy block within us and since our subconscious has the greater power we end up getting the opposite of our conscious intent. The energy system within our body changes polarity - a Psychological Reversal. All self-sabotage results from Psychological Reversal.

We can compare Psychological Reversal to positive and negative batteries in a flashlight. They need to be properly installed for the flashlight to work. Polarity change means the positive and negative energy systems in our body have been switched and we get the opposite of our conscious choices.

Psychological Reversal occurs when our subconscious mind believes it is better for us to keep our chronic pain, extra weight, or bad habit rather than change.

The following explains in brief detail how our inner child, Shadow, or victim consciousness may sabotage our success.

Cathryn Taylor a counselor and author of *The Inner Child Workbook* explains how our inner child can sabotage us. Our inner child sabotages our efforts to succeed in an attempt to protect us from failure . . . it fears our success! It fears our being too powerful. It is frightened we will get hurt.

Our Shadow sabotages us when we deny it and push feelings and behaviors we dislike down into our subconscious. As Carl Jung said the Shadow is, *The negative side of the personality, the sum of all those unpleasant qualities we like to hide, together with the insufficiently developed functions.* For example, intense reactions to others may indicate the same qualities within ourselves we refuse to face.

According to John O'Neill, *The Paradox of Success, our Shadow can sabotage success by an imbalanced focus on acquiring power, inappropriate sexual relations, overly pursuing money, or addictive behavior.* Do any famous people come to mind?

Finally, our victim mentality sabotages us through subconscious thoughts of being unworthy and powerless. Victims fail to recognize themselves as victims to their own critical thoughts and beliefs.

CREATING STRESS and SELF-SABOTAGE

Janie Behr, a life coach, talks about ways we create self-sabotage. She says, *Over reacting to stressful situations is a form of self-sabotage that causes emotional stress.* Do you know people who create unnecessary conflicts and emotional drama?

Do you engage in a lot of negative self-talk inside your head? Do you interpret positive events as negative? Do you sabotage yourself by creating self-fulfilling prophecies to prove your negative beliefs? You can learn how to change the negative self-talk into positive self-talk

Do you sabotage your relationships by being aggressive rather than assertive? Do you know the difference between aggressive and assertive? Do you let others walk all over you for fear of saying no and sabotage your own self-esteem? You can learn how to be assertive and also speak up and say no to begin establishing good personal boundaries.

Do you sabotage yourself by taking a pessimistic view and seeing things worse than they are? This undermines your esteem, health, and success.

Which of the self-sabotage methods apply to you? Do you want to reduce the stress in your life and quit sabotaging yourself? If so break through your denials, discover and express your unmet needs, strive to uncover your unconscious patterns of pain, face your fears, and take back your power.

SELF-SABOTAGE: GETTING to BE RIGHT

We all have a critical voice in our heads, which reminds us we lack something or other. That little voice coming from the subconscious drills a black hole of doubt, worry, and self- pity into the back of

your mind that seems to swallow up all the positive ideas that should be there instead, says Randolph Fabian Directo, Oriental Sports Trainer.

We all have our ways of perceiving the world from our core beliefs, our paradigms. We create our experiences to confirm the truth of our perceptions. We may have a core belief that we will never succeed at anything we do. So we set up our outcomes to prove that we will never succeed and thereby sabotage any possibility of success and we keep creating obstacles to our success on an unconscious level.

If for example we start a new relationship, expecting it to fail like all our previous ones than it probably will and we get to be right. Rather than continuing to create a false paradigm, we could choose to look at our core beliefs and "truths" to assess their rightness.

We might also examine our negative self-talk and our tendency to view life through the paradigm of a negative lens. As our perceptions shift, so may our outcomes. Could our rightness have a positive outcome rather than our past paradigm of failure?

SABOTAGE: DOUBTS and FEARS

We all have fears and doubts. Kishori Aird, a professional naturopath and a medical-intuitive, says, *It is far better to acknowledge those fears and doubts straight up and use that energy to propel us towards our goals than it is to have that energy, unexpressed, oppose those goals.*

Aird recommends the use of any positive statements needs to also recognize our doubts. When we add even if . . . to our statements, this gives our saboteur a voice. An example might be, I choose to improve my self-esteem even if I doubt it will get better.

TIPS to MOVE BEYOND SABOTAGE

1. Do you tend to focus on what is wrong or missing in your life? Does this attract more of the same? Instead focus on all the things that do work. The Law of Attraction says, "Where your attention goes, your energy flows."

2. Do you spend a lot of time worrying about or fearing the future? Instead focus on solutions and take action when you can. Even small actions can make a difference.

3. Do you sabotage by comparing yourself to others and then feel bad? Instead think about, write out, and focus on daily qualities or strengths you have or can develop.

4. Do you feel worthless or less than? Do you make excuses for yourself? Begin looking in the mirror, morning and evening, and say, I love myself. Your critical thoughts will emerge. Pay attention to them and continue the mirror exercise for a minimum of

twenty-one days straight. What do you notice has changed? Do you value and appreciate yourself more?

5. Do you live in the past, in past failures? How can you learn from your failures and grow?

OVERCOMING SABOTAGE

We can choose to become aware of our unconscious beliefs through reprogramming methods such as the one explained in Carolyn Ball's book, *Claiming Your Self-Esteem*.

We can also use ways to dissolve and release these beliefs once we become aware of them. One way is Byron Katie's, *The Work*, which has questions for releasing beliefs which no longer serve us. The four questions include:

1. Is this belief true?

2. Who would I be without the thought?

3. Could I let this go?

4. Would I let this go? When?

Then like Carolyn Ball's reprogramming choose a new belief.

Joe Vitale in *The Key* also has a method of reprogramming unconscious beliefs, which block attracting our intents. Joe says, *We are unconsciously attracting the wrong things.* The Key tells of Joe's journey out of poverty.

The Emotional Freedom Technique – EFT – also has a method for dealing with subconscious objections or yes-buts that may arise to sabotage the positive affirmations used as part of the EFT. Gary Craig, the founder of EFT, calls the yes-buts "tail enders."

EFT combines tapping certain acupressure points on the body while repeating a specific choice statement to release physical or emotional issues. The method would include the original statement and an antidote to the tail ender. For example, the original choice: "I choose to be successful in my business." The tail ender: But if I am successful other people will ridicule me the way my father used to." The antidote: I choose to feel respected even when I am successful." The final statement: I choose to feel respected even when I am successful in my business."

Recently it has been brought to my attention that the pattern of sabotage may be part of our DNA.

SELF-SABOTAGE in the DNA

Is self-sabotage built into our DNA through our fight or flight response? Because of fear of intimacy, lack of self-worth or insecurity, do we sabotage our relationships by fighting or fleeing?

Do patterns of sabotage lurk in our DNA from our family lineage? Theresa Dale, Ph.D., *Transform Your Emotional DNA*, has researched this and says, *NeuroPhysical Reprogramming allows you to explore DNA consciousness, locating and eliminating sabotaging energy patterns that create illness and depression.*

Lyn O'Hara, a radiatory healer, radiates energy from the divine through her heart chakra into the auric field and body of the client. She then asks permission to enter the clients DNA into held patterns of trauma. The trauma then releases without any pain. Lyn further assists by asking questions for the client to gain realizations.

HEALING SABOTAGE in the DNA

Three of us, Lyn, Mark, and I gathered in a group as Lyn guided us. Lyn asked if we wanted to heal the pattern of sabotage in our DNA. The emotions held by our inner child or Shadow continues to sabotage us until we identify them and energetically hold them in the Light of the Divine allowing them to transform.

Yes, I said and Lyn commented she sensed my inner child saying "No" as he girded himself with protective armor. I had remained unconscious of my child's reaction.

Lyn explained, *When we have a negative emotional reaction or we respond with a "No," conscious or unconscious, this means that our wounded inner child or an aspect of our Shadow self has been triggered.*

Lyn continued. *Ask permission of your body to receive the incoming divine energy. Focus in your heart.*

Lyn told me, *Michael you have a lot of old beliefs like cobble stones taking up space in your heart.*

I continued feeling and containing the divine energy coming into my body as I sensed the old beliefs releasing.

Then Lyn said, *Aspects of our inner Shadows are coming up for each of us. For the Shadow to release it has to be named or else it becomes slippery and sneaks away.*

Naming our Shadow means we identify the emotions the Shadow carries within itself as it comes forth. When we do this the Shadow no longer has any power over us.

Lyn commented, *Mark and Michael both your Shadows carry the cross of the martyr.*

I recognized the pattern of victim, powerlessness, and unworthiness that I had struggled with for most of my life.

Lyn said to Mark and me, *When the Shadow has been identified, then it melts and power returns to our bodies.*

In response to Lyn's remark I felt an increase of energy filling my body. She told us that our bodies would need extra water and minerals as our DNA continued to change as we focused in our hearts and allowed the divine energy to continue coming in. Be aware it takes time to heal our past patterns.

I believe most of us would like to heal our pain or suffering. We may, however, have been unaware of the causes or methods to do so. Even further, we may be unaware of how sabotage occurs to thwart our best intentions. We may fail to recognize or heal our wounded inner child. We may deny the Shadow parts of our personalities. We may choose to allow our victim mentality to keep us powerless and feeling unworthy. In **Part 3** we begin by exploring how our Power of Choice keeps us locked in suffering or lessens it.

PART THREE

- **Making conscious choices**
  - **Path of the heart**
  - **Paths of service**
- **Global paradigm shift**
- **Spiritual awakening**

CHAPTER 22

DO YOU MAKE CONSCIOUS or UN-CONSCIOUS CHOICES?

Man's power of choice enables him to think like an angel or a devil, a king or a slave. Whatever he chooses, mind will create and manifest.

Frederick Bailes, *teacher of Science of Mind*

Choices can be conscious or unconscious. In our relationships when we explode in anger or blame others, do we recognize this as an unconscious reaction?

How do we teach our children to make choices? If as a parent or role model to other children, do we react without thinking from our emotions such as frustration? Perhaps instead of reacting we could sit down with our children or in our relationships and discuss better ways to handle situations. Perhaps we could review our choices daily to realize which ones we make consciously and which come from unconscious emotional reactions.

I believe our unconscious choices come from unresolved emotional pain and conditioned mental beliefs. Do you want less pain and to make more conscious choices?

Next Joanna talks about making a conscious "critical choice."

JOANNA: A CRITICAL CHOICE to HEAL

At the age of twenty-four after a failed effort at suicide, I looked into the bathroom mirror, says Joanna, a retired CEO. So you have not had a nice childhood. I had an "Aha" experience at that moment. In a state of clarity, I became aware, okay, I have a choice. I can continue the rest of my life blaming my parents or I realized the only person who could heal and make changes was me. I then resolved I am going to do anything and everything to heal. I refuse to continue being afraid, lacking confidence, and feeling pain all the time.

Joanna made and committed to a conscious critical choice in her life. A critical choice involves a decision that has a major impact on our lives. We have the freedom to make that decision on a conscious level rather than unconsciously by blaming others or reacting to situations.

Do we want to continue choosing suffering? We will examine this next.

DO WE CHOOSE PAIN or SUFFERING?

Choice implies consciousness - a high degree of consciousness. Without it, you have no choice. Choice begins the moment you disidentify from the mind and its conditioned patterns, the moment you become present.

Eckhart Tolle, *Practicing the Power of Now*

Do we choose suffering? Lyn, an energetic healer, has this to say about pain and suffering. *We tend to avoid pain. Numbness and addictions indicates an avoidance of pain. With suffering, we recycle in the suffering going over and over the same story. Pain lies below suffering. When we choose to go into the suffering the pain can end, otherwise it remains un-ending. When we make the choice for "Yes," the Grace can come in.*

When we can hold and contain the pain, Grace can come in. Containing requires staying present with the pain or specific emotion, without slipping away and becoming unconscious. When we stop con-taining the pain, we fall back into our unconscious "shadow," which feeds on pain like a hungry beast.

Withdrawal into fear, feeling powerless, victim-ized, holding onto anger, or feeling unpresent all in-dicates we have fallen into our shadow selves – parts of ourselves, which we deny. We can hold these parts with compassion.

When we run away from our pain, meant for us to face, it only gets worse. When physical or emotional discomfort arises, our mind activates and spins around all the details. Let the thoughts come and contain them without going over and over them. Then we keep the energy inside ourselves rather than projecting it out onto a person or situation.

We have a choice whether the energy spins inside of us or spins out into blaming or being angry with others. Then the situations will continue to occur repeatedly, creating suffering each time if we choose taking no responsibility for ourselves.

Always say "yes" to the present moment. What could be more futile, more insane, than to create inner resistance to what already is? What could be more insane than to oppose life itself, which is now and always now? Surrender to what is. Say "yes" to life -- and see how life suddenly starts working for you rather than against you.

Eckhart Tolle, *The Power of Now*

Lyn continues. *If we choose, however, to hold a point of inner containment, then we experience more discomfort like a pot of boiling water with a lid on it. The energy builds so it can transform.*

We also can choose to hold no anger towards the thoughts that arise in our minds. This can be a chal-

lenge for when our minds become agitated this indicates some unconscious choice.

Our minds want to stop us feeling. We can bring ourselves back to the present by screaming, exercising, using our breath, or focusing on feelings or sensations in our body.

As we contain, the patterns will dissolve. A truth lies at each layer of the pattern, when we remain present. When all the layers dissolve, we experience joy, peace, or oneness.

When we learn how to contain our pain and emotional reactions, we create a cup like a grail. Then Grace has a place to come into to change our lives and those around us.

Now we will look at making critical choices and new choices.

CHOICE for LIFE

A number of people took part in a weekend seminar examining their past and future critical choices. A critical choice involves a decision, which has a major impact on our lives. Many times our choices, in the past, came from an unconscious emotional reaction, which then leads to suffering. The more conscious our decisions become, then the less suffering we have to endure.

The following examples illustrate how some of the people had handled critical choices in their lives.

In the past when June, an office manager, faced big decisions, seeing no other solution, she run away from them, which resulted in a feeling of emptiness and being a prisoner of her emotions. Tina, in search for liberty, married out of rebellion and now lacked the courage to end an unsatisfying relationship. Another woman, Josie, had moved from a European country to South America. She felt wonderful as her emotional wall tumbled down, yet over the course of her life she underwent fourteen surgeries in her lower body.

Julie, a lawyer, suffered severe depression and thoughts of suicide most of her life until recently. She had repressed her emotions all her life and when she finally chose to leave a codependent relationship of many years where her husband abused her emotionally and financially, she made the decision out of reaction. This left the bank door open for her husband to take further advantage of her financially.

Julie has this to say. *I experienced intense depression and agony since childhood. Even with psychiatrists and medication the depression remained. Every day, I faced the choice to commit suicide or live.*

I went to India to undergo an intense 21-day emotional and spiritual purification. Even after India the depression continued, even though I made a choice in India to start to look at what I had avoided all my life.

My biggest change came when I decided to accept divine help. Then Divine Grace and inner spiritual light started coming into me.

I continued working with an energy healer who assisted me to face and enter my fear. The fear began to dissolve. Afterwards, even though I still felt sadness, my agony changed quickly. Thoughts of suicide no longer overwhelmed me. I began to laugh and make new choices.

It takes great courage to face and choose to go through our fears as voiced by Eleanor Roosevelt, You gain strength, courage, and confidence by every experience in which you really stop to look fear in the face. You must do the thing, which you think you cannot do. The poet Robert Frost states the same in another way, The best way out is always through.

We always have a choice to go through our darkness and come out the other side into the light. Making conscious choices clears the chaos in our lives, says Lyn.

Lyn continues. *We all have a "wall of war" like the Berlin Wall. This wall builds up inside us with all our conscious and unconscious choices of "No" to positive change in our lives. It consists of all we choose to be unwilling to see about our lives. The first step in the coming down of the wall involves a willingness to recognize a wall exists. We can then choose to chip away at the wall, which involves a willingness to see the truth about ourselves. God's Grace can come into our lives when we finally choose to see.*

During the seminar Josie, a business consultant, made a beautiful statement, *When we make the right choices our soul smiles.*

Oprah Winfrey has this to say, *Before you agree to do anything that might add even the smallest amount of stress to your life, ask yourself; What is my truest intention? Give yourself time to let a "Yes" resound within you. When it's right, I guarantee that your entire body will feel it.*

Some people experience suffering in the midst of making a choice, for our minds attempt to take charge. Joanna, a seminar leader, expresses it this way, *Our mind wants to be our best friend, yet it disallows change, which it fears.*

Lyn, as a personal growth seminar leader, reminds us, *We need all parts of ourselves to make choices. When faced with a difficult choice, which affects others, parts of us may split off and leave energetically. A sign such as confusion indicates some part of us has left. Also, when a choice includes someone else we may take them into our energy field as part of ourselves. To make the best choice we need to let them go. In other words, we make the choice to* be in our own sovereignty. *Another important aspect to consider involves the inner child, which has to be open to receiving the choice also or else our hearts desire never occurs.*

Breathe and invite the inner child to breathe in also. When our inner child feels fear then we create fear. Our inner child connects with our power to move forward. Our adult and inner child must feel the same for creation of a new choice to occur.

We can live life as a child. By being the happiness, we show the joy of the child.

Lyn explained another technique to manifest new choices. *Feel your old life. Feel the new life and the inner child. Then step across an imaginary line on the floor into the new life while making a statement such as "I am receiving . . . ." Each day step across the line into a specific activity of your new life while feeling it physically.*

Julie, a lawyer, commented, *Daily I have made choices related to past painful choices.*

Lyn suggested to Julie. *Bring the feeling of the pain into the present. Leave behind everyone else connected to the pain. Just bring yourself forward. Like a newborn baby, cut the cord to the past. Be present now.*

In the following story, a sexually abused woman tells of her choice, shifting from anger into compassion.

POWER of CHOICE: FORGIVENESS

Sylvia Klaere says, As a transpersonal therapist, I help the entire person body, mind, and soul.

The following details a typical example of Sylvia's type of healing for a woman who suffered sexual abuse.

Sylvia said, *A young woman of twenty-seven from Guayaquil, Ecuador, came after a physical violation to ask me for help. Understand Ecuador as a third world country has much poverty and as of November 1998 rape continues as a growing issue.*

The woman described her ordeal. While travelling on a bus to her work a few men entered the bus and pulled out guns. They stole everything valuable from the passengers and then threw out all the men and old women. Then the men begin raping the young women as they forced the bus driver to continue on route.

The abuse filled the young woman with fear, hate, and desolation.

Sylvia describes her therapy. *First, the client agrees to look at the higher reason on the soul level for their difficulties.*

Later I start with Reiki.

A Reiki healer taps into a life force guided by a superior intelligence and the energy flows where a patient needs it.

Sylvia continues talking about her approach. *During a Reiki session, I receive channeled information from the higher guidance of the client, which I then give them.*

In the healing, we also talk about new affirmations, meditation, positive thinking, and the possible deeper causes of physical difficulties.

In this case, the abused woman needed no physical help. Therefore, during and after the Reiki, I gave her channeled information, which said, "Forgive this man."

The woman said, "No!" She feared seeing his face again and reliving the suffering. Then I told her to remember the moment of violation.

When I open to channel Reiki and other Universal energies, I can sense the presence of higher inner beings and I hear words that I repeat to my clients, which I describe as angelic. So when I now refer to the angel, this is what I mean.

After the Reiki, the woman stopped crying. The angel had her look at the man and into his eyes.

In the moment, when I looked into the eyes of the woman, she saw the expression of love and understanding flowing through me. My face reflected the higher angelic vibrations in and around us. I remember I spoke to her with love and compassion and she understood the next step necessary for her well-being.

The woman closed her eyes and remembered the moment in spite of her fear. Then her fear faded so she could withstand the ordeal again, as she looked into the man's soul.

The woman gazed deeply into the eyes of the man. She saw the inner demons, a man without hope. She saw a childhood of always stealing and begging for money. She saw a drunken dad and no love. She saw hate and poverty.

As the woman continued to look deeply, she saw the deep despair and compassion welled up in her for this tortured soul.

The angel now told the woman to send the man love.

The woman refused. How could she do this?

Then the angel told her to connect her heart to the divine and make another effort.

A few moments later the woman did. After a while, she let go of her suffering and released the man.

We talked about her angelic experience

The woman walked out of my office smiling.

All trauma sufferers experience the phenomena of chronic helplessness to some extent, says Peter Levine, Waking the Tiger, Healing Trauma.

I suggest with the above woman that she chose to move out of being a victim to taking charge of her healing and regaining a sense of empowerment. She chose to forgive, connect with a Higher Power, and move from anger and suffering to a higher emotional state of compassion.

Next Jacqueline Stone asks, Will we live by our unconscious programming or make a higher choice?

JACQUELINE STONE: THE GREATEST EXERTION of WILL

Jacqueline Stone, author and personal coach says, *Sometimes it takes the greatest exertion of will to make a higher choice. We know our attitude remains entirely up to us. We know bearing feelings of resentment, regret, and judgment hurt us and bring us down. Yet, the programming in our unconscious* mind toward such reactions exerts a powerful influence difficult to overcome.

As one grows in self-awareness, the realization slowly unfolds that one's own condition is brought about by oneself and one's own choices in life, whether they are gut reactive, knee-jerk choices, or conscious choices.

Melvin D. Saunders, 100% Brain Course

Jacqueline continues. *Life gives us plenty of opportunities to make choices. Every time a situation arises which triggers a first response of judgment or resentment, we get the chance to choose whether we will live by our unconscious programming or make a higher choice. These situations serve as gifts to become more conscious even though we may believe differently at the time.*

I can tell myself all day that I choose to come from love in all things. How I actually feel and react remains the same until I make a conscious choice about my responses.

Some days I am in a tough place emotionally or feel down energetically and I refuse to make the higher choice, or at least put it off. I know, however, if I want to live in a higher vibrational frequency of consciousness with less suffering, I can ill afford the luxury of wallowing in resentments or blame.

If the emotion runs deep, it may take all the spiritual strength I can muster to refuse the negative feelings and redirect my thoughts and emotions. In these times, I can choose to use my spiritual practices. Everything I have learned about letting go, forgiveness, acceptance, and where I focus my attention helps me through these moments.

Gratitude attracts what we desire. The universal law of attraction says that we will attract into our life the things we think about and focus on.

Enoch Tan in article, *Gratitude Attracts More of What you Desire*

Jacqueline continues. *Have you ever tried to forgive someone to whom you hold a lot of resentment? It's a challenge. We can easily get caught up in justifying ourselves and blaming another, which only leads to swimming in a soup of negative emotions.*

Would you like to get out of the soup pot? Then find something you feel good about that makes you feel happy or grateful. Focus on that for a while. Go outside and spend some time in nature or whatever elevates your spirits. When we feel good inside we can revisit our challenge. We will be in a higher vibrational frequency, seeing things more clearly. From this point of being, we will find it easier to make the higher choice.

Next Kathryne-Alexis describes upgrading her consciousness through making conscious choices.

KATHRYNE-ALEXIS: CONSCIOUS CHOICES

Law of Attraction is Universal and every person is affected by it. And it is always true that what I think and what I feel and what I get are always a match.

Abraham-Hicks, *www.abraham-hicks.com*

Kathryne-Alexis a life path consultant talks about her method of transforming emotional suffering. *We can look at fear as the food that feeds separation or redefine and direct it into a feeling of excitement to be, do or experience something better, more loving. I learned to shift the energy I had labeled fear into fuel and courage to make new choices.*

One perception drives us to avoid the fear and the other moves us towards it. David Hawkins M.D., Power vs. Force, has formulated a consciousness scale to calibrate levels of emotion. Fear has a score of 100 while excitement, the other side of fear, rates at a higher level of energy of possibly 310. Courage attunes to 200 on the scale while love calibrates at 500. The average level of human consciousness, according to Hawkins scale functions below 200.

Which way do we choose to use the energy of fear? Would we choose the lower level of energy and be caught up in the fear – false evidence appearing real or consciously choose the excitement, which can be used to drive us forward into positive change.

Just as we can choose to upgrade our thoughts previously referred to as conscious languaging, we can also upgrade our emotions into a higher level of consciousness. Can we be ready to look at our beliefs and emotions and see if they still serve us in the highest truth? Do we have the courage? Can we feel excited in the face of fear? Can we make the conscious choice for the higher level of consciousness, which involves change?

Kathryne-Alexis says, *Yes, if I reach for feeling excited and ready, then the pain and resistance ceases. Conscious choices can be made, understandings come readily. Change can happen quickly. Then truth moves from fear into love. Grace becomes a natural flow towards excitement and joy based on love. We then shift from suffering into love.*

If we choose suffering, then we will suffer. The Law of Attraction illustrates this; I attract to my life whatever I give my attention, energy and focus to, whether positive or negative, says Michael J. Losier in his book *Law of Attraction.*

Kathryne-Alexis describes her use of the Law of Attraction. *When I go to bed, in my mind, I wipe my slate clean for the day of all experiences and energies that no longer serve me. I feel appreciation for the moments and things that made me feel good, that I am enthusiastic about, and reset my magnet of attraction for more of these moments. I wake up feeling new, free, and excited about creating my day.*

For Shivani, a previous nurse, and now a healer and artist, it took many years to shift from making unconscious to conscious choices. She says, *I have made some critical choices in my life from a state of being unconscious. I let others persuade me to make many decisions, I truly disagreed with. A cloud of death hung over my head for 25 years. I lived in chaos. Now I choose to make conscious choices. I make choices in alignment with my life purpose. I choose to live in celebration of life. As a Torchbearer for the Light, I choose to bring harmony out of chaos.*

Shivani continues next by telling of her choice of detachment and surrender.

SHIVANI: CHOOSING SURRENDER

Shivani says, *For seventeen years of my life I poured everything I had into creating and maintaining a meditation center. I did the cleaning, the cooking, and the driving, everything. I felt like no one appreciated me. When a partner came back after being away for six years he did not want to work with me and all the others said it was ok.*

I fell into being the victim. The community had voted me out of my life's work.

I was offered a position working in the best hotel in my area. I realized my pattern of self-destruction, of how I created stress and attachment to the meditation center. I saw how my desire to maintain certain standards at the meditation center created suffering for me.

I saw how I allowed others to victimize me. I had chosen to break the pattern. I established another center in my town. Friends offered to help me. Then I found myself alone again. Why did I create this center? I prayed for a message on an inner level, for a sign. I surrendered. Should I keep this center or let it go?

A group leader called to rent the center one weekend every month. She gave me more than I needed for the monthly rent.

Shivani's experience shows the importance of detachment and surrender. Kahlil Gibran, a Lebanese poet, describes letting go of someone you love. This also applies to attachment to anything. This takes courage and a choice to surrender.

If you love somebody, let them go, for if they return, they were always yours. And if they don't, they never were.

Kahlil Gibran, *The Prophet*

CHAPTER 23

WILL YOU CHOOSE the ROAD LESS TRAVELED: the PATH of the HEART

Next I begin by explaining my myth of unworthiness. As a child, I chose on an unconscious level to take on my father's emotional pain. Like most people I chose to numb this pain as well as my own for about half of my life. I also chose to sink into feeling like a major victim, powerless or angry, for two-thirds of my life.

MICHAEL: CHOICE - UNWORTHINESS or WORTHINESS

Two roads diverged in a wood, and I took the one less traveled by, and that has made all the difference.

Robert Frost, *The Road Not Taken*

For more than forty years, I chose limited beliefs, which locked me into feeling unworthy. Growing up as a poor farm boy, wearing second hand clothes in high school, I felt like the lowest of the low. Being shy and introverted my self-worth drug on the ground.

To complicate my low self-worth, I unconsciously choose to swallow some of my alcoholic father's pain and shame and take it on as my own. Until about the age of thirty I felt like a social outcast, a broken-down bum like my father.

In school, I believed myself to be stupid. After six years of College and additional years of ongoing self-study of psychology and systems of self-development one day a realization hit me, I was smart. From then on I chose to believe in my intelligence and feel more confident.

For, however, another fifteen years I felt like an emotional retard in male-female relationships. Inside, I experienced anger, depression, and hurt. Yet, I felt too vulnerable to express my feelings and chose to numb myself in the false belief I won't experience any more pain. Each failed codependent relationship reinforced the perception, which I chose to believe, of my incapability of expressing love.

Nevertheless throughout my life, even though I felt unworthy, I chose to follow the inner light of my intuitive guidance. Always I seized the highest action leading me into greater light. Through each relationship I chose to learn more about myself. After the age of forty-five my life purpose and creative gifts of energy healing, teaching self-development, and writing about spiritual subjects began manifesting.

Through the difficult emotional relationships and a spiritual dark night of the soul, I chose to follow the highest truth I knew at any particular time. Through these experiences I gained an inner sense of my own self-worth independent of other people's perceptions.

It has taken over forty years of choosing to be healed emotionally and spiritual development to purify the pain of the past. Continuously, I chose the highest and came closer to the divine center within myself.

I have chosen to move out of the myth of my unworthiness into a creative, intelligent, intuitive, loving, and worthy being. In the words of Robert Frost, I chose the road less traveled by most and that has made all the difference.

Have you chosen the myth of unworthiness at times in your life? What have you done to dispel this myth? What do you chose to do now?

I talk next, from my own experience, about taking on other people's pain in an unconscious desire to help them. This can be in regards to our birth families, in relationships, in the work place, and particularly as therapists or energy healers.

I still to some degree take on people's pain when working with groups of people, conducting seminars, or doing energy sessions with clients. I use methods afterwards like conscious intention and Tibetan bells to clear myself and the healing room of energies that have been released. My wife, also an energy healer and ultra-sensitive, reminds me at times that I am carrying some group or an individual's energy that I need to clear.

Are there areas in your life where you unconsciously take on other people's pain?

TAKING on OTHER'S PAIN

Through unconscious choice, we sometimes accept loved one's pain. Out of compassion, knowing no other way to ease the hurt, as a child in our family we may absorb one or both parent's agonies they lacked the capacity of handling. For instance, as an unaware child I imbibed my alcoholic father's shame as my own. Silently, within myself, I struggled to resolve his shame and pain as if it were mine.

Our shouldering another's pain provides a disservice both to that person, as well as ourselves. Is responsibility about choosing to carry the cross of another's emotional load or is it the ability to respond?

In our adult years as we choose to release stored agony from our bodies we may consider all the emotional issues as ours personally. I did. In my experience, both personal and as an energy healer, I discovered some accumulated pain comes from the family. Sometimes the healing of ourselves seems never ending.

When we shoulder the burden of another's pain, we rob them of their learning their life lessons, as well as slowing our own personal development. Psychological and spiritual release of another frees both of us to walk our unique paths of transformation.

We can best help our family by choosing to release our own core issues of emotional pain. As we release, the main family patterns clear from the blood line. We have a link in consciousness with our family through our blood. I have personal experience as well as that of others in this regard.

Any major change in us echoes like a sound vibration into our family's bodies, blood, and consciousness. We can look at the blood of the family as a pool of water. A pebble tossed into a pond creates waves to ripple throughout the whole body of the pond. In a similar way, our ripple of change affects the pool of our family consciousness. This sets a pattern for any particular family member at the time they chose to shift their consciousness. It makes their shift easier.

As mentioned earlier, for most of my life I bore a sense of unworthiness. It has taken over forty years of emotional healing and spiritual self-development to release my issue of unworthiness.

The resolving of my own unworthiness liberates all generations of my family. Unworthiness existed like a string with many knots tied along its length. Each knot represented a generation of the family. Unraveling the unworthiness within one member yanks the string and all the knots on the string get extracted for that person. This releases the pattern of unworthiness for the family as a group. Each member needs to clear his or her, for example, individual unworthiness when ready. It will, however, be much easier for them.

Kathryne-Alexis describes next the path of the heart, loving ourselves.

KATHRYNE-ALEXIS: CHOOSING the PATH of the HEART

Kathryne-Alexis as a life path consultant says, *Choice and intention is another key of living my daily life. What do I invite into my life? What are my heart desires? What intentions do I hold to manifest these choices? Am I willing to receive my highest dreams and creations?*

We are all experts at polarized "negative" learning experiences; are we not? I prefer to shift my learning and living to a more balanced fulfilling path.

If I accept that I create my relationships and experiences, what is my highest choice? What issues or beliefs do I select to let go of when events feel out of balance or overwhelming? What experiences do I choose to expand and create in receiving an abundant, joyful, graceful life?

Be specific in the qualities you invite. Set intentions of how you allow them to come to you. Enjoy and be grateful for what arrives. Ask and question when something does not happen or feel on purpose and then refine your choices, intentions, and desires.

Being in control of my life has gained new meaning since 1989. "Let go, let God." It is not surrender to a force outside me. It is awakening to that God force within me. I call it my course to Source, the path of heart

My first choice is to love myself. This involves integrating all my selves; conscious, unconscious, and higher. Loving myself moves me out of codependency into empowerment. I shift out of the polarity of half Light into Full Light, a spiritual Light that comes from within. Half Light includes all my beliefs, judgments, and repressed emotional pain based on conflict.

I choose to awaken to the Full Light of Unity.

At the beginning Kathryne-Alexis posed the question, *What are my heart desires? Do we consciously choose to live our heart's desires or do we choose to "play it safe?"*

Now Julia Marie tells of some of her critical choices, which had a major impact on her life and also finally choosing the career of her heart's desire.

JULIA MARIE: CRITICAL CHOICES

My spiritual journey toward my Higher Self involves critical choices and actions taken or not taken. One critical choice occurred in October 1969 when I broke my engagement to my high school sweetheart, the All-American boy, captain of the football team; perfect husband material. I dumped him for a skinny, little, baldheaded, Jewish, pool hustler from Ohio. I knew if I married the football hero, I would have a life just like my parents. This I did not want. Of course, I had no idea what I was choosing. I only knew what I was rejecting. The choice had far-reaching consequences.

Standing upon the altar the priest intoned, "Forever and ever and till death do you part". Meanwhile I said to myself, If this lasts two years it will be a miracle.

We stayed together, beyond the two-year mark because my husband's brother, Willis, died in a car race. His death devastated me.

This death is one of those turning points in my life of spiritual growth, of increased consciousness. Willis, a twenty-nine year old surgeon, had a stellar career in medicine ahead of him. My husband Ray idolized him. Willis like a brother made me happy.

The weekend of the accident, we moved from Los Angeles to Bakersfield. I waded, knee deep in uno-

pened boxes, fast food containers, diapers, and bottles for a cranky teething year old daughter. Willis called us several times that week before the races in Phoenix, Arizona, to fly out and cheer him to victory. Ray decided to go while I stayed home unpacking trying to create order out of chaos. There would be other races.

A deeper meaning of chaos hit me when I received Ray's phone call announcing Willis' fatal last race. So many lives now would never be saved or healed because of the snatching of a gifted surgeon. His death brought me the realization of how much I loved him, which I never expressed.

During the time of intense mourning, I began to perceive the entire universe as a finely woven tapestry, intricately linked. What would have happen if I had said yes to Willis' requests? Would that one alteration in the fabric of time and space have moved things around enough so that those particular cars might not have collided? Would someone else have died instead?

Meanwhile back to the saga of my marriage. I stayed married long enough to create two beautiful daughters with Ray the "hustler." He left me for a teenage girl with an eighth grade education. The hussy's IQ matched her bust measurement.

In 1974, the Women's Liberation Movement gained momentum, which supported my being a sin-

*gle parent. My friends advised me to go for the jugu-
lar in a court battle with Ray. Instead, I opted for a
more amicable and informal agreement.*

*Karma or the effect of one's actions was only a
word I had heard. Somehow, I knew life (karma)
would give the "hustler" his due. Consequently, his
hussy spent the next five years making Ray miserable in ways I never imagined.*

*My life is full of critical turning points. Some-
times I feel as though I am many different beings living many lives all at the same time.*

*With the next turning point, Mother Nature knew
my life needed to change direction. She jolted me out
of my complacency. On January 1994, an earthquake
rumbled through the Los Angeles San Fernando Val-
ley. At forty-four years of age, I was already in the
process of change. I put my real estate career on hold
six months before the earthquake to work for a Los
Angeles food bank – L.I.F.E.*

*Finally, I found my purpose in L.I.F.E. - Love Is
Feeding Everyone. However, the Divine Master
Planner had something else in mind for me because
L.I.F.E. ran out of funds by the end of 1993. Out of a
job, I decided whether to return to real estate or seek
employment elsewhere. Applying for unemployment
benefits, I determined to use a six-month period to
find a new path better suited to my shifting lifestyle.*

The new path led me in February 1994, just after the L. A. earthquake, to attending an energy healing training taught by Michael David Lawrience.

I had no idea about energy healing. At the request of my sister, I attended the training to support her. She has had cancer four times. Now she is radiantly alive and healthy thanks to various alternative healing methods.

The choice of energy training took me into a career as a craniosacral therapist, which I have continued to this day.

Like Julia Marie, we make various unconscious and conscious critical choices in our lives. We also have the choice of making more of our unconscious choices conscious and thus, altering our life for the better. As Dr. Kathleen Hall says in *Alter Your Life, In every single thing you do, you are choosing a direction. Your life is a product of choices.*

In this chapter, we see we have the power to change our unconscious choices to conscious ones. Conscious choices involve acceptance, forgiveness, gratitude, and surrender. Most important, conscious choices create less suffering.

We can choose, rather than being immobilized by fear, to take that same energy and use it as courage to take action. As well as choosing to upgrade our emotions, we can also choose to change limiting thoughts and habitual unconscious critical and negative language patterns into positive language, which will support manifesting success rather than self-sabotage.

We can choose to follow our higher inner guidance as well as loving ourselves and living our heart's desire. Finally, we can make choices in alignment with our life purpose rather than being taken off purpose.

In the next chapter, we explore how some people's unique creative gifts assisted in fulfilling their life purpose and also helped others lessen their suffering.

CHAPTER 24

DO YOU WANT to Be of SERVICE in YOUR LIFE ASSISTING OTHERS?

Each act of service is a flower placed at the feet of God.

Discourses of Sathya Sai Baba

*W*e came into this life with a special plan or purpose to help elevate humanity and life on earth through our own unique service. It is our responsibility to be successful in carrying out our plan and to infuse our service with creativity, or our own special God-given talent. Spiritual Quotes for Life* www.teachingvalues.com

A person should strive to use every talent and skill they have, not only for their own benefit, but for the benefit of the whole world, says Sathya Sai Baba, an Avatar or god in human form. He goes on to define service as love made manifest. His simple message is: Love all, Serve all. In what ways have you been of self-less service, made Love manifest? Service is defined as a helpful action to assist others. Alice Bailey says in *A*

Treatise on White Magic, Service is another word for the utilization of soul force for the good of the group.

I will explain the soul more. Our soul as the next level of our spiritual self connects with us through our mind, emotions, and physical body. When we reach a certain level of development in consciousness where we have learned how to take charge of our emotions and thoughts, such as through some of the methods described in this book, then the energy of the soul functioning as higher mind and a compassionate heart can flood our bodies more easily with soul energy for our upliftment, as well as service for the good of others around us. Thus, as Bailey says we can use this "soul force for the good." As our bodies infuse with more soul force, we stimulate and energize those people, animals, and plants around us by our presence.

Do we need to know our purpose to be of service? I have found whether or not we have received clarity on our life purpose or discovered our unique talents, we all can be of service. Clarity about my purpose and creative abilities evolved over sixty years. In my mid-twenties, I first began to get some clarity and I started in the direction of service to others. I am still getting more insights.

The daily events that surround us and relationships will point out areas that we now can assist others, if we choose. One of these areas involves intimate relationships and particularly marriage, as we are asked continually to consider our partner's needs and wellbeing, sometimes over our own. Having children requires even greater acts of selflessness.

Some of us have found ourselves being given opportunities in work or group situations to be of service without being given any recognition. If we crave power and recognition for our actions rather than serving out of the compassion and the recognition of an individual or group need, then this indicates a desire to enhance ourselves rather than selfless service to improve the wellbeing of others.

Alice Bailey says in *A Treatise on White Magic, True service is the spontaneous outflow of a loving heart and an intelligent mind; it is the result of being in the right place and staying there.* In other words, all of us have or can develop the qualities to serve. "Being in the right place" means we see an area to assist and we choose to do so rather than closing our hearts and ignoring the situation or leaving it in hope that someone else will take care of it. Sometimes we may make a judgment that the unfortunate people in need deserve their misery. Can we judge others when we have never been in their situation?

That area of service may be something very small and unglamorous like helping those less fortunate by serving food at a soup kitchen. It may also be in unpleasant situation like the slums where Mother Teresa ministered to the poor, sick, orphaned, and the dying.

Alice Bailey describes a way to define our degree of service in *Discipleship in the New Age Volume 2* with this statement, *You cannot possibly do everything that you see needs to be done; therefore, do that which will bring about the greatest amount of good to the greatest number of seeking souls.*

Bailey goes on to say in *A Treatise on White Magic, A true server gathers around him those whom it is his duty to serve and aid by the force of his life . . . and has no preconceived ideas as to his own value or usefulness.* In other words, whatever life situation we find ourselves represents our area of service. Furthermore, in those situations how many of us can truly serve with no expectation of results or the desire for recognition?

According to Alice Bailey, we grow in selfless service when we handle each situation with love, rather than pursuing ambition, personal power, or allowing separation. As Sai Baba, an East Indian Avatar says about service in his *Discourses, Love all and serve all. Your entire life will be sanctified thereby.*

I believe we also grow towards selfless service as we handle our life challenges. Our acquired strengths then assist us in service to others.

PATHS to SERVICE

The people in this book who have shared their experiences have developed and realized their unique personal abilities through steady perseverance and overcoming life challenges. They now use their strengths and life experience in service to others, fulfilling their life purpose and uplifting the world.

As selfless servers, we need to care for our own physical needs such as getting proper rest and nutritious food. As has been also explained in depth in this book, we have a responsibility to acknowledge all emotions such as self-pity, depression, fear, worry, and anger to heal our wounds and take charge of our emotions as they arise. Also, as has been described in the chapter five on meditation, we can learn to steady our lower mind so that our creative abilities of the higher mind can come through.

How can we use our unique strengths and creative abilities to assist others in lessening their suffering and increasing their awareness to deal more effectively with their life challenges?

Choosing to endure through adversity and our greatest weakness, we uncover and develop our greatest strengths, which than serve to make other people's lives better.

Reviewing people's experiences in this book through severe physical challenges, as well as loss of freedom, innocence, and parts of their souls from various forms of abuse, the following summarizes their paths to service as they emerged stronger in their souls with abilities to heal, inspire, serve, and uplift the spirits of others.

Jacqueline Stone, as a former victim of sexual and emotional violence dug deep into the heart of her life experience to overcome her subconscious fears of power. Jacqueline chose to face her life challenges rather than avoid them and stay stuck in victimhood. She learned to trust, be grateful for what material blessings she did have after losing a home, being forced to leave another residence, and also suffering from a stroke. She chose to persevere, developing a positive attitude throughout her trials, as she shifted from codependence to independence and empowerment as well as freedom from abuse. She now expresses her life purpose as a self-help author and personal coach teaching others recovering from abuse, as well as those interested in greater self-awareness.

Joanna repressed memories of the sexual abuse she received at age three to nine from her father, for two thirds of her life. She grew into adulthood lacking confidence and greatly afraid of expressing herself. With her childhood legacy of trauma, she married three times into major codependent relationships.

At the age of forty, Joanna had her first inkling of sexual abuse in a therapy session when she saw her father's face and she curled up into a fetal position. About ten years later in a sweat lodge, she had a full vision of the abuse and broke down in tears.

Joanna has faced and healed the emotional wounds of the past rather than continue to avoid them. She has learned from her three marriages about codependency and grown into a self-reliant leader who inspires others by her presence, compassion, and regard for their welfare. As Gandhi said, My life is my teaching, this applies to Joanna.

Joanna has shifted in a forty year journey of healing, into unity consciousness, where her life purpose like Gandhi is bigger than herself. She uses her positive influence to assist others to have a better life. For instance, she provides housing and schooling for a mother and her daughter unrelated to her. Joanna also financially supports the local school so poor students have books and better facilities. She pays for and hosts self-development seminars for her employees and friends, as well as having sent and paid for some of them to go to India to the Oneness University.

Like Gandhi, Joanna has a world mission, which has yet to unfold.

Julianne first suffered sexual abuse as a child of two and again at the age of sixteen. She blanked out these memories into her forties. At the age of twenty-seven she began a path of meditation with a spiritual master to begin mastering her mind. Julianne finally regained and released, after forty years, her memory of abuse as a child of two with EMDR - Eye Movement

Desensitization and Reprocessing, as well as various other natural healing methods.

Over the years Julianne also underwent psycho-therapy, experienced various forms of bodywork, as well as other forms of inner work to develop greater self-awareness. All these methods assisted in healing her fear and trauma, codependency and esteem issues, as well as opening her emotional heart. Today Julianne, as a licensed therapist, with a combination of analytical ability plus a refined intuition assists teenage girls with issues of sexual abuse, drug and food addictions, low self-esteem and codependency.

Kathryne-Alexis as a child experienced sexual abuse and also intuitively knew facts about people, which she repressed because her parents refused to understand her.

Throughout her life Kathryne-Alexis learned over a dozen energy healing methods, which she practiced, mastered, and also used for her own healing. As a result she learned she could chose to shift the feeling of fear into courage, moving forward in her life rather than staying stuck. Through silent meditation she would observe her thoughts and how they wanted to run her. She found when she allowed unconscious thoughts and feelings to flow into her awareness, she then had the choice to change her critical self-talk to conscious language, increase positive outcomes, and also neutralize the charge on her emotions.

Emotions of suffering when held and contained in the moment become neutral. In other words, their emotional charge dissipates once we learn to stay present with a particular feeling. This takes understanding and practice.

Kathryne-Alexis, as an energy healer and life path consultant since 1989, shares her wisdom through consultations and the vibrational energies of personalized flower essences made by her company, Gaia's Own. She has a gift of bringing depths of knowledge to her clients for awakening of their creative gifts, empowerment, soul integration, and life transformation.

Lana grew up in a family with an alcoholic mother and her parents constantly arguing. In her first marriage, of ten years, she repressed any emotional expression and lived in misery. Self-doubt plagued her and for two-thirds of her life she had no sense of life purpose and limited expression of creativity.

Through ongoing steps of self-discovery and personal inner healing, over fifteen years, Lana began to awaken to her creative gifts and inner self. She eased and healed the pain from her mother's wounding, as she began to understand with compassion her mother's own childhood agony.

Lana created a stable home foundation from which she could work to share her creative expression and developing intuition with clients through energy healing, as she facilitated their healing journeys.

For over ten years, Lana as a clairvoyant counselor, energy healer, and life coach with a blend of mental clarity and integrated heart intuition has assisted clients, national and internationally.

I will now tell a little about my path to service. I struggled most of my life with frustrated creative energies. I lacked self-esteem and trust in myself and my abilities, repressed my anger and depression, and most of all feared exposing any emotion or vulnerability for dread of being rejected by women.

For twenty years, before I developed trust in my own inner knowing over a period of fifteen years, I looked outside myself for knowledge from psychologists, clairvoyants, energy healers, and spiritual teachers. I learned from experiencing their limitations, as well as strengths, and I am grateful to all of them. Dan Millman in *The Life You Were Born to Live* sums it up, *We can only get in touch with our own source of intuition and wisdom when we no longer depend upon others' opinions for our sense of identity or worth.*

In the last one third of my life, I have developed the courage to better express my emotions and needs and set personal boundaries, as I recovered from codependency. I have also discovered and developed my creative expression through energy healing, teaching self-development seminars, and writing. I feel a closer connection within, as well as with others, as my emotional heart continues opening and deepening.

Now we return to more stories of people overcoming life challenges as a path to service.

Pat Gurnick rebuilt her health persevering through years of suffering as the result of aerial pesticides, black mold in her apartment, Chronic Fatigue Syndrome, and fibromyalgia. She learned over time positive ways to manage her energy levels, as well as loving herself and her body.

Today as a psychotherapist and certified lifestyle counselor, Pat uses her life experience and learning in service for the easing of pain and suffering in others with similar conditions.

Rob Gonzalez, a poet and musician, says, *In 2006 a doctor diagnosed me with something called psoriatic arthritis, similar to rheumatoid arthritis without the extensive deformation of joints.* Rob struggles daily with joint and muscle pain and extreme fatigue.

How would you handle a chronic illness? Would you give up or choose to look deeper into the inner message within the pain?

Rob chose his suffering as a path to service. He developed compassion, seeing the depth of suffering in others who also endure chronic illness. Strangers talk to him about their troubles in malls. He listens, says little, and often wonders whether he made a difference. Sometime later, however, someone may write thanking him for what he said or did and how much it meant.

Rob has this to share. *I have found the best reliever of pain and suffering is in loving others on this difficult earth path. I think we can all find some way to serve even though it may seem insignificant.*

Do we really know how much we touch the lives of others through our actions, words and the presence of our being?

One of my areas of service involves being a Residential Coach at a therapeutic boarding school for about eighty teenage girls who have deep issues of emotional pain. After about two years, administration told me I would be transferred to another residential unit, on the larger campus, which would eventually house about one hundred and twenty in its three units.

I believed I had little effect on the group of twenty teens I had worked with, until on my last evening when I told them I would be leaving and had enjoyed working with them. Their responses amazed me and brought tears to my eyes. I had no idea that my presence as a healthy male role figure had touched so many. Simply being present in the moment, listening, and playing card games or saying something as I listened to their emotional turmoil's had a significant effect.

Over eight years later at the same school, I have occasional moments when I know what I say or do has a significant impact. For the most part, however, I still have little idea of who I have affected and that's okay for I do the best I can every day with the intent of being a positive influence.

Returning to people's experiences in this book, Shannon Nelson through steady perseverance learned to deal with a severe life challenge.

Breaking her neck, in a swimming pool accident, changed her life as an active twenty-four year old to a quadriplegic in a wheelchair. She struggled with chronic pain, depression, and health issues for twelve years until a friend introduced Shannon to energy medicine and psychology.

Shannon began regular sessions of EFT – the emotional freedom technique of acupressure and also Reiki energy healing. As a result, she gradually eliminated her pain and anti-depressant medications. She overcame depression and powerlessness to reclaim her power and found her mission in life.

Shannon says, *My mission involves reaching out to people experiencing despair due to health problems, especially chronic pain and depression.*

Sharon Lund's grandfather sexually abused her as a child for nine years. As an adult she felt deep anger towards men, unlovable, helpless, and ashamed. Losing the will to live she sought the oblivion of suicide twice.

Instead of giving up, however, she conquered childhood abuse, betrayal by a former husband, life-threatening AIDS, and chose in a second near death experience to come back. She made a documentary of her NDE, Dying to Live.

In 1984, Sharon encountered her first near-death experience resulting in the gift of her life purpose - to be a healer, teach around the world, and write books. Sharon has taken all the healing techniques, she has learned and taught around the world since 1986, and shares her wisdom in The Integrated Being: Techniques to Heal Your Mind-Body-Spirit.

As an author, international speaker, and producer, Sharon makes service her life. Her compassion, love, and understanding motivate people of all ages to overcome illness, grief, and life challenges.

Shivani learned a powerful life lesson from the death of her five year old son. She had told him to stay away from the waterfall. He drowned.

She became a work alcoholic and never shed a tear for years. She practiced various forms of meditation and experienced many types of healing therapies, yet avoided the pain and never took a deep breath. As she says, *A cloud of death hung over my head for 25 years. I lived in chaos.*

It took her twenty-five years to finally surrender and take a deep breath in a rebirthing therapy session and let go of the pain of her son's death.

Shivani's personal agony developed her compassion for others suffering. In acts of service, she assisted three girlfriends through their suffering when their children committed suicide.

For most of her life, Shivani made critical choices from a state of being unconscious. She now makes choices in alignment with her life purpose as a healer and artist. She has learned the life lessons of detachment, surrender, and harmony through chaos.

Sinnet Olina Tiwaz endured physical illnesses as a child, psychological abuse from her family, and violence from a husband. She coped with stress by working out and starving herself.

She, however, through her interaction with horses while learning natural horsemanship discovered that horses mirrored back her fears and emotional states. Fearful and attracted at the same time, one day after a month she realized that the rearing bucking horse in front of her represented herself and as she froze with the understanding so did the horse.

Sinnet continued working with horses realizing they mirrored all her weaknesses as well as strengths. They assisted her to regain her self-worth she had lost, as a child as well as ending her eating disorder.

Sinnet, as a horse whisper for over ten years, now uses horses to assist humans in their personal development and healing.

Viola Bergeron encountered physical and emotional abuse from her alcoholic husband for ten years until she divorced. Through her journey of abuse to empowerment she handled her unhappy memories, afterwards, by letting them go and remembering only the happy times. In other words, she chose to focus on the positive rather than the negative. This assisted in teaching her children to forgive and love as she taught them to speak only of their love for their father, as they had known him before he became an alcoholic. What a wonderful service for a mother to provide for her children. My family still carries bitterness and wounds as the result of my father's alcoholism.

Rather than allowing her husband to continue to control the family's life as he had before the divorce, Viola and her children forgave him, which freed them to live their life in peace rather than hatred.

Viola, as a wife and mother, learned from the challenges of her marriage as she shifted from codependency to independence, finally gaining freedom - freedom for her and her children to be themselves, freedom from self-doubt, and freedom from fear.

I believe we all have special talents, whether we realize them or not. My life experience shows that within our areas of greatest challenges lies the dormant seed of our creative talents. When we discover and develop these talents in selfless service to elevate others with similar challenges, we then walk the road fulfilling our life purpose.

According to Adyashanti, author of *The End of Your World*, Our greatest contribution – service to humanity – is to heal the illusory divisions within ourselves. In other words, when we choose to recognize and heal the pain and suffering within ourselves that keeps us locked in separation, this becomes our area of service to others as demonstrated by people who have share parts of their lives in this book.

Do you believe you have incarnated on this earth to learn lessons about choices, empowerment, or abundance, etc.? If you believe our experience on earth holds the opportunity for spiritual growth and expansion of consciousness, then at some point in our development we also have the ability to share our spiritual gifts in service to ease the suffering of others and to assist them in their growth.

As the spiritual master Sai Baba says, *A person should strive to use every talent and skill they have, not only for their own benefit, but for the benefit of the whole world.*

Many of us want to make a positive difference in the lives of others, yet have little or no sense of our life purpose. First, look at the needs of people around you.

Where do you feel a desire to help? What talents do you have which would help others?

Next, a medical doctor gives us a summary of the teachings of Buddha with a practical explanation of yet another way we can all be of service to those around us.

JAMES OLIVER CYR, M.D.: LOVE as SERVICE

Love all and serve all. Your entire life will be sanctified thereby.

Sathya Sai Baba, East India Spiritual Master

James sums up the teachings of Buddha and takes these teachings a step further to show how we all can be of service. We can still be of service in the way James describes whether or not we believe in the concepts of past lives or karma that he mentions.

James talks about our responsibility to help the less fortunate. Our service becomes the love and compassion that flows through us towards those in need that we find around us.

James says, *What have the Great Ones from the Spiritual Hierarchy of humanity to say about the alleviation of suffering? The Buddha, for instance, after he reached enlightenment tended to be clear and specific. Suffering, after all, caused Him to leave his privileged life as a prince to seek a higher conscious-ness, which might reveal a more illumined under-standing about the suffering of his brothers and sis-ters. His disciples and followers called his precepts the Four Noble Truths.*

The Buddha taught suffering existed while in in-carnate human form and He taught the attachments humans have for the things of the material world -- possessions, family, friends, pleasures, desires, long-ings, and the identification of oneself with the physi-cal form rather than the Higher Self caused suffer-ing. Suffering ceased with the elimination of all at-tachments and desires of any kind. His Eight-fold path outlined the way to detachment. This path re-mains as useful today.

I'd like to take a step further though. There can be a little more involved. Much of the suffering of humanity may be a matter of karmic indebtedness. That is to say that the original cause of the present day suffering originated in another lifetime. For eve-ry cause an effect occurs, the Law of Cause and Ef-fect. When a person imposes limitation, pain, or suf-fering upon another human or life form, then they must endure similar conditions either in this life or another. Our Higher Self balances all of its human experiences for its own evolutionary progress with no punishment involved. The self meets the Higher Self by taking a glance into the mirror of the uni-verse.

Suffering still exists, even when we reach a state of non-desire. Should we look on the suffering of others and turn away with the thought that they are receiving their just rewards? I believe our responsibility lies in reaching out a helping hand to the less fortunate, the needy, the sick, the homeless, and the suffering. How can we know the karmic cause or if one really exists?

By demonstrating the compassion and love that flows through our being, we can do a world of good to our own karmic balance sheet as well as ease the suffering of another of God's creations, be they human or another life form. The impulses which become manifest as giving, caring, kindness, and helpfulness arise out of the most Powerful Force in Creation, Love. As humans we can best serve as a conduit for that Love toward all other life forms that only appear to be separate from ourselves.

SPIRITUAL TEACHERS SERVING HUMANITY

A wave of service, if it sweeps over the land catching everyone in its enthusiasm, will be able to wipe off the mounds of hatred, malice and greed that infest the world.
Quotation from the discourses of Sathya Sai Baba

Tiara Kumara, founder of the Children of the Sun, like James Oliver Cyr has a similar message; spiritual teachers serve by radiating love, which assists humanity to shift into higher consciousness.

Tiara says, *The true spiritual leaders and teachers of wisdom emerge today in greater numbers to help guide humanity across the bridge and into the new consciousness reality. These common people from every race, religion, nation, and culture have liberated their Higher Self from personal identity and from desire. With divine indifference and deep inner peace, these light bearers stand humbly at the center of their being radiating love and selfless aspiration to simply serve as an extension of the divine. They only emanate love and great wisdom as a result of the realization that all comes from Universal Divine Mind.*

Next, let us look at the affect and possible dangers service can have on our bodies, emotions, and mind.

TRAINING and CARING for OUR PHYSICAL, EMOTIONAL, and MENTAL BODIES for EFFECTIVE SERVICE

As we grow in service, we shift our focus away from satisfying only our personal self to the larger issues of service as a group in regards to some of the world's problems. This indicates an increasing effect of the power our soul entering our physical, emotional, and mental bodies. Alice Bailey says in *Esoteric Psychology Volume II, This stage will in some cases fan into flame the latent seeds of ambition. This ambition is, in the last analysis, only the personality urge towards betterment, and in its right place and time is a divine asset, but it has to be rooted out when the personality becomes the instrument of the soul. On the other hand, we may begin focusing less on our own ambition and work in greater harmony with our chosen groups. This foreshadows the beginning of true service where we lose sense of self for the greater good of the group purpose, which can serve a world purpose.*

When increased soul force enters our physical body increasing our ability to be of service, we need to see we get sufficient sleep, wholesome food, and rest when necessary or else we may experience illness or nervous strain.

The next step requires healing and taking charge of our emotional body or else we stay trapped and spinning round and round in emotional suffering or caught up in endless power plays or emotional dramas with other individuals or group members. We learn how to flow with our angers, fears, or agony without either suppressing or drowning in them, as has been demonstrated by methods in this book. Methods have also been given to heal emotions such as depression, grief or self-pity that have been repressed in the past and trapped in our physical bodies. This training and purification of our emotional body allows it to become still, clear, and calm as a pool without any ripples. Then we can proceed in a state of neutrality on our path of service without the upset of emotional reactions.

Finally, we need to develop our mental body for service with knowledge, which in time will become a stable foundation for the wisdom from our soul. In addition, we develop steadying and focus of our lower mind through regular meditation practice. As Alice Bailey says in *Esoteric Psychology Volume II, As the work of learning to serve proceeds, and the inner contact becomes more sure, the next thing which will occur, will be a deepening of the life of meditation, and a more frequent illumining of the mind by the light of the soul. Thereby the Plan is revealed.*

Without the illumination of the soul, we stay stuck in our mental illusions and limited paradigms of un-reality.

Stilling our emotional body creates receptivity to compassion from our soul. Stilling our mental body creates receptivity to our higher mind of intuition and inspiration.

IN CONCLUSION:

When a sufficient number of humanity can align with their souls and act in unity, then we, as one human family, will enter upon the greater plan of planetary service. Its mission is to act as a bridge between the world of spirit and the world of material forms. All grades of matter meet in man, and all the states of consciousness are possible to him. Mankind can work in all directions, and lift the subhuman kingdoms into heaven, and bring heaven down to earth, Alice Bailey, *A Treatise on White Magic.*

CHAPTER 25

HOW WILL the GLOBAL PARADIGM SHIFTS AFFECT YOU?

Due to massive cosmic events, growth is no longer the linear, slow process that inches its way forward, hurdle by hurdle . . . Like the vertical ascension, this "growth through grace" changes any linear predictions moment by moment.

Almine, Toltec Nagual mystic

PARADIGM SHIFTS

Has the Universe thrown down the gauntlet challenging us to face our mental and emotional conditioning, which has only created suffering for us in the past, and open to see new levels of reality and possibilities?

Are we being asked to shift from a grasping for survival to opening to a way to supply all of the world's people's basic needs for food, shelter, and health care?

Are we being asked to shift from consuming the Earth's resources for destructive purposes to constructive solutions to humanity's challenges to live on the planet in peace?

Are we being asked to shift from harming others, injustice, and violence to ending the pain and suffering of humanity and establishing goodwill for all?

Massive infusions of gamma-ray light have pulsed through our planet and bodies for years. On December 2004 scientists recorded the largest gamma-ray burst ever to penetrate the Earth. It came from a neutron star with an enormous magnetic field 50,000 light years distant.

American astronomer Carl Sagan wrote in 1973 that human evolution resulted from incoming cosmic rays from a distant neutron star. Consider this statement by Celia Fenn, a spiritual facilitator and writer, *In January of 2006 it was decided by Spirit that the planet was ready for recalibration and reconnection with the Galactic grid. This reference to the Galactic Grid means creative energy from the center of the Milky Way pulsed through our sun and into our planet. The light energy from the higher dimensions . . . enters the physical body at the pineal gland, replied Celia. Astronomers call these creative energies gamma rays.*

How do these massive doses of gamma ray light affect us? Like Carl Sagan believes does this light signal a shift in evolution, a possible opportunity for enlightenment or spiritual awakening of humanity?

A paradigm describes the way we perceive our reality. What makes up our paradigm? Do we see a vase or two faces? Depending on the way we choose to perceive information determines how our brains organize it. Is it possible to see both images at the same time? On another level, do we believe in only the third dimensional world or in multi-dimensions containing many levels of light and energy? A paradigm shift occurs when new information changes our belief about the truth of our reality. This invites us to view our world with a new perspective.

A paradigm shift signals the transition from one model of perception to another. We gain an expansion of vision by seeing through a new lens. Old barriers, which limit our thoughts, give way to new realms of possibility because the new paradigm replaces the old assumptions.

As our planet adjusts to a higher quotient of light/love/energy, so do our physical bodies. The increased spin of our light bodies brings more light into our physical bodies, increasing the percentage of light we hold until more and more white light radiates throughout our auric fields. See *You and Your Crystalline Body: Part Two* by Celia Fenn.

The article has aura chakra images of the recalibration of the body, which produces more white light. Once our light body and physical body rewires, we adjust from 30 - 40 – 50 % light to eventually 100%. We progress from the regular quotient of light to the light body of increasing white light to the crystalline body of clear light. I believe the crystalline light body appears at 100% quotient of light and emits rays of clear light because many previous emotional and mental patterns of pain, illusion, and resistance have dissolved through willingness, effort, and the choice to say Yes to Divine Will. Remember gamma-rays pulse huge doses of light into our physical bodies to en-light-en them.

During our transition embodying our light body into the physical body, we experience many symptoms. Ongoing daily fatigue can manifest for many months or years as higher dimensional light pours into us. The fatigue occurs as the light increases in frequency and bumps into our resistances: fixed beliefs in the mental body, emotional pain and unresolved trauma, and toxins in the physical body. These resistances create an off tone in the clarity of the light's frequency. More energy flows as the resistances dissolve through our conscious effort to heal and grow in consciousness, to awaken. As we live in a higher light quotient, we may feel waves of energy moving through our physical bodies.

Just as individuals choose to increase their quotients of light, so do groups of individuals make the choice together. Each individual who has a light quotient of over 50% can with willingness, effort, and conscious choices, set aside conscious and unconscious resistance, and move into a higher level of group creation dedicated to the service of humanity and the planet. Thus, the group shifts out of an old paradigm into a new paradigm of expanded vision. All of the bodies emotional, mental, spiritual, and physical, which serve to ground the energies, become involved in the choice of creating a new foundation of light for the group.

One of our group members described our new foundation vehicle as a Divine Mechanism viewed as a hub with spokes like a wheel or gears. Our group vehicle, as a geometric form, spiraled to a new level and spun in 360 degrees, unlimited, as a multi-faceted, inter-dimensional, galactic container ready for co-creating in service to humanity.

With the paradigm shift because of increased light flooding the planet the shadow rears its head more often. The shadow, which exists in us, in groups, in institutional bodies, and in humanity as a group, resists the new frequencies entering our planet and our bodies. This shadow aspect as defined by the psycho-analyst Carl Jung makes up a part of the unconscious mind consisting of weaknesses and instincts. *Everyone carries a shadow,* Jung wrote, *and the less it is embodied in the individual's – and nations - conscious life, the blacker and denser it is.*

Look how an aspect of the United States shadow – the greed of financial giants, banks, and mortgage companies – had emerged into the light in 2009.

To confront a person with his shadow is to show him his own light. Once one has experienced a few times what it is like to stand judgingly between the opposites, one begins to understand what is meant by the self. Anyone who perceives his shadow and his light simultaneously sees himself from two sides and thus gets in the middle. Carl Jung

The shadow's face has never seen the light and fears exposure. It shows it's self through our projections unto others and our resistance to saying Yes to Life and the Divine Will. Many of us deny that these unacceptable or unwanted thoughts or emotions belong to us. As we increase our light quotient, everything in our shadow aspects rises up into the light of day. If we choose to increase our light quotient, we can choose to allow our shadow aspects to rise to the surface of our awareness, recognize them, and permit the light to dissolve them. Blaming others only keeps the shadow imprisoned within us. First contain the resistance and then through conscious breathing through our whole bodies and our heart chakras and by intent, we can allow the Light of the Divine Fire to burn through all parts of us. Intent means we release all emotions, judgments, and old paradigms into the fire to dissolve.

We can support the paradigm shifts and increased frequency of light in our physical bodies through regular exercise such as walking, running, and methods such as yoga to stretch and open the body's energy channels. Support also includes conscious breathing to fill the whole body - it brings more light, eating organic fruits and vegetables, which contain higher life force, drinking sufficient and pure water, and choosing to heal our emotions and shadow aspects. Regular energy sessions such as Angelic Reiki, Bowen Therapy, Network Chiropractic, or Thai Massage, etc. also assist to open the denser parts of the body, which may be in pain or discomfort.

RELEASING the MIND and ATTACHMENT to SELF

Rest in natural great peace this exhausted mind,
Beaten helpless by karma and neurotic thoughts
Like the relentless fury of the pounding waves
In the infinite ocean of samsara
Rest in natural great peace

Sogyal Rinpoche, author, *The Tibetan Book of Living and Dying*

The Buddha taught the only way to end suffering requires the ending samsara – the wheel of suffering – through enlightenment. On a mental level this requires a paradigm shift, a different way of seeing reality and accepting new truths.

I teach one thing and one only: that is, suffering and the end of suffering.

Buddha

When we do finally awaken to our true nature, our world will change in ways that we can now hardly imagine – a paradigm shift, Pete Russell, computer scientist and futurist.

As a species, as new cosmic energies of light enter our planet and bodies. Our brains will undergo rewiring to open to the grace and absorb it. Our emotions require purification. Our fear conditioning strengthened by the control of our minds resists with stubbornness the changes sweeping like a tsunami across our planet. Our lack of surrender rather than ending suffering creates even greater misery for us.

We all can recognize and face our fears and resistance to change. We can make a conscious choice to let go of our mental beliefs, which keep us locked upon our personal wheel of suffering.

Do you have an investment in keeping your suffering? I have in the past. I suffered under the false belief, as a victim, for most of my life; my life had to be hard and I had little or no power. This belief had been forged through the centuries by my family lineage. I am dissolving that.

Tiara Kumara and Celia Fenn, both verify the paradigm shift occurring on a global level.

Tiara Kumara, founder of Children of the Sun Foundation writes about the necessary of shifting our paradigms. The Children of the Sun Foundation is a global platform serving as a bridge between consciousness paradigms by helping others into the higher dimensional system of New Earth energy. www. childrenofthesun.tv

Tiara says, *Our advancement into the new Golden Age continues in greater acceleration. The strengthening grids and continuing influx of solar energies, galactic alignments and other cosmic influence greatly affect energy system recalibration, on both a human and planetary level. As the holographic energy field of our New Earth anchors, the old grids and foundational base from which we previously attached our reality perceptions becomes nearly obsolete. Without this past plane of perception, old paradigm rules no longer apply. As a result, we now boldly confront major life choices in order to advance at this evolutionary pace.*

Celia Fenn, spiritual facilitator & writer, in July 2008 describes the Grace of the Golden Light entering the Earth's grids, opening us to new paradigms. *We now can integrate the new Light Codes received from the Great Central Sun at the time of Solstices. This Golden Light of Ascended Compassionate Love enters*

the Earth's grids and creates a Radiance that acti-
vates old memories and new directions in those of us
open to receiving these waves of Golden Love from
Source.

How does your everyday life challenge your attachment to past paradigms, ways you perceived reality? What new life choices confront you now?

The next section gives some steps we can choose,
to shift our paradigms from the illusion about reality
to the truth by allowing more spiritual light into our
bodies, by our willingness to enter our pain, and
through the grace of awakened beings in physical bodies.

FROM the UNREAL to the REAL

Lead me from Darkness into Light, from the Unreal
to the Real, from Death to Immortality.

Sanskrit Prayer

The voices of all of humanity thunder in an agonizing roar, clamoring for the unreal upon our planet.
In this din a voice like that of the Golem from Lord of
the Rings raises above all sounds, *My precious . . .*
mine . . . all mine, which echoes the voice inside us
that clutches at having more and more material stuff.

Inside each of us lurks a facade of illusion. Within
this facade we believe we know our real selves. We,

CHAPTER 26

THE TRUTH ABOUT DIVINE GRACE: GENTLE or FIERCE

Life is full of grace – sometimes it's wonderful grace, beautiful grace, moments of bliss and happiness and joy, and sometimes it's fierce grace, like illness, losing a job, losing someone we love, or a divorce.

Adyashanti, a spiritual teacher

We would all prefer to experience only moments of gentle grace rather than the pain of fierce grace as Adyashanti has called it. Yet, in times of challenge we experience our greatest learning and growth in our consciousness. This has been the truth in my own life, as well as the clients I coach.

Ram Dass, author of *Be Here Now* and a spiritual teacher, suffered a stroke in 1997, which left his left arm and leg paralyzed. Ram Dass used the trauma of this fierce grace as a calling to serve others to come to terms with old age and death. He created a DVD, *Fierce Grace,* of his recovery from his stroke.

Ram Dass commented in an interview, *That's the two perspectives on suffering. The ego perspective, that suffering stinks. The soul perspective, that it's sandpaper.* He also said the stroke opened him *to deeper levels of my own being.*

Although we have no control over the type of grace which enters our lives, we do have a choice whether to meet fierce grace with resistance and thus encounter more suffering or to look for the meaning and positive gift within it. We can ask, "What am I to learn from this experience?" We can look to see what part of our soul has applied the sandpaper, burnishing our personality into greater brilliance for its next level of service.

Have we reached a state of consciousness where we see each event in our lives as neither "good" or "bad," only as an act of grace? Can we experience the event without any emotional reaction? Remember although we may have learned how to contain our emotions; we still feel them with intensity. We, however, have the choice to accept the truth or reality of the moment for what it is, without any resistance. I confess I still meet resistances within myself at times.

A number of stories have been shared in this book. About three times as many people encountered fierce rather than gentle grace. OceAnna, a soul keeper, felt the gentle grace of the dolphins and had two gentle heart openings. I would call Joanna's ordeal of being kidnapped, horrendous, yet also gentle grace as she emerged unharmed. Some may say the Grace of Spirit protected her.

After reviewing people's experiences of fierce grace through severe physical challenges, as well as loss of freedom, innocence, and parts of their souls from various forms of abuse, the following summarizes their path as they emerged stronger in their souls with developed abilities to heal, inspire, serve, and uplift the spirits of others.

Jacqueline Stone, author and spiritual coach, as a former victim of sexual and emotional abuse overcame her fears and found freedom and liberation. She now commits herself to assist others recovering from abuse through coaching and writing.

Julianne, who came from an alcoholic family, as well as being sexually abused, now uses her gifts as a therapist to help teenage girls raise their levels of awareness.

Kathryne – Alexis, as a life path consultant, uses her background of abuse and suffering to transform critical thoughts, emotional suffering, and the unconscious shadow with her clients.

Pat Gurnick suffered for years with CFS and fibromyalgia and has learned how to manage her energy levels, as well as loving herself and her body – an important lesson for most of us. As a psychotherapist, she serves her clients by easing their pain and suffering.

Rob Gonzalez as a musician and poet who suffers from the pain of arthritis has learned to tap the flow of grace beyond pain to play instruments. In his unassuming encounter with others in daily life, compassion flows from his presence and people begin to unburden themselves where ever he may be.

Shannon Nelson had a doctor tell her she would never walk again. As a quadriplegic she struggled with chronic pain, depression, and severe health issues. With the grace of Energy Medicine she overcame depression and reclaimed her power to assist others with physical and emotional pain.

Sharon Lund journeyed through trauma, death, and AIDS. As an international speaker, spiritual teacher, and writer, she helps people overcome emotional and physical challenges.

Shivani, an artist and healer, learned a powerful life lesson after the death of her son. *A cloud of death hung over my head for 25 years. I lived in chaos. Now I choose to make conscious choices. I make choices in alignment with my life purpose. I choose to live in celebration of life.*

Sinnet Olina Tiwaz endured physical illnesses, psychological abuse, and violence. As a horse whisper she healed, learning how horses can serve as mirrors of our strengths and weaknesses.

Finally, Viola Bergeron traveled a path from abuse into empowerment, which liberated her from doubt, fear, and unhappy memories.

What have you experienced – gentle or fierce grace? How have your paradigms shifted? What life challenges have you encountered? What lessons have you learned? How can you be of service to others?

PERSONAL EXPERIENCES of GRACE

People usually consider walking on water or on thin air a miracle.

But I think the real miracle

is not to walk either on water or in thin air,

but to walk on earth.

Thich Nhat Hanh, Buddhist monk

I will give an overview of my experiences of grace and a life changing one of fierce grace after visiting Sathya Sai Baba in India.

As an assistant spiritual teacher, I spent a month in June 1990 travelling with three other instructors. We escorted a small group of people to various outdoor sacred energy sites including Sedona, Mount Shasta, and various other areas in Colorado and Arizona. The purpose of the spiritual journeys involved awakening higher emotional and spiritual aspects of each person. This occurred with instruction in practical spiritual techniques magnified by the natural energy of the particular sacred area.

These journeys and subsequent ones over the next five months exhilarated me as I began to perceive Spirit manifest visibly through nature. I had read about various spiritual phenomena in *The Keys of Enoch* by J.J. Hurtak and now actual Pillars of Light, Light radiations, and Beings of Light materialized in cloud formations in the sky as a heightened state of perception enveloped me. The spiritual journeying and experiences of Divine Grace granted me one of the most fulfilling times of my life.

I now recognize the materializations as aspects of grace or synchronicity. We can describe grace as events from the divine appearing in our lives, without any effort on our part. Carl Jung termed the word synchronicity to describe meaningful coincidences or mystical experiences. With Divine Grace or synchronicity, we feel or see the invisible connection between us and others, nature, or the universe. *Synchronicity reveals the meaningful connections between the subjective and objective world,* said Carl Jung.

Divine Grace refers to the divine's power of loving kindness by which we as souls awaken to our inner divine nature. Divine Grace manifests as our power to meditate, pray, the spiritual urge, which drives us to know our inner nature, or as an awakening of love for the divine. Divine Grace ever flows as love and compassion.

When our souls and minds reach a certain level of maturity grace can enter our lives through a spiritual initiation, shaktipat, from a spiritual teacher who transmits a spiritual power or awakening. This transmission comes through a sacred word, look, thought, or by touch. We can choose to accept or reject this grace.

I have experienced five forms of shaktipat, one through initiation into sacred words, three through touch, and one though touch as well as gazing into the eyes of Mother Meera. These occurred over a period of over thirty-five years. The most profound shaktipat descended through the grace of Satya Sai Baba when I visited his ashram in India in December of 1990, as the final event in my five months of spiritual journeying.

Sai Baba's ashram called the abode of highest peace attracts hundreds of thousands of pilgrims from all over the world. Twice daily, Sai Baba in his flowing orange robe treads barefoot amongst thousands of eager seekers, bestowing blessings through outstretched arms and uplifted hands. Sai Baba radiates Divine Light, which assists in purifying our suffering if we open and allow the grace.

Millions of people around the world accept Sathya Sai Baba as an avatar, an incarnation of divinity in human form like Krishna, Buddha, and Jesus. By our touching His lotus feet or His touching us, there is a descent of divine energy, shaktipat.

The feet of a divine one are considered especially precious as they represent the point of contact of the Divine and the physical, and are thus revered as the source of grace.

Himalayan Academy

Within the first week of my arrival, I got the rare opportunity to sit in the first row after Sai Baba's first round of morning blessings. Positioned cross-legged in meditation on the hard concrete, I opened my eyes to see Sai Baba's small frame emerging from his temple to give a second blessing. He glided to the right of the first row where I sat. Floating closer, his orange-robed figure alighted directly in front of me. Realizing this gesture as granting permission to touch his feet, I bowed my head to the gritty concrete. My mind blank, I raised my hands to rest upon his warm insteps. Seconds later as I lifted my hands off his feet, Sai Baba wordlessly slipped away to my left. On impulse, I touched the ground where His feet had just rested. The concrete tingled and vibrated as though it had a life of its own as Sai Baba's spiritual presence lingered, transmitted to the concrete.

One of Sai Baba's divine powers manifests as healing touch or shaktipat. Whatever part of our body Sai Baba touches awakens that area spiritually. By His allowing us to touch lotus His feet, grace descends. At the time I remained unaware of the power of the sacred transmission.

Upon my return to Los Angeles, in spite of a decade of constant inner healing, I experienced a few months of deep emotional releasing. Sai Baba's activation of increased spiritual Light within me brought to the surface emotional agonies which I had unconsciously harbored all my life. This rapid cleansing of emotional poisons caused painful boils to break out on my skin.

For a few months, my buttocks and fingers broke out. My body exuded poisons from every cell, and symptoms of heart congestion and inflammation of the joints of the hands, arms, legs, and hips released. Grace burned through my resistance to god. Without this fierce grace of Sai Baba, I intuitively know this purification would have taken at least an additional ten years.

After my own intense purification, the gift of healing touch buried within me surfaced. Sai Baba says, *My burning Love touches the hearts of incarnate people and ignites the souls. One has to bring people to the threshold where they come in touch with Me. If a soul, after touching Me, continues to shine for others — then this is the true burning.*

Before Sai Baba's touch, I received my first experience of grace in 1970 by being initiated into Kirpal Singh's Surat Shabd Yoga, which included the repetition of sacred mantras while focusing on the chakra center between the eyebrows. I practiced this form meditation most days for a minimum of two hours for ten years and glimpsed the inner light at times.

Sri Bhagavan and Sri Amma, founders of the Oneness University have said, *The solution to humanity's suffering can only be found through each individual being awakened to a state of Oneness.*

I have been fortunate in receiving the grace of Deeksha also known as the Oneness Blessing since August of 2007 from my wife, Lyn, who attended the Oneness University in India twice. Lyn transfers divine energy through her hands held on my head. This energy enters my brain and body, eventually dissolving any tension, stress, or congested energies in my body. I feel more balanced and energized afterwards.

In 2009 I had the good fortunate of receiving the blessings of grace from two awakened beings, Mother Meera and Sri Karunamayi, who travel to the U.S. and came to Sedona, Arizona. Mother Meera held the two sides of my head while I touched her feet. Then as I opened my eyes and gazed into hers I saw sorrow reflected back to me – my own. After leaving, a few minutes later a pain left from inside my right brain. My wife, Lyn, saw only neutrality mirrored in Mother Meera's eyes and the experience of the shak- tipat/darshan flowed as bliss throughout her whole body.

Sri Karunamayi, as an embodiment of the Divine Mother, entered the Creative Life Center smiling say- ing, *My sweet babies*. I felt a softening within myself. I remained in and out of meditation for three and one half hours as I waited for a blessing from Karunamayi. During meditation I felt sensations of heaviness and hunger, as well as energy pulsing in parts of my body. Underlying bliss also permeated my being. When my time came to stand before Karunamayi, I closed my eyes after handing her a card with written requests. She placed vibhuti – sacred ash - on the center be- tween my eyebrows and stroked my head as she trans- ferred the grace of the divine through her. Afterwards, I sensed a quickening or enlivening within.

Next OceAnna, a soul keeper, shares her encoun- ters with the gentle grace of the dolphins and two ex- periences of her heart flowering.

Having had the opportunity to swim with wild spinner and spotted dolphins in the Pacific Ocean waters surrounding the Hawaiian Islands has been one of the most breath-taking examples of Grace in Motion, comments OceAnna.

Boating or swimming out from shore, I hear the dolphins beckoning us to play with them. Dolphins use sonar, their version of music, to bounce sound off objects to see what lies ahead of them.

I believe the dolphin's purpose with human's lies in teaching us about love and light, laughter and joy, and about living in a synchronized way. So to hear them calling out to those who have the keen sense to hear them remains heartwarming and precious.

I have been given the opportunity on several occasions to swim with these majestic sea angels. They certainly have a lot to teach and share. My first encounter with dolphins came thru a week-long dolphin retreat to the Big Island of Hawaii with a group of energetic healers. Our co-facilitators, Laura and Lawrence of Dolphin Dimensions, would take us out daily for dolphin swims, either off the shore at designated spots or off a boat. We would rise early each day, meditate, and then hit the surf in search of friendly fins. All of our week long adventures with dolphins proved to be exquisite.

We enjoyed the unusual experience of encountering dolphins every outing. We all loved the new heights of achievement.

One of our trips included a boating trip off the Northern Kona Coast area. We ventured out early that morning full of anticipation of what the day would bring. We never quite knew what to expect be-

cause every day brought different and new types of adventures, today being no exception.

We moved along at a nice clip in the boat. Then we spotted them, a pod the size of a small city. Almost 300 in number started to form with our boat headed straight for them. The excitement mounted as we all chomped at the bit to enter the warm waters and begin communing with the dolphins.

The pods of spinner dolphins had many babies. We loved watching the little ones learning to spin out of the water and do flips as they expressed themselves with pure joy. As we cheered them on, the more they flipped and flopped.

We finally stopped the boat and began to enter the water. No words describe the exhilaration we felt jumping into the semi-temperate ocean water. Both fear and exhilaration propelled us forward into the blissful unknown territory we'll call "dolphin paradise."

Once we all gathered, accounted for as a human pod, we moved toward our dolphin counterparts, who eagerly awaited our arrival. We swam with our arms at our sides to counter any misunderstanding by the dolphins of aggression. We bobbed our bodies up and down like dolphins as we continued swimming towards them.

Now the grace entered as we moved as if in meditation. As we swam closer and the pods allowed us entry into their groupings, they graced us with the honor of swimming side-by-side with and among them. Shoulder to shoulder, they begin incorporating us into their formations and synchronized swimming.

No human words describe the feeling that rises from swimming with these incredible beings. As they swam with us, they looked into our eyes and we looked into theirs. So much energy and love transmits through this interaction and the opening our energy field, as well as the pores of our body to receive the energetics of the dolphins. You could describe it as poetry in motion as we swam without realizing our differences.

Dolphins allow us to feel comfortable with all boundaries dropped away. We can swim amongst them as one in harmony and peace. Somewhere along the swim we realize the overwhelming enormity of what's happening, and then the mind creeps back in and we suddenly find ourselves coming up for air and off the pod goes without us. It's staggering, exquisite, and simply beyond words just like the power of grace.

Synergism . . . in regeneration there is cooperation of Divine Grace & human activity. They — dolphins - become a wonderful mirror to our state, while stimulating in us a tremendous awakening of our inherently natural state of joy & love . . . as we align with our higher, collective, unified field, often embracing the oneness of all life, says Daniel McCulloch of Synergy Dolphin.

HEART OPENING: SAI BABA'S DAR-SHAN/BLESSING of GRACE

Darshan is the blessings communicated through being in the presence of a holy person . . . .

Global Oneness

I view the dolphins' energy to be very similar to Sai Baba's, pure love, radiating everywhere like an Ocean of Devotion, literally saturating our energy field with all we need to create change and transformation for ourselves and others while having the sensation of being held in a frequency of love and grace, says OceAnna, a spiritual alchemist.

Sai Baba resides in South India as a spiritual teacher and avatar who manifests all forms of the Divine.

OceAnna continues with her description of her experience of Grace. *While staying at Sai Baba's ashram in India a group of us who had gone to visit Sai Baba for his 75th Birthday Celebration experienced every day as different, unique, and special, just like the dolphin swims in Hawaii.*

The external world is a reflection of the inner world. To change the world we must begin with ourselves, with the flowering of the heart.

Sri Bhagavan – Oneness University

One day in particular, our group of women sat awaiting entry into the mandir meditation hall. On this special day millions of people gathered to participate, so we had to wait outside.

Baba had yet to make his entrance from the side where we women sat in direct route to the entrance of the mandir. All of us sat in lines on the outer concrete waiting in silence. While we waited my heart chakra began to break wide open. Baba remained out of sight, yet I felt his effects deeply in my heart. In this most auspicious day of my life, my group leader explained to me my readiness to be a "world server."

We never gained entry into the mandir that day; however, by the Grace of God Baba gifted me with a true heart awakening.

HEART OPENING: GIFT of GRACE

I attended an energetic healing school in Sedona, Arizona called the School of Energy Mastery and during one of our class gathering I received the most precious gift of all, the gift of an open heart, says OceAnna, a Living Water Medicine Woman.

It happened rather simply. I started the morning sharing a hands-on healing with a fellow student prior to our group forming and then our group began the morning session with a mediation period. During the meditation session, I began to physically feel like a total flip-flopping occurring in my heart center, however, I experienced no distress.

After the meditation session completed, I opened my eyes and began to feel a distinct difference in my entire being, nothing off the charts, just a very subtle feeling of being altered in some way. The group went on to explore a new healing technique and as we sat amongst one another on the floor my teacher, David, looked over at me and tears started rolling down his face. This started a chain reaction as each person who looked over to me began to share the same emotion, tears of joy, the most delicious feeling, almost a non-feeling, I have ever experienced.

Man learns through experience, and the spiritual path is full of different kinds of experiences. He will encounter many difficulties and obstacles, and they are the very experiences he needs to encourage and complete the cleansing process. And when the cleansing is finally complete, the evolved soul ceases to react to anything. All emotions are perfectly balanced. He lives in a state of permanent happiness, regardless of prevailing circumstances.

Sathya Sai Baba

OceAnna continues describing her heart opening. *The open heart becomes a space wherein anything occurring around us creates neither a push nor pull within us. It consists of a complete space of unity, compassion, love, peace and joy, subtle, yet simple.*

Without me getting up in front of the class, we broke up into healing triads. I knew, instinctively, where to place my hands for healing. In the flow of grace, I remember saying to my teacher, David, I now will be able to assist others with their healing as well as healing myself.

This gift of grace lasted in intensity for twenty-four hours. I still call upon it in times of pain and suffering. With Divine Grace, healing becomes effortless and gracious.

Rob Gonzalez, a musician and poet, who suffers from the pain of arthritis, shares a poem on grace.

My Heart is Thawing

Winter has passed
My heart is thawing
In the warmth of the Light

Whispers from above
Something is calling
To those who will Love
Love is our Being
Nothing less, nothing more

The soul's expressive singing
All that is necessary
Is a simple state of Being
Realizing all things fall into place

Forgiveness follows Love
Unnecessary in Its Light
The graceful flight of a dove

Living in Grace
Released from earthly bonds
Spirit shines upon our face.

Throughout this book you have read about becoming more aware of your emotional/mental conditioning and making a choice as reactions arise to either remain trapped in the reaction or practice being in the moment. Learning to be in the moment and accepting the reality of what manifests allows the flow of grace, fierce or gentle.

Mention has been made of spiritual awakening – the dissolving of the illusion of our separation from life – which has been the goal of most spiritual practices. Chapter 27 explains how awakening no longer remains the exclusive achievement of a few. Awakening has become available to us all, if we choose.

Do you choose to awaken?

CHAPTER 27

WHAT is SPIRITUAL AWAKENING?

Spiritual awakening is no longer the domain of elite practitioners, but is suddenly within the reach of all of us.

Tami Simon, *Sounds True*

WHAT is AWAKENING/ENLIGHTENMENT?

Spiritual Awakening and Enlightenment is the primary goal of almost all *spiritual practices*, traditions and *religions*, and for any spiritual seeker.

www.experiencefestival.com/spiritual_awakening

A s I said at the end of chapter 26, spiritual awakening refers to the dissolving of the illusion of our separation from life. That apparent feeling of being separate is at the root of the suffering, inadequacy, and sense of loss that drives people to search for escape or resolution, says Tony Parsons author of *The Open Secret*.

Overcoming suffering requires the use of previously mentioned methods as well as others that we discover. Then grace can flow into and through our lives as we begin to awaken from separation and experience moments of oneness. *Awakening . . . is a shift in ones perception* - a paradigm shift . . . *Full awakening simply means that we perceive . . . from the view of oneness,* comments Adyashanti, author of *The End of Your World.*

Sri Bhagavan, an Avatar for Enlightenment, talks about awakening/enlightenment as, *Complete liberation of the senses without control of the mind or thought. Experience reality as it is, no longer separate. Joy means being connected to everybody.* See Bhagavan, *What is Enlightenment,* on YouTube.

Enlightenment, for a wave in the ocean, is the moment the wave realizes it is water, says Zen master, Thich Nhat Hanh.

Let us examine more *the moment the wave realizes it is water.* The Buddha achieved bodhi – awakening – which freed him from the cycle of human suffering. Bodhi when translated also means enlightenment. We have seen images of enlightenment, the halos of spiritual light around saint's heads. So the two terms tend to be used interchangeably for the same state of consciousness, some of the time.

According to Buddhism bodhi only needs to be uncovered for it already exists in perfection like gold within us all. Our misperceptions and emotional/mental conditioning and reactions blind us, however, to this gold. The Buddha taught in the *Sutra of*

Perfect Awakening, Good sons, it is like smelting gold ore. The gold does not come into being because of smelting . . . Even though it passes through endless time; the nature of the gold is never corrupted. It is wrong to say that it is not originally perfect.

When we recognize our gold, we realize the illusion of being a separate wave as false and shift our paradigms to know ourselves as always having been within an ocean of the oneness all the time.

BEFORE AWAKENING/AFTER AWAKENING

Before awakening we perceive from separation, after awakening, we perceive from unity.

The path after awakening, then, is a path of dissolving our remaining fixations – our hang-ups ... So it's not that much different from the path to awakening which is a path of dissolving certain delusions . . . .

Adyashanti, *The End of Your World.*

We can only hint at the experience of awakening for it goes beyond the mind and mental understanding. For a few, it occurs quickly and produces a permanent state. Yet, others experience partial awakening and later undergo further deepening states. Adyashanti, a teacher of awakening, says, *As I've mentioned, this experience of awakening can be just a glimpse or it can be sustained over time.*

Maybe some of the confusion about awakening/enlightenment stems from the fact that it will be different for each one of us. Bhagavan has said that given over seven billion people on the planet in 2011 means over seven billion different awakenings, each unique. Sri Amma/Bhagavan, as Avatars of Enlightenment, as well as other awakened beings hold Divine Grace for all of us to awaken to the Oneness within.

With awakening, parts of our body can awaken such as the emotional heart, the navel chakra, the solar plexus chakra or other chakras over a period of time in a continuing integration.

One of the major changes occurs in our emotions, people move from emotional reaction to being in a more neutral state. They love without attachment, a new way of relating for most of us. People also experience their personality sense of being a separate self dissolving and as a result their body may, at times, feel foreign to them.

Before awakening, we face our emotional and mental conditioning mirrored back to us through life situations. After awakening, we face our remaining conditioning. The difference being we now have more awareness and thus the choice to stay in reaction or shift to neutrality. Sometimes we still have to discover the core to dissolve the remaining conditioning.

I next discuss a few people's personal experiences before awakening.

PERSONAL EXPERIENCES on the ROAD to AWAKENING

LANA: DISSOLVING EMOTIONAL REACTIONS

Lana, an energetic healer, has experienced integration towards awakening over the last 1½ years after she spent some time at the Oneness University in India. Most of her life she reacted with great emotion to everything. She called herself, *A person with a big emotion body.*

Lana explained, *Now I feel everything around me – people and situations – and many times I experience no reaction. I am neutral. When I do react I am more conscious and know I have a choice.*

My emotions no longer take me out of myself, even when I am upset because I still have personality crises. Doubt use to hound me as I reviewed where I may have gone wrong. Doubt seldom raises its head now and I doubted myself most of my life.

I have been plagued by migraines for over thirty years. My body would lock up as I reacted to situations in the outer world. Now I react less to the outer world. I focus on the changes occurring in my inner world.

I have learned to remain calm rather than angry or frightened when my mind fears losing control.

Some of my clients, however, become threatened when they start to lose control.

GROUNDING: STAYING PRESENT in the BODY

Lana says, *Before, I use to have to ground myself, often, with intent by visualizing a grounding cord connecting me into the earth. Now I am always grounded without thinking about it.*

LOVE WITHOUT ATTACHMENT

Lana continues. *I am no longer attached to someone behaving a certain way or being different than who they are. My old relationships have been falling away; I now can only be in relationship with people willing to be in the flow. I see more with compassion and understanding.*

CHAKRAS AWAKENING

The etheric body – energy body - is a body composed entirely of lines of force, and of points where these lines of force cross each other, and thus form in crossing - centers of energy - chakras.

Djwhal Khul, Tibetan Master of Wisdom

Lana says, *I use to have to keep opening my chakras as they kept shutting down. Since the beginning of my integration, various chakras continue to awaken in their own order. My third chakra, the so-*

lar plexus chakra in the area of the stomach, which relates to personal will and power, has been shifting over a number of months into Divine Will. I broke through this chakra in a day long meditation retreat with the Awakened Being, Karunamayi, who sat in meditation for eleven years in a forest in India. I held a focus for eight hours allowing God's Will to come into me all the while my personality battered me like a tornado. I refused to let this stand in my way. Fortunately, the presence of Karunamayi contained me like a child in a womb.

I needed to know how to meditate, hold a focus. I believe the ability to hold a focus through the discipline from the practice of meditation contains a crucial key to be able to awaken.

The breakthrough went beyond my mind deciding how to do it. I had to hold God's Will then the breakthrough could occur otherwise, I would have only become exhausted.

JUDGMENT and BLAME

After awakening – What is required is the willingness to let life impact you: or let yourself see when life impacts you; to see if you go into any sort of separation about it, if you go into judgment, if you go into blame . . . .

Adyashanti, *The End of Your World*

Lana describes her experience with her clients. *If we go into judgment or blame, we get caught in personal will, which stops the divine from working through us. We may be emotionally triggered by outside influences, friends, etc. and go into judgment. We can take any type of judgments we make as a sign of the divine talking to us. We now have a choice to become aware, hold, and contain like in meditation and flow with the situation.*

These triggering situations challenge us to stay out of reacting, self-judgment, blame, or shame. These take us out of being God

I consider nonjudgment as a state of being. It remains beyond a decision for it occurs very quickly with the speed of thought.

I AM MORE THAN MY BODY

As we progress through spiritual initiations and awakening, we reach breakthroughs of realization: I am more than my body, I am more than my emotions, or I am more than my mind.

Lana received a Bowen Therapy session, a form of energetic bodywork, after she awoke with a stiff neck and a sore throat. She suffered agony throughout her body, in her heart chakra, and she sensed it in her DNA.

For some time Lana had an awareness of wanting to be alone and also finding it increasingly difficult to talk to people. She knew this to be unhealthy. When she looked into the feeling with her inner sight she saw the vibration of this feeling throughout the other four children in the family she grew up with. She saw it in her mother rather than in her father.

Lana's mother had an extremely painful childhood as her three sisters before her had all died, burned to death or aborted. Lana saw her mother's trauma carried in the DNA and passed down to the family. Lana commented, *Any strong emotion gets imprinted into the DNA. The trauma of wars and mass destruction of groups of people also get stamped into the DNA, which requires clearing and healing.*

At the beginning of the Bowen session Lana contained her agony, the sensations, and thought forms that emerged. She felt strengthened and the agony began to burn off. Lana said, *I feel something dead in my DNA* – her mother's agony of death.

After the second set of Bowen moves, Lana went to sleep for fifty minutes.

With Bowen the body integrates after each move. The body requires a minimum of two minutes and sometimes longer. When a client goes into a deep rest mode, such as sleep, this indicates major healing and they should be left for as long as they need, sometimes

up to twenty minutes. Lana needed fifty minutes because of the intensity of the issue moving through her.

Before Lana went to sleep she said, *I had the
awareness, my body isn't mine. I only inhabit this
body.*

After the third set of Bowen moves Lana said,
*Something's breaking open. Every part of my body
aches. I am going through the Seed of Evil – greed,
destruction - within humanities blood.*

Once we reach a certain stage in our own spiritual
development, we begin clearing and healing group
and humanities karma. We can ask the question.
What percentage of this issue is mine? Usually ours is
very small. What percentage is humanities? So the
Seed of Evil being burned off through Lana pertained
mostly to humanity.

Lana said, *I trust I can go through it. I see things
rising up out of the ooze – the dead – spirits being set
free. They've been unaware of being dead. I sense a
guidance assisting me. My body's like a homeopathic
– very small amounts of a substance create healing –
going into the earth and changing the Land of the
Dead. I see spirits dead for eons, waking up and
looking around. I feel something coming out of the
back of my heart chakra.*

After the final Bowen move Lana said, *I feel a lot of stuff coming out. If I felt the same amount of emotions I used to, I would be screaming in absolute agony now.*

Because of Lana's choice of being aware, containing her emotional reactions, and healing them over a period of 1 ½ years, she had mastered her emotional body sufficiently to stay in the center of the tornado of her emotions rather than being caught in the violent rotating column of agony. Healing her mother's agony imprinted in her DNA, which in the larger part connected to the agony of death in humanities DNA, freed her to realize, I am not my body, an important realization in spiritual development.

MICHAEL: PERSONAL EXPERIENCES on the ROAD to AWAKENING

My daily experience, like most people, involves seeing my past emotional and mental conditioning being mirrored back to me. I will describe a few instances relating to handling emotional situations over about 1 ½ years from August 07 to April 09. I have an advantage receiving feedback, Oneness Blessings every few days from my wife, Lyn, and some energetic healings.

JUST SAY YES

A major aspect of my emotional/mental conditioning involves an unconscious resistance which shows up by me voicing an automatic "No" to any new requests asked of me. In the past, I have had rigid mental patterns of fear which said "I can't, it's too hard." This of course closes the door to exploring new possibilities, experiencing my present reality, and also leaves no room for Divine Grace to enter and assist to dissolve suffering.

In the past, when I have allowed light into the victim aspect of myself, this "Yes" to life entered the resistance and I felt a shift and a change in my consciousness. Lyn said the aura of my whole energetic field shifted.

Through Lyn's persistent feedback, my resistant "No" becomes more conscious to me and I am now gradually choosing to open to the possibilities of "Yes" to life situations.

DISSOLVING EMOTIONAL REACTIONS

I have tended over the years to carry tension in my shoulders, neck, and the back of my head in the area of the occipitals. One day, as I felt a lot of tension in my occipitals, Lyn assisted by giving me an Oneness Blessing.

I held intense anger at American politicians for their disregard to act for the highest good for the public. My tendency to get stuck in my rage dammed up the energy in my head. Lyn guided me to contain and feel my anger and sadness rather than directing it outward at certain politicians. She later had me feel and radiate compassion from my heart towards myself as well as the politicians.

Lyn's assistance provided valuable training for me to continue to practice to disengage from automatic emotional reactions, which in the past left me feeling like a victim, powerless. With emotional reactions, enter into and feel everything about them rather than resisting them. Once we do this our emotions take us through a still point of balance to the other side to the opposite higher emotion. For example, at the high end of anger lies forgiveness and empowerment. At the low end of anger the victim hides out. When I become of aware of my victim and stand in the middle – the still point – then healing can occur.

Note: Feeling everything about our emotions means riding them like a wave rather than getting trapped in the quagmire of the emotion like a victim.

INNER CHILD RETRIEVAL/HEALING

It is through healing our inner child, our inner children, by grieving the wounds that we suffered, that we can change our behavior patterns and clear our emotional process. We can release the grief with its pent-up rage, shame, terror, and pain from those feeling places which exist within us.

Robert Burney, *The Dance of Wounded Souls.*

My inner child has felt unsafe for most of my life. He has hidden away attached to his suffering. At least with the suffering he felt something rather than a void of nothingness.

I have learned to connect with my inner child and invite him to assist to retrieve and hold our pain in a container, to be present with it, and feel it in our heart or body.

There may be a core belief holding the suffering in place. We can ask this to be revealed to us through intuitive awareness or with the assistance of a healer. Then have your inner child breathe with you into the belief as you contain it.

The pain may lessen or intensify at first. Continue bringing back all parts of yourself rather than slipping back into the suffering. Imagine, visualize, or see the divine entering the breath and burning up all the pain.

MY CHILD

By Michael

Locked in pain,

Lost in a sea of suffering

Falsely believing the illusion

It's my duty to suffer.

I am all alone.

The Angels have abandoned me

Flown to the heights above and beyond

Swords pierce my heart,

Tearing asunder all joy

Wait.

Something glows,

Like an ember.

It's in my heart.

A Voice,

Of the divine says, *Breathe.*

I breathe.

Divine Fire enters.

The pain increases, and then lessens.

I come out of hiding,

Unafraid, safe

An Angel's wing caresses my body.

Joy returns.

LIGHT QUOTIENT – WHITE LIGHT

I have personal experience plus that of two people with the light quotient – the amount of light our physical bodies can hold, increasing. The two friends light quotient increased to 100 %. They still continued integrating the awakening experience; however, their body of emotional reactions began to dissolve more quickly.

Lyn sees the light as white to crystalline clear. I believe when we hold a 100 % quotient of light it appears clear because many previous emotional and mental patterns of pain, illusion, and resistance have dissolved through willingness, effort, and the choice to say "Yes" to Divine Will.

Our physical body rewires as we adjust to embodying more light. Over 1½ years my light quotient increased from 57 % to 97 %. I still have lots of emotional patterns; however, I am becoming more aware of them which gives me the choice to disengage from their clutches.

PERSONAL EXPERIENCES on the ROAD to AWAKENING

To offer no resistance to life is to be in a state of grace, ease, and lightness.

Eckhart Tolle, *The Power of Now*

JOANNA: DISSOLVING EMOTIONAL REACTIONS

Joanna, a retired CEO, has spent over 40 years becoming aware and mastering her emotions. During the last 1½ years she has been to the Oneness University in India three times, preparing for her purpose of being on the forefront assisting in the awakening of humanity.

Years ago, I learned in meditation to be with my emotions, regardless of the situation. I stopped figuring them out or pushing them away.

Slowly, little by little, I went from being in emotional reaction to being more conscious of my state. Then I could choose to stay in the reaction or become more neutral. Nothing much triggers me now.

LOVE WITHOUT ATTACHMENT

My son suffered a near fatal car accident a few years ago. Most mothers would be sick with worry, fearing paralysis or death as the outcome. I, howev-

er, remained unemotional. I stayed in peaceful acceptance of whatever happened. Meanwhile, the rest of the family and relatives clamored about in emotional upheaval.

Same may say I appeared as unloving. I care deeply for my son and I am also unattached to this care as an emotion. I have no expectations, no fear of what may happen tomorrow.

Perhaps we can understand Joanna's state of emotional neutrality, through the Serenity Prayer by theologian Reinhold Niebuhr. This prayer has been adopted by Alcoholics Anonymous.

Joanna had no power to change the fact her son suffered an accident or the extent of his injuries. Any fears projected onto her son would only have created more harm than good. So instead she sent out calm, unworried thoughts for his recovery.

Joanna best served her son through staying in an emotional state of no attachment – serenity. She did take all the actions possible such as providing a helicopter to evacuate him to the best hospital and doctors in the country. The rest remained out of her hands.

Her son had a miraculous recovery with no paralysis or disfigurement. As a matter of fact, the accident shifted his focus and he became more aware of his life purpose.

CHAKRAS AWAKENING

In 1994, I woke up with a burning sensation at the top of my head. At the time, I had little experience with energy work said Joanna. *An intense burning like a million ants swarming about occurred. I went into the bathroom to look into the mirror. My hair stood straight up like static electricity pulled on it and each hair strand split. It looked and felt like straw on the top and sides.*

I consulted my gynecologist in case hormones could be the cause. Neither, my hairdresser, medical doctor, nor gynecologist had a clue about this strange occurrence.

One year later in Poona, India I got an answer. One of the people familiar with energetic healing told me, "Your crown chakra opened."

I had another chakra awakening, in August 2007, at my first 21 day experience at the Oneness University in India. All of a sudden while lying on my bed, I felt a strong explosion in my heart. The electrical energy came out of my chest in waves and I felt it for about fifteen minutes.

PERSONALITY/EGO DISSOLVING

But with real awakening, the whole structure of separation begins to dissolve under one's feet. Adyashanti, *The End of Your World*

A Christ Consciousness grid of Unity energetically connects above the Earth. Each person who moves into awakening connects into this grid, strengthening it. This grid assists human consciousness to shift into Oneness and has been talked about by people involved with the study of sacred geometry such as Ronald Holt director of the Flower of Life.

Joanna describes an experience of Unity/Oneness. *In November 2008, I prepared to attend my daughter in-laws birthday party. At the airport I felt an expansion of energy from out of my chest. It filled the entire terminal. My whole body energetically expanded as far as the eye could see.*

I looked at a woman and realized that she was just another manifestation of me. Then I looked at a man, and then a baby, both manifestations of me. This continued for a long time with no judgment, only total acceptance.

Then my mind said, Where is me? I had no sense of a "me" in the body, just something, it was not Joanna.

I stood up to board the plane and walked on the granite floor when I realized I was also walking on another manifestation of me.

On the plane one man rudely informed another man, "Get out of my seat."

I observed another manifestation of me hurting another manifestation of me.

I remained in the experience, with my eyes closed, for the next 1½ hours. The total experience of unity lasted 3½ hours.

Before this experience, I have had other momentary sensations of being startled when I looked in a mirror and didn't recognize the person looking back at me or looking at my hand, which appeared foreign.

In summary, it has taken years and years of diligent effort to arrive where I am today. Before, I used to get stuck on an emotion and spin away like a car mired down in mud, going nowhere. Now after years of suffering and much learning, I can distinguish when I am stuck in suffering or just allowing what is. Now when strong emotions arise I sit with them until they pass.

I have less intensity of longing, of "working" on myself, of seeking.

Adyashanti says, *In this way, one of the hallmarks of a true awakening is the end of seeking.*

PERSONAL EXPERIENCES on the ROAD to AWAKENING

TIARA KUMARA: PERSONALITY BREAK-DOWN

Tiara comments, *I returned, early in 2009, to the United States from a six month solo pilgrimage in India. I am still in awe of the experience, without a doubt the most challenging initiatory period of my spiritual life.*

Walking in familiar footholds, witnessing horrific suffering and being exposed to certain sacred signatures of an ancient homeland triggered an immense personality dissolve. The levees of the illusory mind and its glamoured life finally broke free from its selfish holds. Amidst the great flood, codes downloaded, a reprogramming occurred, and internal crystalline seals opened with access to the new blueprint of the DNA.

Canceling all previous understandings, this feels like a permanent and quantum shift, which happened because of the necessary preparation to endure an intense accelerated breakdown on all levels of my personality.

The aspects of shadow self had to be boldly called up and faced head on. An authentic and conscious choice relinquished all self-identity and the hold to material reality without knowing what would hap-

pen next. I had no idea if I would even physically survive.

I felt as though blindfolded in these travels, constantly prodded, provoked, and even sickened. This breakdown – scary many times - could never have happened without the guidance and support from many spiritual forces and overlighting Masters, all held within the constancy of Krishna's dancing flute.

We are never alone, ever. The Divine orchestrates all.

Tiara endured an intense initiation becoming aware and dissolving her glamour's, as well as facing aspects of her shadow. This requires complete surrender of our personality will to Divine Will, to trust the divine even in our darkest hour. When we surrender, than the Breath of the Divine, known as grace, can flow through us for we become as the hollow flute of Krishna.

We are as the flute, and the music in us is from thee, Rumi, mystic & poet.

AMMA/BHAGAVAN: PLANETARY AWAKEN-ING to GRACE

Once there is a certain degree of Presence, of still and alert attention in human beings' perceptions, they can sense the divine life essence, the one indwelling consciousness or spirit in every creature, every life-form, recognize it as one with their own essence and so love it as themselves, says Eckhart Tolle, *A New Earth.* He also says, *This is a time for awakening for humans on the planet.*

In regards to awakening/enlightenment, something different has been occurring since 2003 when Bhagavan, founder of the Oneness University in India, began giving enlightenment to the public. Dasas, guides at the Oneness University, give Oneness Blessings or Deeksha, as well as others from around the world after having attended the Oneness University.

Arjuna Ardagh, *Awakening into Oneness*, describes the Oneness Blessing as a transfer of Divine Energy from one person to another. The Blessing can be given by touch, through the eyes, or through the power of intention, resulting in healing, peace, and overall well-being.

Both Bhagavan and his wife Amma hold the Divine Grace, which powers the Oneness Blessings. Bhagavan says that awakening can only occur through a change in brain functioning - *an activation of the frontal lobes, and a deactivation of the parietal lobes,* which happens over time through the Oneness Blessings. *A type of rewiring occurs in the mind, at the mental level, and there is a rewiring of how we sense and perceive on an emotional level,* states Bhagavan.

Christian Opitz, Neurophysicist, confirms that Deeksha initiates a neurobiological change in the brain. He states, *With the blocking of the parietal lobes a feeling of expanded consciousness is produced. The stimulation of the frontal lobes also releases dopamine, the essential neurotransmitter that creates a feeling of bliss.*

The divine purpose behind the birth of the avatars Sri Amma/Bhagavan is to help every individual awaken to a state of Oneness within himself, says Radhakrishna, a Dasa, at Oneness University.

The vision of Bhagavan and Amma involves enlightening at least 1% of the world's population – 70,000 people - by the year 2012. This would allow for a shift of mass consciousness to occur.

David Hawkins, a psychiatrist, author of *Power vs. Force* has devised a scale of consciousness from 0 to 1000. He says that a person holding a state of joy or enlightenment counterbalances millions of others in guilt, shame, or fear. So, a few people high on the consciousness scale can create a wave of enlightenment. *That is why we believe that once we have 70,000 people that will be enough for transforming the whole of mankind,* Bhagavan says.

Bhagavan and Amma have built an Oneness Temple in India to amplify the meditative energy of 8000 highly conscious meditators focused in deep meditation 24 hours a day. As smaller meditating groups around the earth connect, the energy rises and allows for the shift of human consciousness into a state of oneness.

Quantum physicist, John Hagelin, verifies that 8000 highly vibrational meditators, calculated after years of research on the effects of meditation, as the minimum number of people necessary to affect the fields of human consciousness worldwide and trigger a paradigm shift. See www.experiencefestival.com for articles on enlightenment.

OVERCOMING SUFFERING

At the beginning of chapter one, I talked about both personal effort and Divine Grace as necessary for lessening suffering.

Overcoming suffering requires courage, the courage to face our fears, the courage to speak our truth.

Overcoming suffering requires becoming more aware of our emotional reactions. It requires examining the thoughts that activated the emotions and reprogramming these thoughts. It requires learning and choosing to contain our emotions with love.

Overcoming suffering requires conscious choice rather than a desire to avoid suffering. Once we learn how to stand in the middle of any two reactions, in a state of neutrality, we begin to heal, which allows grace to enter our lives.

In this chapter and others, personal experiences involved both effort and grace. On a bigger planetary scale our path can take us now – for the first time in human history - from just the easing of personal suffering to awakening by a paradigm shift into greater consciousness through Divine Grace and a change in our brains.

The question remains of how much lessening pain and awakening requires effort and how much can be surrendered to grace. The answer depends on what we need at any particular time on our path. Only our own inner teacher or higher intuition knows the answer, which we can develop through effort.

Adyashanti, *The End of Your World,* sums it up by saying, *You will know from the inside whether it is necessary to investigate a fixation – i.e., your past mental or emotional conditioning . . . Connect to your intuition, which gives direction as your own inner teacher . . . If we're listening deeply, we'll also feel when it is time to let go, when it is time to let grace do what only grace can do . . . It may take effort to get you to the point where you are willing to let go into grace.*

I sincerely intend that this book has inspired you to heal your emotions, increase your self-awareness, and happiness. Continue to practice the art of embracing your feelings. Choose to notice and transform your critical self-talk into positive self-talk for increasing success in your life. Keep connecting with your inner child and listening to his or her needs and satisfying these needs. This child will bring greater joy to you. If you still need to overcome codependency keep becoming aware of your needs and feelings and express them. Also practice setting healthy personal boundaries.

I bless you with increasing physical, emotional, and spiritual health, joy, mental peace, and fulfillment in your life purpose.

REFERENCES and RESOURCES – PART 1,2, 3

REFERENCES and RESOURCES – PART ONE

Jacqueline Stone, author of *Awakening Consciousness* and *Rising from Ashes,* and spiritual coach. http://recoveringfromabuse.blogspot.com

Building the Antahkarana bridge http://soul1.org/invocation_of_the_soul.htm

Book on antahkarana <u>Rainbow Bridge: First and Second Phases Link With the Soul Purification</u> by Two Disciples

Byron Katie, Spiritual Teacher & author, *Loving What Is – Four Questions That Can Change Your Life.* http://www.thework.com/index.php

Gangaji, a spiritual teacher & author, *The Diamond in Your Pocket* www.gangaji.org

Eugene Gendlin, *Focusing* teaches us six steps how to be mindful through paying attention to our body awareness. www.focusing.org

Carolyn Ball's, *Claiming Your Self-Esteem: A Guide Out of Codependency, Addiction, and Other Useless Habits.*

REFERENCES and RESOURCES – PART TWO

Eckhart Tolle, *The Power of Now*

Pia Melody, *Facing Codependency*

Charlotte Kasl, *If the Buddha Married*

Melody Beattie, *Codependent No More*

Dr. Heyward Ewart Ph.D., *The Lies That Bind: The Permanence of Child Abuse*

Dan Millman, *The Life You Were Born to Live*

Pat Wyman, *Three Keys to Self-Understanding*

Robert Burney, www.joy2meu.com – Codependency

Yogananda, *The Bhagavad Gita* – a commentary

Pat Gurnick, www.caringcounselor.com

Maria Mann, author, *Verity Red's Diary: A Story of Surviving M. E., and CFS sufferer*

Peter Novak, *End Tiredness Program*

Michael E. Rosenbaum & Murray Susser, *Solving the Puzzle of Chronic Fatigue*

Dr. David Bell, MD, *Cellular Hypoxia and Neuro-Immune Fatigue* www.chronicfatiguerelapse.com

Dr. Barry Weinberg, *A Clear Path to Healing*

Dr. Bruce H. Lipton, *The Biology of Belief*

Greg Braden, *The Spontaneous Healing of Belief*

David Feinstein, Donna Eden, and Gary Craig, *The Promise of Energy Psychology*

www.emofree.com – EFT – Emotional Freedom Technique

Dr. Bradley Nelson, *The Emotion Code*

Robert Stevens, *Consciousness Language*

Gangaji, *Diamond in your Pocket*

Richard Gerber M.D., *Vibrational Medicine*

Alice Bailey, *Esoteric Healing*

Chris Irwin, *Horses Don't Lie*

Carl Jung, *Collected Works, Volume 17*

John Bradshaw, *Homecoming: Reclaiming and Championing Your Inner Child*

REFERENCES and RESOURCES – PART TWO

Carl Jung, *Psychology and Religion*

Alice Bailey, *Glamour: A World Problem*

St. John of the Cross, *Dark Night of the Soul*

Gregg Braden, *Walking Between the Worlds*

Wayne Dyer, *Power of Intention*

Cathryn Taylor, *The Inner Child Workbook*

Carolyn Ball, *Claiming Your Self-Esteem*

Byron Katie, *The Work*

Theresa Dale, Ph.D., *Transform Your Emotional DN*

ADDITIONAL RESOURCES: CHRONIC FA-TIQUE SYNDROME and FIBROMYALGIA: A FEW PROGRAMS YOU COULD DO at HOME

Pat Gurnick recommends these books. One hopeful and helpful free resource you can access online is the book "*Recovering from Chronic Fatigue Syndrome: A Guide to Self-Empowerment*" by Dr. William Collinge, PhD, in collaboration with Dr. Daniel Peterson.

Another encouraging self-care book that can be purchased inexpensively used or new and is particularly helpful for those of us who suffer from allergic reactions and sensitivities is "The Rebellious Body: Reclaim Your Life from Environmental Illness or Chronic Fatigue Syndrome" by Janice Strubbe Wittenberg, RN.

SOME FEE-BASED RELAXATION and EDU-CATIONAL PROGRAMS YOU CAN DO at HOME:

CD, Learn to Breathe by Anna Coy, http://www.inspiringyourlife.com , I want to help you understand how breathing effectively and fully can change your life.

DVD, Healing Rhythms - *biofeedback guides by Wild Divine Project*, http://www.wilddivine.com

DVD, *The Advanced CFS/ME Recovery Programme* by Ashok Gupta, http://www.cfsrecovery.com Ashok Gupta, a CFS therapist believes the amygdala in the brain keeps the body in an imbalanced state creating the CFS symptoms. He offers a drug free therapy to retrain the amygdala.

DVD, Heartmath, stress reduction techniques, http://www.heartmath.org

HeartMath institute shows the affects of emotions on the body through technology measuring heart rate variability. Learning to create positive emotions saves your body energy.

CD's to change brainwaves for health, http://www.centerpointe.com

Holosync from Centerpointe has a direct impact on the nervous system. Specifically, it saturates the nervous system with stimulus, producing enhancements in the way the system functions.

CD's for breathe, meditation ,visualization, http://www.collinge.org/CFSaudios.htm *Recovering from Chronic Fatigue Syndrome* by Dr. William Collinge, PhD.

Dr. Collinge stresses successful treatment of CFIDS requires many approaches including medical evaluation and intervention, psychotherapy, and self-help. Patients heal themselves using methods of body awareness, inner dialogue, deep relaxation, guided imagery, etc.

Note*: This information has been unevaluated by the FDA. It is generic and is unintended to prevent, diagnose, ameliorate, treat, or cure any condition, illness, or disease. It is important you make no change in your personal healthcare plan or health support regiment without researching and discussing it with your professional healthcare team.*

REFERENCES and RESOURCES – PART THREE

Eckhart Tolle, *The Power of Now*

Peter Levine, *Waking the Tiger, Healing Trauma*

Abraham-Hicks, www.abraham-hicks.com

Alice Bailey, *A Treatise on White Magic*

Alice Bailey, *Discipleship in the New Age Volume 2*

Sharon Lund, *Dying to Live* - documentary of her NDE

Sharon Lund, *The Integrated Being: Techniques to Heal Your Mind-Body-Spirit.*

Dan Millman, *The Life You Were Born to Live*

Adyashanti, *The End of Your World*

Alice Bailey, *Esoteric Psychology Volume II*

Celia Fenn, http://starchildglobal.com/

Sogyal Rinpoche, *The Tibetan Book of Living and Dying*

Tiara Kumara www. childrenofthesun.tv

Ram Dass, *Be Here Now*

Ram Dass, *Fierce Grace* – DVD

J.J. Hurtak, *The Keys of Enoch*

Global Oneness -
www.experiencefestival.com/spiritual_awakening -
articles on enlightenment

Robert Burney, *The Dance of Wounded Souls*

Eckhart Tolle, *A New Earth*

Arjuna Ardagh, *Awakening into Oneness*

ABOUT the AUTHOR

Michael David Lawrience

Michael David Lawrience travels a path of Awakening from separation into Oneness. He has dedicated his life for over 35 years, discovering and healing himself and others physically, emotionally, mentally, and spiritually.

Michael's spirit radiates healing, inspiration, love, and peace as an energy healer and a Professional Bowenwork Practitioner. As a personal development seminar leader for over 20 years, he has taught professionals as well as nonprofessionals in the United States, Canada, and Brazil. He also has experience as a Residential Coach mentoring and teaching teenage girls.

Michael is a certified Residential Coach III with over 13 years' experience teaching teen's self-awareness, self-esteem, and self-reliance. He has over 35 years' experience as a holistic health practitioner with a B.A in Sacred Healing and has been a certified Bowenwork Practitioner since 2005. His niche is emotional health with extensive personal experience related to codependency recovery, strengthening self-esteem, healing the inner child, stress management, and meditation which he has practiced for over 40 years.

Michael offers top emotional health tips on his blog
http://www.emotionalhealthtips.com

Facebook fan page
http://www.facebook.com/pages/Emotional-Health-Tips/308508762330

http://twitter.com/#!/unity3

Michael also offers Bowen Therapy in person in Sedona, Arizona.